D0929993

# Salt City and Its Black Community

# Salt City
## and Its Black Community

A SOCIOLOGICAL STUDY OF SYRACUSE, NEW YORK

## S. David Stamps & Miriam Burney Stamps

 SYRACUSE UNIVERSITY PRESS

The paper used in this publication meets the minimum requirements of American National Standard
for Information Sciences—Permanence of Paper for Printed Library Materials, ANSI Z39.48–1984.∞™

For a listing of books published and distributed by Syracuse University Press, visit our Web site at
SyracuseUniversityPress.syr.edu.

ISBN-13: 978-0-8156-3180-4 (cloth)
ISBN-10: 0-8156-3180-4 (cloth)

**Library of Congress Cataloging-in-Publication Data**

Stamps, Spurgeon Martin David, 1937–
    Salt city and its black community : a sociological study of Syracuse, New York / S. David Stamps and
Miriam Burney Stamps. — 1st ed.
        p. cm.
    Includes bibliographical references and index.
    ISBN 978-0-8156-3180-4 (cloth : alk. paper)
    1. African Americans—New York (State)—Syracuse—History.   2. African Americans—New York
(State)—Syracuse—Social conditions.   3. Syracuse (N.Y.)—Race relations.   4. Syracuse (N.Y.)—
History.   5. Syracuse (N.Y.)—Social conditions.   I. Stamps, Miriam Burney, 1941–  II. Title.
F129.S8S73 2008
305.896'073074766—dc22
2007036645

*Manufactured in the United States of America*

We dedicate this book to the late Miriam Cunningham Burney, mother of Miriam Burney Stamps. A 1932 graduate of Mount Holyoke College with honors in history, she stressed the need to understand a community's past before you can fully understand its present. Her insight led us to include a sociohistorical section in this book.

**S. David Stamps** (Ph.D., Washington State University, 1974) is a professor of sociology at the University of South Florida. He has also served in various administrative positions there: special assistant to the president, associate dean and dean of arts and sciences, as well as provost and vice president of academic affairs. Prior to coming to the University South Florida, he served on the faculty at Norfolk State University and was both a professor of Afro-American studies and sociology and the chair of Afro-American studies at Syracuse University. He has published in the areas of community engagement, crime victimization, and leisure.

**Miriam Burney Stamps** (Ph.D., Syracuse University, 1982) is an associate professor and the chair of marketing at the University of South Florida. Prior to coming to the University of South Florida, she was an assistant professor of marketing at Le Moyne College in Syracuse, New York, and served on the faculty at Norfolk State University. She has published in the areas of leisure, sales, market segmentation, and the impact of ethnicity on consumption.

# Contents

# Illustrations

# Tables

# Preface

A LITERATURE REVIEW reveals that in recent years only a few community studies have focused on minority communities and none has looked at black community life in a midsize northern urban community. This lack of attention is reason enough to justify this study. Not only are communities constantly changing, but minority communities are playing much more significant roles in the larger communities of which they are a part than they did prior to the civil rights movement.

Having grown up in the South, we were intrigued by some of our observations of the Syracuse black community when we began to live there. When we first arrived in Syracuse, other professional blacks attempted to introduce us to the black professional community, as they did with most newcomers. Throughout the Syracuse metropolitan community, however, many of these black professionals gave the impression that they were only temporarily located in the area. We later found out, however, that they had lived in the area for ten to fifteen years. This observation led us to conclude that although many professional blacks lived in the greater Syracuse area, they did not identify with the black community. We began to wonder whether they really felt a part of that community, which led us to the question: Were suburban blacks a factor in the growth and development of the Syracuse black community? That is, did they identify with problems and issues confronting Syracuse and its black community? We also observed that there was a low voter turnout among black professionals as well as other blacks in local elections. We began to wonder whether this lack of identification had an effect on political participation as well as on voter turnout. In addition, we observed that a critical mass of professional blacks did not arrive in Syracuse until about 1967, primarily the result of affirmative action initiated by the business community;

local, state, and federal governmental agencies; and K–12 schools and institutions of higher education. We became interested in how the Syracuse black community differed prior to the arrival of this critical mass of professional blacks. As social scientists, we had to ask: What factors led to the early growth and development of a black community in Syracuse, and how did the later growth and development differ with the arrival of professional blacks?

Recognizing the limited focus of previous studies, this monograph looks at a total black community in an urban northeastern city and analyzes how it has functioned as a subset of a larger community. It also analyzes the various factors interrelated to the black community's growth and development. We use conflict theory as a framework in the analysis of this community from its inception through the 1980s.

More specifically, this monograph focuses on the following questions: What structural factors affected the black community, but were external to the community itself? What internal cultural factors have played and will play a role in the past, present, and future progress of the black community, and to what degree have these factors been effective or ineffective? Did the black community develop naturally outside the conscious efforts of the larger society, or was it a social creation of that society? If it was a social creation of the larger society, then what role did the members of the black community play in its creation? This study attempts to address these questions, among others, in looking at an urban black community in the northeast through a detailed sociological analysis.

We used various collection techniques in amassing the large quantity of data on both the black community and the larger Syracuse community: personal interviews with key local residents, census data, newspaper articles, local documents, previous studies on the local black community, and surveys we conducted on our own. One of the surveys, a cross-sectional random sample of 750 households within Syracuse, provided primary data.

We hope that this study provides valuable insights into how minority communities grow and develop. In the final chapter, we offer an analysis of the future of black communities. We attempt to address how black communities and other minority communities can take charge and determine their destiny.

# Acknowledgments

WE ARE INDEBTED to the reviewers and others whose critiques were extremely helpful in revising the final manuscript. The late Jack Bell was also very helpful in the early stages of writing this manuscript. And our adult children, Monique Y. Stamps and S. David Stamps III, often added insightful observations as we discussed the book during its preparation.

# Salt City and Its Black Community

# 1

# Perspective on Studies of Urban Black Communities

## The Changing Nature of Black Communities

THE BLACK COMMUNITY TODAY is different from that portrayed in earlier studies, such as W. E. B. DuBois's *The Philadelphia Negro* in 1899, John Dollard's *Caste and Class in a Southern Town* in 1957, St. Clair Drake and Horace Cayton's *Black Metropolis* in 1945, Hylan Lewis's *Blackways of Kent* in 1955, E. Franklin Frazier's *Black Bourgeoisie* in 1957, Elaine Burgess's *Negro Leadership in a Southern City* in 1960, and Kenneth Clark's *Dark Ghetto* in 1965. Like the rest of society, black communities are constantly changing. Yet these early studies, along with more recent studies by Carol Stack (1974), James Blackwell (1975, 1985), William J. Wilson (1978, 1987, 1996a, 1996b, 2001), James Borchet (1980), Douglas Daniels (1980), James Blackwell and Philip Hart (1982), Joe Trotter (1985), Adelaide Cromwell (1994), Bobby Lovett (1999), Kimberly Battle-Walter (2004), and Frank Wilson (2004), provide baseline data that assist in understanding the interrelationships between blacks and whites as well as the intrarelationships among blacks. These more recent studies have addressed themselves to specific issues: the family, social classes, education, lower-class behavior, working-class women, political powerlessness, and inner-city joblessness.

Trotter's (1985) historical treatment of blacks in Milwaukee, Wilson's (1978, 1987, 1996a, 1996b, 2001) analyses of the underclass, and Battle-Walter's (2004) ethnographic study of working-class African American women are among the few new studies of the black community that utilize new approaches and perspectives. We hope to meet a part of this need by providing in this study an

1

objective and analytical treatment of how a black community developed and grew in a northeastern city. Although this study seeks to displace some of the myths and inaccuracies about black community life, it endeavors to do so by presenting a sound analysis of relevant data rather than by making an expository defense. An analysis of many of the post–World War II studies that focused on black community life in the urban North reveals an attempt to refute the findings and perspectives of earlier studies by utilizing a "ghetto" theoretical framework. The later studies include Gilbert Osofsky's *Harlem: The Making of a Ghetto, 1890–1930* (1971, originally published in 1963); Allen H. Spear's *Black Chicago: The Making of a Negro Ghetto, 1890–1920* (1967); David M. Katzman's *Before the Ghetto: Black Detroit in the Nineteenth Century* (1973); Kenneth L. Kusmer's *A Ghetto Takes Shape: Black Cleveland, 1870–1930* (1976); and Thomas Philpott's *The Slum and the Ghetto* (1978). Ghetto-formation studies were reactions to the earlier assimilation studies and their contention that black life in urban slums was comparable to that of European immigrant groups before them. Although ghetto-formation studies served to dispel some of the notions attributing slum life to personal inadequacies inherent in blacks, the ghetto orientation itself was too narrow to provide an adequate sociological analysis of black life in northern urban communities.

Studies by Frazier (1957), Billingsley (1968), Stack (1974), Blackwell and Hart (1982), and others point to the dynamic nature of the black community. As William Wilson (1996a) points out, most of these studies were designed in part as a reaction to Daniel Patrick Moynihan's (1967) public-policy report on the pathologies of the black family in inner-city neighborhoods. However, the manner in which the black community is different from the descriptions provided in early studies can be gleaned from these later studies. Despite these scholars' work, it is evident that there is a need for continuing community studies. Over the past forty years, the black community has undergone radical changes as the social order of American society has drastically altered. Changes within the black community and the society at large have been neither smooth nor rapid. Blacks and others believe that many of the changes that took place during the late 1960s and 1970s were not sustained during the remainder of the twentieth century, as evidenced in the following measures: (1) abolishing forced busing as a measure to achieve school integration, (2) allowing tax credits to private schools that discriminate on the bases of race, (3) relaxing enforcement of affirmative action legislation, and (4) tolerating record heights in unemployment within the black community that more than doubles that of the white community. A closer look at unemployment shows that for black adults in the United States in recent years the rate has been 20 percent, and among black teenagers it has been approximately 50 percent. High unemployment, coupled with a drastic cutback in social programs, has had a devastating effect on the economy of the black community, as Wilson (1996a) has pointed out. Given this state of affairs, the whole issue of equality and progress, as related to the black community, is being questioned in that government and social interest and concern seem to have diminished.

Studies of the black community over the past few years have investigated myriad new problems and issues. As mentioned, some studies have looked into the rather tenuous state of so-called black progress of the 1960s and 1970s (Hill 1978, 1981; Newman et al. 1978; Blackwell 1981a, 1981b; Blackwell and Hart 1982). Other studies have highlighted the growth and progress of middle-class blacks or outlined the dim future of the growing underclass (Kriesberg 1970; Kronus 1971; W. Wilson 1978, 1987, 1996a; Blackwell 1981; Glasgow 1981; Ropers 1991). They also show the increase in number of black public officials, but the elusiveness of real power to influence public policy (Baron 1968; Nelson and Meranto 1977).

Debate certainly has an important role in research and scholarship; however, such motivation puts the researcher constantly in a defensive position and does not allow for the introduction of new ideas or perspectives. To this end, we see as our task the development of a theoretical model for the analysis of the emergence, growth, and present status of individual black communities.

Both "community studies" and "race relation studies" have had, at one time or other, varying degrees of emphasis within the discipline of sociology. Cyclical periods in race relations in the United States have influenced both the type of social research sponsored and the choice of subjects selected by sociologists. Immigration trends, for example, caused an upswing in the number of studies on ethnicity and the community (see Sowell 1981; Portes and Rambout 1996) as sociologists tried to better understand these new groups, just as they have tried to understand the relationship between blacks and whites.

As the nation became more concerned with international issues, transportation issues, the environment, aging, sexism, and health, and as both the

civil rights movement of the 1960s and its aftermath, the Black Power movement, died down, the attention paid to the study of black Americans diminished somewhat. Only a few sociologists continued a concentrated study of
black Americans and the black community.[1]

Demographic changes during the 1980s and 1990s, coupled with demographic projections for the twenty-first century, brought about a refocusing on
minority issues, in particular those related to black Americans and Hispanics
(Blauner 2001; Suarez-Orozco and Paez 2002). Recognition that minorities
and women would play an increasingly vital role in American economic and
political pictures escalated efforts to educate those who had been traditionally ignored. The fact that a new emphasis on education and skill training
was needed is not debatable. However, for this new emphasis on minorities
to bear fruit, a better understanding of the effects of structural changes that
have taken place in society and of their impact on the social fabric of minority life is needed. Changes that have already occurred and that are currently
taking place within minority communities as well as between minority and
majority communities need to be the focus of serious study. Insightful analysis and detailed inspections of everyday life in minority communities during
the latter half of the twentieth century would test old theories and provide a
foundation for new theories.

Despite these demographic changes and future projections, there is still
a need to look at the total black community as it functions as a subset of the
larger society and to see how various factors interrelate in determining the
direction that this community has taken and will take.

What structural factors affect the black community but are external to
the community itself? What internal cultural factors play a role in the present
state and future progress of the black community, and to what degree are these
factors effective or ineffective? Was the development of the black community
a natural progression that took place outside the conscious efforts of the larger
society, or is the black community a social creation of that society? If it is a
social creation of the larger society, then what role did the members of the

---

1. The most notable studies among sociologists include Blackwell 1975, 1981a, 1981b;
Staples 1976, 1981; Willie 1976; Hill 1978, 1981; W. Wilson 1978; Glasgow 1981; Blackwell and
Hart 1982.

black community play in its creation? These questions remain unanswered but are important to understanding the emergence of any black community. This study attempts to address these questions, among others, in looking at the urban black community in Syracuse through a detailed investigation that includes a sociological analysis.

## Social Reality of the Community: Basic Assumptions

For the purpose of this study, conflict theory as developed by Richard Quinney (1970) is broadened to analyze community life, especially the relationship of the black community to the larger community of which it is a part. We utilize basic premises conceived by Quinney and others (Erikson 1962; Kitsuse 1962; Akers 1963; Becker 1963; Gibbs 1966; Bordua 1969) to explain social forces that have had an effect on the status of a black community in a white society.[2]

In keeping with Quinney's (1970, 8–15) treatment of conflict theory, we rely heavily on certain basic assumptions about society and the community that include process, conflict, power, and social action. The first assumption is that the society is constantly changing or is in a dynamic state. By looking at social processes, one can observe phenomena over time and analyze the social changes that have taken place. The second assumption is that conflict is a consequence of group interaction, particularly within communities where there is a high degree of diversity among inhabitants. *Diversity* in this case refers to race, ethnicity, socioeconomic status, and political affiliation. The conflict model sees change as a dominant aspect of society. Conflict results from the coercion or constraint of some groups within the society by other groups (Dahrendorf 1959). The third assumption says that "power" stems from conflict. When groups are coerced or constrained, power is being utilized. As Quinney states, "The differential distribution of power produces conflict between competing groups, and conflict, in turn, is rooted in the competition for power" (1970, 11). Social behavior can be looked upon in terms of power and values. Those groups who are in positions of power attempt to guard their values through coercing or constraining less-powerful groups with divergent values. The ability of any group within the community to influence public

2. This section draws heavily from Richard Quinney's narrative (1970, 8–15).

policy is dependent on that group's political power. The fourth and final assumption that deals with social action is in consonance with the basic premises inherent in conflict and power: social behavior is not haphazard in nature, but oriented toward achieving specific goals. Each group selects from various alternatives those courses of action that best serve the group's interest. Therefore, social reality is created as a result of social action taken by groups.

## The Formal Theory

The four assumptions just outlined allow us to present the theory of the social reality of community life. The interrelationship between social institutions is a product of social processes enacted by groups. Those groups having the most power at a particular point in time are the primary creators and shapers of social institutions and, to a certain degree, control how institutions relate to each other. Thus, the roles, statuses, norms, and values that make up social institutions are created, and, hence, the social community is created, as is the physical community. Although an assumption is made, particularly in democracies such as the United States, that all groups share in the creation of a community, in fact all groups do not share in this activity, and those that do are not equally powerful. Through power and constraints placed on groups with little or no power, certain groups create social institutions in such a way that roles, statuses, values, and norms are shaped to serve their own self-interest. The degree that norms constrain groups with less power is in direct relationship to the degree of conflict within the community (Quinney 1970, 17). Groups in power perceive other groups that maintain a somewhat passive state and that do not challenge them as being less conflictual, and therefore they make fewer attempts to place constraints on these passive groups. However, in instances where other groups attempt to bring about social change or are perceived as having the potential to induce change, constraints are placed on them to curtail their actions.

It should be understood that power groups perceive or find it convenient to perceive that their constraining action is necessary for the good of society and not as an attempt to maintain the status quo or to retain their power. According to the perspective of power groups, their position of power, their values, the roles they play, and the sanctions they induce represent the future and the progress of the society. As an example of this point, one can look at the policies put forth by the Reagan and Bush administrations during the 1980s and again by the George W. Bush administration of the early 2000s that were geared toward giving more to power groups by providing tax breaks for the wealthy, reducing the enforcement of antitrust laws, eliminating environmental restrictions on businesses, deemphasizing affirmative action, and generally moving toward deregulation. The rationale offered for such actions was not that they provided more latitude for the powerful, but that they provided a more viable economy for the larger society. Some people in power may even believe their own rationalizations.

Social change occurs as a result of social action. And social action is initiated by groups with power as a result of conflict or a felt need to redefine their priorities.

Politicians at all levels, national, state, and local, and public bureaucrats are legalized agents through which power groups work. Values "are constructed and diffused . . . [to] all segments of society by various means of communication" (Quinney 1970, 22). Through the diffusion of values and through social action initiated primarily by power groups, the community becomes a social construction. How individuals, groups, and institutions relate to one another is shaped by those in power through all forms of communication. Even the coerced and the constrained serve as vehicles of communication because their experiences and hence their values are shaped to a large degree by the powerful. "The 'real world' is a social construction: [individuals] with the help of others create the world in which [they] live. Social reality is thus the world a group of people create and believe in as their own. This reality is constructed according to the kind of 'knowledge' they develop, the ideas they are exposed to, the manner in which they select information to fit the world they are shaping, and the manner in which they interpret these conceptions" (Quinney 1970, 22).

A part of what is constructed within society is how one racial or ethnic group is regarded in relationship to another. Basic to the interactionist perspective is the position that attributes are determining factors in how certain groups are regarded, until they have been recognized as such by society. Race, ethnicity, color, and other ascribed statuses come to be associated with or are criteria of one's status when they are so defined by society.

Therefore, through the diffusion of values and through social action, primarily initiated by groups in power, the community becomes a social construction. Characteristics evident within communities—such as status hierarchies, value systems, legitimate and illegitimate structures, racial and ethnic neighborhoods, inequality, and discrimination, among other things—are all social constructions.

## The Dominant Groups

In the creation of society, social groups with the most power are able to generate structures that assist them in maintaining their advantage over groups with less power. Although social institutions are not defined in terms of specific groups or specific individuals, but in terms of an entire system of values, norms, statuses, and roles, they are organized in such a fashion that their functions and relationships to each other protect the interests of those groups in power (Federico 1975, 2, 12). Analyzing the interrelationships between social institutions reveals that the economy and the government are dominant and that family, religion, and education play supporting roles. In their supportive roles, families, churches, and schools adapt to the trends of society, whereas the economic and political institutions shape society.

There is not "one" dominant or powerful group in a society, with all other groups placed in a completely submissive position. If there were but one dominant group, there would be little need to discuss power or to recognize the importance of conflict. American society can be characterized as a hierarchy of power groups extending from those in dominant positions down to those that are virtually powerless. Separate hierarchies are present on international, national, state, and local levels. Individuals or groups may have power both on the local level and in the state. The reverse, of course, is also true, wherein powerful groups on the national level exercise influence on the state and local levels.

## The Relationship Between Levels

If one can assume that power groups, although not completely coordinated in social action, are somewhat loosely tied together by philosophical principles of economic gain, prestige, and the accumulation of additional power, then it can also be assumed that these groups participate in social action geared toward mutual goals. This is not to say that conflict between power groups on different levels and within levels does not occur (Quinney 1970). Conflict often arises within the hierarchy of powerful groups when those at the very top or at a high level institute social policy directed toward their own self-interest, but in doing so negatively impact those groups with somewhat less power. For example, the middle class, which represents a faction within society, has to be dealt with because it, although loosely organized, has power. This is especially true on the local level, where the middle class is often in complete control with regard to internal or local issues. More powerful groups that are external to the local community have to be conscious of the power held by local groups because they depend on the collective support of various local groups to carry out programs and support policies instituted external to local communities. However, local community power groups must perceive a mutual benefit, or at least no immediate negative consequence, for them to cooperate. When these local groups' economic or political gains are curtailed, they move to constrain those at higher levels (state, national, or international).

The largest power group numerically are the poor, but the poor are made up of diverse groups within society who have been labeled negatively. Those who are poor, black, white, Hispanic, Native American, or female face not only racism, ethnic dislike, and sexism, but also a contempt or disdain that usually renders them ineffective. Although the overall goals of these various poor groups might be advantageously perceived as common and mutual, the fact is that each group has defined its goals more narrowly in light of its particular immediate difficulties. Therefore, it has come to believe that any one group's ability to attain its goals is predicated only on other groups' being constrained from goal attainment. For example, racism is such a pervasive factor in the fabric of American society that nonblack groups (even Hispanics and Native Americans) who have similar problems see the attainment of economic and political gains only through the constrainment of blacks, and the converse is also true. Ironically, minority groups with little or no power do not see powerful majority groups as having an impact on their status. Therefore, the poor and powerless often play supporting roles when more powerful groups coalesce to constrain any powerless group. This phenomenon occurs on all levels: local, state, national, and international.

In terms of the social construction of the community, it might be useful to categorize power groups in terms of those that exert internal influence on the community and those that exert external influence. Those from within the local community are the ones who exert internal influence, which can be defined as both informal and formal influence imposed by power groups that results in policy decisions or customs that affect the local community's social construction. External influence, in contrast, results in actions or decisions imposed on the local community from the outside. Public policy set by the federal or state government that directly or indirectly has an impact on the local community in terms of compliance is external influence—for example, affirmative action laws, school integration rulings, fair housing policies, policies covering the administration of justice, coordination of health delivery, and manpower training.

Another type of influence might be a combination of internal and external influences. These combined influences may pose alternatives to action, such as policies wherein compliance is not mandatory, but optional. These policies are set by external agencies, but have to be initiated by the local jurisdiction. Such influences fall under the close scrutiny of local power groups and often result from the interplay between local and external power groups. When a local power group's vested interest is threatened, that group utilizes the mass media to unite other groups of varying power to block the action within the community. However, where local power groups are to receive economic gain, the mass media is again utilized, but this time to sell the idea to the rest of the community. Examples of the latter scenario include policies for model cities, urban renewal, empowerment zones, urban mass transportation, urban highways, employment and training, housing, and community health.

The Housing Act of 1949, with its urban-development section, assisted local business and government leaders to clear the rapidly spreading slums adjacent to central business districts. This external public policy had to be initiated on the local level, therefore qualifying it as both an external influence and an internal influence. Local power groups saw the clearing of urban slums as a mechanism for developing a buffer zone, or cordon sanitaire, between the downtown area and the inner-city slums (Palen 2005, 238).

## Community Versus Black Community

The main focus here is the emergence of a community within a community. Such a focus first has to raise the question: What is a community in the first place? Defining the concept "community" is no easy task. However, certain important dimensions in the idea of "community" can be identified. A community incorporates the dimensions of territoriality, social interaction, interrelationships between institutions, and shared values and interests. Based on these dimensions, the following definition seems appropriate. A community can be looked upon as "a . . . combination of social unity and systems that perform the major social functions having locality relevance" (Warren 1972, 9). However, within societies, such as the American society, diverse groups of people often live in segregated neighborhoods, have special interests that transcend the larger community, participate at least partially in parallel structures, and interact differently among themselves than within the larger community. Such groups have to be looked upon as being a part of their own community as well as a part of the larger community. Such is the status of black Americans within American society. Although blacks have made enormous gains in making the larger society accessible to themselves, it is readily apparent that throughout American society, in varying degrees, black communities exist within nonblack larger communities. Although black-constructed communities arose both as a response to and as a defense against racism, they have continued their existence as an important aspect of black life in America. In some cases, blacks are able to cope with the problems of discrimination, racism, and social isolation only through membership in the black community, which acts as a buffer that keeps them from being destroyed by their situation within the larger community and society. The black community provides blacks with social support that oftentimes obviates feelings of alienation (Kramer 1970, 39).

The black community does not embrace the dimension of "territoriality" basic to the concept of community in general. In order for a black community to exist, blacks do not have to reside in racial ghettoes; or, stated differently, blacks who live in integrated areas are not excluded from membership in the black community. However, the black community is looked upon as a subset of the community of which it is a part. "People are brought together in community because they happen to share common interests and values. They have accepted sets of definitions of situations, life experiences, or other conditions that give them uniqueness apart from others whose views, values, and experiences are dissimilar. Shared values, in the formation of a community, may supersede geographic boundaries" (Blackwell 1975, 16).

## Emergence of the Black Community

As has been stated in reference to communities in general, the black community did not arise out of some natural progression, but developed from social action on the part of its members and from conscious action on the part of those external to the community itself. The black community originally emerged as a reaction to and a protection against racism. From the inception of slavery until today, "racism," in varying degrees, has been an external force that has had an impact on the black community. "Racism" has been and continues to be a prevailing force that affects social action oriented toward the black community. It thus has been a factor in the social creation of the black community. At the moment that the system of separatism became formalized within American society, the black community emerged. Given that this system of separatism was forced upon blacks, it can be concluded that the black community emerged as a result of social action external to the community itself. The black community was generated as a result of the castelike structure of society. Therefore, as a phenomenon of study it is unique among communities in general. Its development and growth has been influenced by factors external to it as well as by factors from within it. Because black Americans held less power before the civil rights movement, white American groups on all levels (international, national, state, and local) had some influence on the early direction, development, and growth of black communities at these levels.

From a national, state, and local prospective, the philosophy of "separate but equal," which in reality translated into "separate but unequal," provided the societal justification for the formation of a black community. A segregated community for blacks that was supposedly separate but equal tended to lessen the harsh realities of a society engulfed by racism. North, south, east, and west represented sections of America that sometimes differed in degrees of racism, but racism existed in all of them.

Because the doctrine of segregation existed on all levels and was supported by prevailing power groups and maintained even by groups with less power, a brief summary of its impact on the black community is important here. Although many of the formal laws and sanctions that supported segregation no longer exist, they still have some influence on the condition of the black community, just as they gave rise to its existence. From the doctrine of segregation came parallel structures within the black community: the black family, the black school, the black economic institution, the black church, black politics, and a black stratification system. In denying blacks accessibility to institutions in the larger society, segregation forced blacks to establish parallel structures to meet their needs (Blackwell 1975, 6). A multitude of public-policy decisions were concomitantly being made that influenced the shape, development, and growth of the black community. The so-called separate-but-equal education system resulted in hiring inferior teachers at schools with predominantly black populations; in providing black schools with discarded books from white schools; in not providing equipment and materials required for chemistry, business, technology, physics, and other subject areas; in paying black teachers lower salaries; and in using only dilapidated school buildings for blacks. This inferior system of education within the black community helped national, state, and local power groups justify a system of segregation predicated upon racism by producing an inferior product.

The internal colonist perspective, introduced by Robert Blauner (1969), maintains that the black community served as a domestic colony that is economically exploited by white power groups. From that perspective, it is not unreasonable to assume that these power groups would seek to influence social institutions in the black community, such as education, the family, and religion, to the extent that they themselves would support the exploitative economic arrangement. Although not true today, social institutions in the black community before the civil rights movement supported, to some degree, the community's economic exploitation by whites. Education provided support by producing an inferior product; religion by teaching that those who suffer the injustices of this earth will receive their rewards in heaven; and the family by socializing the young to accept segregation. This explanation is not meant to blame the victim—that is, to claim that black Americans consciously and graciously supported segregation—but to state that blacks, given the structural constraints placed on them, perceived that their only alternative was to accept or to adapt to the prevailing conditions.

As mentioned earlier, public policy instituted on a national, state, and local level helped maintain a segregated black community as well as the status and condition of its physical and social being. Housing discrimination and the practice of redlining derived from the federal government had a major impact on housing conditions for the black community.[3] Federal and local policies provided the historical bases for housing conditions and inequities that can be seen today (see Blackwell 1975, 151). The redistricting of voters, or "gerrymandering," that was supported on all levels of government helped dilute the black vote. Gerrymandering, the grandfather clause, white primaries, the poll tax, and literacy tests virtually disfranchised blacks in the South (Blackwell 1975, 194–95).

As a result of the civil rights movement, most of these policies no longer exist, but they still have an influence on the black community today. Redlining is no longer legal, but it has given rise to disinvestment.[4] Insurance companies often refuse to provide insurance in black low-income areas, or they provide less coverage for exorbitant fees. Segregated schools have been outlawed, but inner-city schools remain less funded and black, whereas suburban schools are better funded and white (Macionis and Parrillo 2004, 354). Although affirmative action has helped eradicate some of the inequalities that exist for members of the black community, unequal salaries still exist, inaccessibility to high-status jobs remain, and the unemployment rate for black Americans is approximately twice that for white Americans. These inequalities have a major impact on the black community and do much to define the status of black Americans. Without the black community, many black Americans both

3. Redlining is the practice of designating an area unfit or "high risk" for home loans and mortgages.

4. Disinvestment means the withdrawal of investments, both loans and reinvestments, from an area or neighborhood, allowing the physical structures (homes, apartments, and buildings in general) to deteriorate.

inside and outside black ghettoes would be unable to cope with racism and the continuing inequalities that result from it.

## Social Reality of the Black Community

It is of vital importance that social scientists, policymakers, businesspersons, educators, and others study the black community extensively. However, before they can glean an understanding of the dynamics operating within the black community, they need a good understanding of those forces that effected its emergence and of those forces that continue to influence its structure and composition. We attempt here to provide a framework that explains why the black community arose and, once it arose, what factors influenced its dynamic state. This framework is predicated on the assumptions that the black community is a social creation and that its growth and development have resulted from social action on the part of external groups as well as of internal groups. The civil rights movement and other political and economic actions assisted the black community in its growth and development. But external groups on the international, national, state, and local levels have exerted an equal influence. Public policy, private business, and economic decisions have had continuing influence on the growth and development of the black community. Public policies made by power groups on all levels have been supported by individuals and groups external to the black community, but with little or no power.

As noted earlier, although blacks and other groups with little or no power have common interests and goals, they define them differently and in such a way that the goal seeking of one powerless group is perceived as counterproductive to the goal seeking of other powerless groups. Therefore, powerless groups tend to join with those in power to constrain other powerless groups in their attempts at goal attainment. Power groups control the mass media and so are able to influence the definitions internalized by groups of less power. Through the mass media, power groups have been able to defend policies that have directly or indirectly affected the black community and to constrain the black community when conflict arises that is viewed as not in the best interest of the power groups. Social action on the part of power groups on all levels has thus had direct and indirect influence on the emergence, development, and growth of the black community.

Utilizing the framework just summarized provides much needed insight into the dynamics of black community life. This framework is needed because of the paucity of data available on the emergence, development, and contemporary status of black communities. It (1) investigates the dynamics involved in the emergence of a black community, (2) reviews the role played by external factors (power groups and national, state, and local governments) in the black community's emergence, (3) identifies factors within the local white community that led to the present status of the black community within the overall scheme of community life, (4) points out factors within the black community that lent themselves to the present state of affairs, (5) compares the black and white communities on selected issues, and (6) provides a descriptive analysis of the black community in the 1980s. It seeks to keep in mind that the emergence of a black community does not represent a universal phenomenon. One can safely assume that different black communities have varied greatly in the influence they have had on themselves. This perspective, however, should provide a framework that will allow for the analysis of the emergence, development, and growth of diverse communities. In addition, this perspective allows for explanations of differentiation in power and influence.

Syracuse as a research site to study the black community provides an excellent opportunity in that a significant population growth within the black community there is relatively recent, occurring only within the past few decades. Also, a most important segment of the black community politically and economically—the black middle class—is an even more recent arrival to Syracuse and its suburban areas. These factors make for a more accessible analysis of the interaction between black and white communities since the black community became a social reality in Syracuse.

## Demographic Characteristics of Syracuse

Syracuse is located in the central region of New York State. It lies about midway between Binghamton to the south and the Canadian border on the north, along Interstate 81, and approximately midway between Albany, the state capital, to the east and Buffalo, along Interstate 90 to the west. Located at the intersection of two major arterials, Syracuse is easily accessible and heavily trafficked, except for during the rather long snow season. Snow has a major impact on the lives of Syracuse residents, for the snow season can range from November through the end of April.

The Syracuse standard metropolitan area (SMA) includes 3,083 square miles; covers four counties (Cayuga, Madison, Onondaga, and Oswego); and serves as the business, educational, recreational, and cultural hub for its residents. The 2000 population figure for the SMA was 732,117, up from the 1990 figure of 659,864. Population density for the SMA was 278 persons per square mile. More than 71 percent of the SMA population was classified as urban and only 5.9 percent as black (U.S. Department of Commerce 2000).

Syracuse is located in Onondaga County, which has 780.3 square miles. Onondaga County had a population of 458,336 in the year 2000, a slight decrease over the 1990 population of 468,973. The county population was 9.4 percent black in 2000, up from 8 percent in 1990.

Syracuse itself occupies 25.1 square miles, with a 2000 population of 147,306, less than the 163,860 figure in 1990. Although 71 percent of the Syracuse SMA population is classified as urban, these individuals are basically located in urban pockets scattered throughout the area. Needless to say, Syracuse makes up one of the largest pockets. By comparing the population density of Syracuse, 6,528 persons per square mile, with that of the SMA, 278 per square mile, it can be seen that the city represents the largest urban pocket (U.S. Department of Commerce 2000). As is true for most urban central cities within the United States, there has been a steady decrease in the Syracuse population over the past four decades. In 1920, Syracuse had a population of 210,000 and reached its peak population of 221,000 in 1950. By 1960, the population had decreased by 2.2 percent to 216,038. Between 1960 and 1970, it decreased even further to 197,243, or by 8.7 percent (Sacks and Andrew 1974, 3), and between 1970 and 2000 by another 49,937, or 25.3 percent. Other population characteristics for 2000 reveal that Syracuse had 52.9 percent females; 47.6 percent males; 62.4 percent whites; 23.3 percent blacks; 5.3 percent Hispanics; 2.2 percent American Indians, Eskimos, and Aleutians; and 6.8 percent "others."

Table 1.1 shows that blacks constituted the largest racial minority in Syracuse, the county, and the SMA in 2000. It is also apparent that the largest concentration of blacks was in the city proper. Blacks living outside of the core city, within the SMA and mostly in suburban areas, were made up largely of those holding professional or white-collar positions. Clay, Salina, Manlius, and other smaller incorporated towns were all part of a contiguous string of towns that made up the suburban area.

It should be noted that although the population of Syracuse in general has declined since 1950, the population of the black community has increased. From 1950 to 1960, it increased by 144.4 percent, and between 1960 and 1970 by 90.7 percent (Sacks and Andrew 1974, 20). The percentage increase in the black community between 1970 and 1980 was 21.5 percent, between 1980 and 1990 was slightly higher at 26 percent, and between 1990 and 2000 was 11 percent (from U.S. Bureau of Census 1970, 1980, 1990, and 2000). Although the latter was a drastic decrease from the near record increases in the black population over the previous three decades, it points out that the decline in Syracuse's overall population was because of shifts in the white population. The black population, as a percentage of the overall Syracuse population, rose from 20.3 percent in 1990 to 25.4 percent in 2000. This increase was owing, in part, to the increase in black migration to Syracuse. However, the major factor contributing to the percentage increase was the movement of whites out of the city into suburban and outersuburban communities. As with other U.S. cities, intrametropolitan shifting has resulted in an exodus of relatively young, middle-income, white families from core cities to suburban areas (Sacks and Andrew 1974, 24). In Syracuse, relatively young, middle-income blacks migrating to the city also took up residence in suburban communities. Table 1.1 indicates that blacks were present in small towns surrounding Syracuse in Onondaga County. The end result was that, over time, relatively affluent and young families were increasingly populating the suburban communities around Syracuse. Although these families were overwhelmingly white in numbers, there was strong evidence that blacks were also becoming a part of suburban community life in increasing numbers. The big difference in Syracuse was that white movement into suburbia was owing primarily to intrametropolitan shifting, whereas black movement was owing primarily to in-migration.

Studies have shown that the migration of blacks to Syracuse in the twentieth century was primarily from the South (Sacks and Andrew 1974; Stamps 1982). Sacks and Andrew point out that for the last half of the 1960s, black

**Table 1.1**
**Syracuse Standard Metropolitan Area (SMA): Population by Race for 2000**

| SMA, County, and Cities | | Total Population | Black | American Indian & Eskimo Aleut. | Asian & Pacific Islander | Spanish Origin | Other |
|---|---|---|---|---|---|---|---|
| Syracuse SMA | (N) | 732,117 | 47,916 | 5,057 | 11,006 | 15,112 | 5,560 |
| | (%) | 100.00 | 5.9 | 0.60 | 1.2 | 1.4 | 0.5 |
| Onondaga County | (N) | 458,336 | 43,011 | 3,945 | 9,569 | 11,175 | 4,076 |
| | (%) | 100.00 | 0.8 | 0.70 | 1.5 | 1.5 | 0.6 |
| Syracuse | (N) | 147,306 | 37,336 | 1,670 | 4,961 | 7,768 | 3,284 |
| | (%) | 100.00 | 25.4 | 1.10 | 3.4 | 5.3 | 2.2 |
| Clay | (N) | 58,805 | 2,060 | 279 | 1,196 | 816 | 224 |
| | (%) | 100.00 | 3.5 | .05 | 2.0 | 1.4 | 0.4 |
| Salina | (N) | 33,290 | 718 | 173 | 546 | 466 | 136 |
| | (%) | 100.00 | 2.2 | 0.50 | 1.6 | 1.4 | 0.4 |
| Manlius | (N) | 31,872 | 277 | 75 | 941 | 310 | 55 |
| | (%) | 100.00 | 0.9 | 0.20 | 2.9 | 1.0 | 0.2 |
| Cicero | (N) | 27,982 | 333 | 107 | 205 | 245 | 61 |
| | (%) | 100.00 | 1.2 | 0.50 | 0.7 | 0.9 | 0.2 |
| DeWitt | (N) | 24,071 | 1,177 | 135 | 724 | 324 | 63 |
| | (%) | 100.00 | 4.9 | 0.60 | 3.0 | 1.3 | 0.2 |

*Sources:* "Current Geography Selection" 2004; for Clay, Salina, Manlius, Cicero, and DeWitt, we used U.S. Bureau of the Census 2000.

migration from the South to Syracuse was comparably higher than for most other U.S. cities (1974, 19). However, a closer scrutiny of migration trends indicates that these conclusions were based primarily on "birthplace" as an indicator of origin. Using place of birth when looking at "current" migration patterns can provide misleading results in a highly mobile society, especially a society in which place of residence is dictated by job opportunities or career patterns that cause people to move often during a lifetime. Within the five years prior to 1981, approximately 8 percent of blacks in a random sample drawn from the Syracuse community had migrated there from out of New York State (Stamps 1982, 35–36). It is reasonable to assume that many of these blacks migrated from states other than the South, in particular middle-class blacks who were recent migrants to Syracuse. These families moved to Syracuse as a result of being transferred by their employers. This is not to say they were not originally from the South, but before moving to Syracuse, they had lived somewhere other than the South. The importance of this observation is that many new blacks arriving in Syracuse could no longer be characterized as poor, uneducated, or from rural backgrounds, as were the earlier black arrivals. These migrants tended to be college graduates, some with advanced degrees, who assumed professional or white-collar positions. Although many were born in the South, they were educated at northern or southern colleges and universities, and upon graduation took jobs in education, social services, industry, the medical profession, and government outside of their region of birth (Stamps 1982).

Syracuse was basically a blue-collar community up through the 1970s, with a significant number of corporate executives and midlevel managers who, along with other professionals from the public and private sectors, made up the white-collar strata. Syracuse's blue-collar stratum is represented by a mosaic of white ethnic communities made up of Irish, Italian, German, and Polish second- and third-generation immigrants.[5]

Blue-collar ethnic neighborhoods were spread throughout the northern part of Syracuse. These neighborhoods provided ethnic clubs, food, entertainment and recreation, churches, and funeral homes. Workers from these

---

5. For a discussion of white ethnics, see Thomas Sowell's *Ethnic America* (1981).

neighborhoods traditionally commuted to the northern suburban industrial section to work at such major industries as Crouse Hinds, General Electric, Chrysler's New Process Gear, General Motors, and many lesser-known or local industries until the late 1960s, when Syracuse and other northern and midwestern cities began to lose private-sector (manufacturing) jobs (see Staley 2003).

White-collar and professional groups were derived from corporate executives employed by industries just mentioned, the university and college communities; the large medical complex; city, county, state, and federal offices; and the business community. Although many of these individuals and their families resided in suburban towns, they were also found in residential pockets within Syracuse itself. Individuals from the city's three institutions of higher education and the medical school largely inhabited the eastern section of the city. White-collar and professional blacks, who lived within Syracuse itself, resided almost exclusively on the eastern side of town. Lower-class and working-class blacks, as a group, lived within the city limits of Syracuse and were integrated with poor whites in a large area that extended from the eastern perimeter of the downtown section throughout the south side of the city.

Although Syracuse has been traditionally characterized as a blue-collar community, its black community was, until recent years, represented in blue-collar jobs to a lesser degree than was the city as a whole. Blue-collar skilled jobs have always been difficult for blacks to obtain. Of course, lack of education and competitive skills were an inhibiting factor for the largely rural southern migrants, but discrimination in job opportunities played an important role as white ethnics gained controls of unions. Because the educational and occupational status of a significant proportion of the black community had traditionally been low, the white power structure often disregarded it as a political and economical resource. The fact that the educational and occupational status structure within the black community expanded during the 1970s and 1980s, as white-collar and professional blacks migrated to Syracuse, went virtually unnoticed by the white community. One statement white administrators often made when asked about attracting blacks to Syracuse to fill professional positions was, "It is next to impossible to attract good, qualified blacks because there is not a critical mass of black professionals in place within the city; therefore, social contacts that are so important in the recruitment of blacks are lacking." Although this statement is not entirely true, it does shed light on white outsiders' perceptions of the socioeconomic status structure within the black community.

As Hyland Lewis (1955) observed five decades ago and E. Elaine Burgess (1960) a little more than four decades ago, when investigating the relationship between the black and white communities in a southern city, the black community serves as a subset of the larger community. In addition, the black community can be looked on as a separate community with its own structure and behavior patterns. Although the Syracuse black community cannot be characterized as a separate community to the degree that Lewis and Burgess characterized the black community in the "Crescent City," it is often perceived as a somewhat separate entity by outsiders as well as by its own members. This brief overview of Syracuse and its black community is provided so the reader can glean some preliminary insights into the area of study. We present a more detailed and systematic analysis in subsequent chapters.

## The Investigation

William B. Sanders, in *The Sociologist as Detective: An Introduction to Research Methods* (1976), makes the following statement: "We should not confine ourselves to a single method in doing research. Both quantitative and qualitative methodologies can be used in a single project, and one can employ experimental, survey, ethnographic, and content analysis methods in one piece of research. . . . If we want to have the strongest possible validity, we should not limit ourselves to a single methodology" (x).

In keeping with Sanders's assertion, our investigation utilized a variety of methodological techniques and many different sources. We collected data through other studies, newspapers, archives, theses, government documents, interviews, oral histories, observation, and surveys. Data derived from all sources other than surveys are integrated throughout the monograph and are not discussed in detail. Other than U.S. census reports, survey data presented in this monograph were derived primarily from an Urban League survey conducted in 1981.

The purpose of the survey was to determine the attitudes and behavior patterns of a representative sample of 750 households. Data from this study were originally published in a report entitled *Urban League Community Survey 1982* (Stamps 1982). Census data from 1970 (1980 data were not available at the time the survey was conducted) indicated that 80 percent of Syracuse's black population was located in twelve census tracts in the southwest and southeast quadrants (U.S. Bureau of the Census 1970/1980). Within those census tracts, blacks made up from 25 to 75 percent of the population. These twelve tracts were labeled as integrated tracts for the Urban League survey. Although there were all-white census tracts in Syracuse at this time, there were no all-black census tracts. However, economic ghettoes existed throughout the city, with middle-income blacks residing in predominantly white middle-income and upper-income areas and with lower-income blacks residing in predominantly white lower-income areas or in predominantly black lower-income areas. A two-stage random-sampling procedure was used. Of the twelve integrated census tracts, a random sample of six census tracts was selected during the first stage. Of the six census tracts selected, four were lower income and two were middle income and upper income. Utilizing the 1979 city directory, we constructed a sampling frame from those six census tracts to be used in the second stage. From this sampling frame, a random sample of 750 households was selected that reflected the population proportion for each of the six census tracts. In addition, an alternate sample of households was drawn so that when an interview was not obtained from the primary sample, a corresponding household could be randomly selected from the alternate sample.

A total of twenty-six trained student interviewers were used to collect the data from the 750 households. Each interviewer was instructed to interview the head of the household or, if the head was not available, to interview the spouse. If after the second visit the head or spouse was still not available, an adult member of the household was interviewed, if present. If an adult member was not present or refused to be interviewed, a household from the alternative sample was selected.

An interview schedule consisting of 111 questions was utilized. These questions focused on background data, opinions on the general situation in the United States, housing, organization membership, types of credit, types of savings, employment, education, leisure activities, newspapers and magazines read, consumer behavior, and general attitudes.

Some interesting insights emerged from the data-collection phase that should be mentioned here. Before the start of the interviewing phase, it had been anticipated that obtaining interviews would be most difficult in the middle-income and upper-income census tracts. The assumption was made that these residents would be too busy and less interested in participating in such a survey because of their income status. In actuality, this was not the case. The interviews in these tracts went relatively smoothly and quickly. The major difficulties encountered in collecting data occurred in lower-income census tracts, where the research team had originally assumed that the residents would have a vested interest in being interviewed. In these census tracts, interviewers were often refused interviews. Residents denied young black male interviewers access to their homes because of a fear of being victimized, especially by households where elderly residents lived. White interviewers were also refused interviews in some cases because the residents, mostly black, feared they represented some agency or administrative power that would use the information against them. Only in the case of Asian ethnicity interviewers did neither of these two fears manifest themselves. It seems as if the Asian interviewers were not perceived as a threat: either as a potential robber or mugger or as a representative of the power structure. During the spring and summer months, residents overcame their fear of being victimized by allowing themselves to be interviewed on their front porches or in their front yards. Although this study did not look at victimization, these observations provide an indirect measure of the problem.

# 2

# The Black Community
# in Syracuse

*Origins and Early History*

MELVIN HERSKOVITS, in the preface to the second edition of his monograph *The Myth of the Negro Past* (1958), states that although numerous studies in the black community were completed during the seventeen-year span between the first edition and the second, a statement given in the original edition remained as valid in 1958 as in 1941. "In this country, the greatest need is for research in Negro communities wherein the life will be studied in all its phases and with all regard for the implications of those traditional values that . . . may be considered in light of similarities in the African background" (xx).

Herskovits further makes the point that researchers on the black community have by and large ignored the sociohistorical context within which current attitudes and behaviors lie. Our study, coming fifty years after the 1958 edition of Herskovits's monograph, also sees no need to alter his statement. True, several memorable studies have been done during the interim; however, they have not developed a sociohistorical base for the analysis of current phenomena. That is, to understand fully the social processes that are taking place within the black community today, it is necessary to look at them within their sociohistorical context. Such a treatise will provide an invaluable foundation for better understanding the social processes at work today within the black community of Syracuse.

This community can be said to have gone through five somewhat distinct eras from its inception until the 1980s, which we label the periods of defiance (1796–1870), exploitation (1870–1910), segregation (1910–60), protest

25

(1960–75), and diminishing expectations (1975 through the 1980s). This chapter provides an analysis of the first three periods in order to determine how internal and external factors impacted social conditions that influenced the emergence, development, and growth of the Syracuse black community. The protest period is covered in chapters 3 and 4, and the remainder of the book is devoted to the period of diminishing expectations. It should be kept in mind that internal factors include social actions on the part of groups within the black community itself that have had an effect on its growth and development. External factors consist of social actions taken by groups outside of the community (local, state, national, and international) that have had a direct or indirect effect on the community.

## Period of Defiance, 1796–1870

This period, which extends throughout most of the 1800s, might be labeled the "period of contradiction" as well.[1] It was contradictory in that it began with the arrival of slaves owned by Syracuse residents and ended with local participation in the Underground Railroad and support for the abolition of slavery. During this period, major confrontations took place between abolitionists and supporters of slavery.

One of the major factors that probably had an effect on how blacks were treated in Syracuse during the defiance period and that served to support slavery was the English Poor Laws. Robert Bogdan (1971) points out that the early settlers in Onondaga County were primarily from England. Hence, their attitudes and ways of handling the poor can be traced directly to the Poor Laws. This system of dealing with the poor held that those who were "needy" were the responsibility of someone else. In Onondaga County, the justice of the peace or the poormaster was given the responsibility of administering funds provided for the relief of the poor.

Important to understanding how this system of handling the poor supported the pro-slavery movement in Syracuse was the value system of early English setters in the county and city. This value system, reflected in how

1. For a more detailed account of this period, see Barbara S. Davis, *A History of the Black Community of Syracuse* (1980).

they provided for the poor, emphasized frugality and a strong work ethic, with humanitarianism running a distant third. The very poor were sold at public auction to the highest bidder once every year. Interestingly, the highest bid represented not the highest price one was willing to pay for a poor person, but what the justice of the peace or poormaster was willing to pay the bidder to clothe, feed, and house the poor person for a year. These auctions were popular both for the bidders and the county. Bidders received money from the county to care for individuals who were required to work for them. The county had found the cheapest way of caring for the poor, and the fear and humiliation associated with being auctioned off deterred all but the most destitute from applying for public assistance (Bogdan 1971). It can readily be seen that such a system devised for "poor whites" in Syracuse served also to justify the system of slavery that existed within the area.

The first two blacks recorded as residing in Syracuse were runaway slaves. Their names are unknown, but it was reported that state senator Silas Bowker saw them mining salt in 1774. However, this incident was recorded as a historical note on a state petition in 1823 as an estimate for improving navigation on the Oswego River so salt could be better distributed ("Early Black Settlers" 1982, B5). Before the involvement of whites in the manufacture of salt, these two black runaway slaves were the only makers of salt in the area. Although Syracuse later became a major supplier of salt for the region, it was ironic that the only market for the salt processed by the two blacks was the neighboring Native American community (B. Davis 1980, 5).

Isaac "Uncle Ike" Wales was one of the first free black persons in Syracuse. Born in Maryland as a slave, Wales came to Syracuse as the property of John Fleming in 1810. He became a friend of Fleming and bought his way out of slavery for $80 before New York State freed all slaves in 1827. During the fifty-five years that Wales lived in Syracuse, he married, purchased a home, and ran a sewerage business. Later, it was reported in the local *Daily Standard* newspaper that Wales saved Fleming, his former slave owner, from death as a "street alcoholic" ("Early Black Settlers" 1982, B5). This account shows that although slavery did exist in Syracuse, blacks could reside as free persons and own property. However, the number of blacks in Syracuse at this time was small and consisted almost exclusively of slaves purchased by local residents to carry out domestic functions and hard labor (Darby 1937, 7).

Accurate counts of the number of blacks in Syracuse were not available until 1810. Table 2.1 reveals that by 1830 all slaves in Syracuse had been freed as decreed by New York State. Included among the free blacks were runaway slaves who had taken up permanent residence in the city. Table 2.1 also shows the steady increase in the number of blacks within the population throughout these three decades. Of course, the outlawing of slavery by New York State had an impact on the black population of Syracuse. Between 1827, when slavery was outlawed, and 1840, the black population increased from 176 to 234.

By 1830, Syracuse had become recognized as a national center for the abolition of slavery. Between 1845 and 1850, abolitionists in Syracuse held twelve major conventions and twenty-five smaller meetings. More than three hundred slaves reportedly passed through the city because it served as a northern terminus of the Underground Railroad, which transported slaves from the South into Canada ("Early Black Settlers" 1982, B5).

Although Syracuse was recognized as being antislavery, pro-slavery sentiments abounded in a rather vocal portion of the community. Gerrit Smith, a leading abolitionist, was verbally harassed and underwent the indignity of being pelted with eggs in 1831 when he attempted to hold an antislavery meeting. The pro-slavery sentiment was so strong that the meeting had to be moved to neighboring Fayetteville, New York. As abolitionists stepped up their efforts within New York State and in the Syracuse area, confrontations spread to churches, with abolitionists splitting off from antiabolitionist-dominated churches to form their own congregations (B. Davis 1980, 5).

**Table 2.1**

**Number of Blacks in Syracuse, 1810–1840**

| Year | Total | Black Free | Black Slave | % of Total |
| --- | --- | --- | --- | --- |
| 1810 | 1,299 | 5 | 2 | 0.5 |
| 1820 | 2,284 | 15 | 4 | 0.8 |
| 1830 | 6,924 | 176 | 0 | 2.5 |
| 1840 | 4,012 | 234 | 0 | 5.8 |

*Source:* Adapted from B. Davis 1980, 5.

The first of two major events that forced Syracuse to face the issue of slavery head on was the freeing of Harriet Powell from her Mississippi slaveholders during their visit to the local community and the now famous "Jerry Rescue." Harriet Powell was rescued and concealed in a nearby village until she was led into Canada via the Underground Railroad. Public sentiment against slavery had shifted significantly by 1842, so that county and state

2.1. Jerry Rescue monument, Clinton Square, Syracuse, 2007. Photograph by Paul Malo.

antislavery conventions could again be held in Syracuse (B. Davis 1980). The emergence of public sentiment favorable to the abolition movement was short-lived, however. Although New York State had passed a law abolishing slavery in 1827, the Compromise of 1850 had a tremendous impact on black fugitive slaves living in Syracuse. Congress, in an effort to appease southern states, passed the Fugitive Slave Law as a part of the Compromise of 1850. Before this point, slave owners experienced extreme difficulty in reclaiming runaway slaves because the Supreme Court, in the 1842 case *Prigg v. Pennsylvania*, had ruled that state government officials could not be compelled to assist in their recovery (Franklin 1980, 200). The Fugitive Slave Law passed by Congress, an entity external to the local community, thus had a major impact on fugitive slaves living as free persons in Syracuse.

This legal change led to the second major confrontation between pro- and antislavery factions in Syracuse, the Jerry Rescue. Slaveholders quickly launched massive manhunts to recover those fugitive slaves that had been living as free persons (Franklin 1980, 200). One such individual was Jerry Henry, a runaway slave from Missouri. Henry allowed himself to be arrested without incident under the impression that he was being arrested for a theft he knew he did not commit. Once arrested, however, he was informed that he had really been arrested under the Fugitive Slave Law (B. Davis 1980, 10). His arrest soon came to the attention of the Anti-Slavery Society. Along with members of the Liberal Party who were meeting in Syracuse, the society rescued Jerry Henry and secured his passage to Kingston, Ontario (B. Davis 1980, 10–11; Franklin 1980, 200). Although Syracuse made history in its repudiation of the Fugitive Slave Law, the abolition issue remained in debate until the system of slavery was abolished at the end of the Civil War in 1870. By that time, it could be said that the black community of Syracuse had emerged as a relatively stable community of 435 individuals (Brown 1943, 11).

## Period of Exploitation, 1870–1910

If the period of defiance was fraught with contradictions, as local abolitionists confronted local antiabolitionists and defied federal slave laws, the period of exploitation was straightforward in its attitudes toward and treatment of the black community, which was neither fair nor equal following the Civil War and passage of the Emancipation Proclamation. As was true in many other sections of the country, the freed slaves were often misused and exploited. During this period, new norms emerged that stipulated the conditions for white-black relationships. Many local whites, in particular the working class, viewed blacks as an economic threat. This attitude was coupled with whites' abandonment of the felt need to ensure that black rights were protected. Thus, blacks were faced with ill-treatment in most facets of their daily life. Yet the black population in Syracuse almost doubled right after the Civil War. However, the black community's percentage of the total city population slowly declined from a high of 5.8 percent in 1840 (see table 2.1) to a low of 0.8 percent in 1910 (see table 2.2). The increase in the black community in the first part of this period was owing to the return of many black families from Canada to the United States and to their settling in Syracuse rather than going back to the South. Another reason for the increase was black southerners' movement north to find work (B. Davis 1980, 14). Contractors brought black workers in from Virginia and North Carolina to assist in the construction of a city reservoir. These male workers, finding conditions in Syracuse better than in their native states, sent for their families (Darby 1937, 8). The decrease in the percentage of blacks in the total Syracuse population later in the period was created by the large increase in the number of whites.

**Table 2.2**
**Syracuse Population by Race, 1870–1910**

| Year | Total Population | White | Black | Black % of Total |
|------|------------------|---------|--------|------------------|
| 1870 | 43,051 | 42,616 | 435 | 1.0 |
| 1880 | 51,792 | 51,202 | 590 | 1.1 |
| 1890 | 88,143 | 87,300 | 843 | 1.0 |
| 1900 | 108,374 | 107,340 | 1,034 | 1.0 |
| 1910 | 137,249 | 136,125 | 1,124 | 0.8 |

*Source:* Adapted from Brown 1943, 11.

*Geographic Area*

The Syracuse black community was confined to a relatively small geographical area within the city, located south of the Erie Canal and made up of the Sixth, Seventh, and Eighth Wards. A few blacks lived outside of this area in white neighborhoods, but they were so few in number that the black community can be described as being physically segregated at that time (B. Davis 1980, 14). Even in the early emergence of the community, external influences served to constrain its geographical growth and direction as blacks were restricted in where they could live.

*Employment*

As mentioned earlier, working-class whites viewed blacks as economic threats and hence did much to limit their employment opportunities. By the end of the nineteenth century, employment for blacks was restricted to domestic and casual labor or to low-skilled trades such as whitewashing and cutting and dressing hair (B. Davis 1980, 15). Black men worked as waiters in Syracuse hotels and on the New York Central Railroad. Although de jure discrimination in employment did not exist, de facto discrimination was widespread. It was impossible for black professionals to obtain employment commensurate with their training (B. Davis 1980, 15). In a speech delivered in 1903, William H. Johnson, the first black man to graduate from Syracuse University College of Law, made a statement that epitomizes the general feeling of black professionals at that time: "It seems strange that there are not more of the [black] students taking up the legal professions and especially when what few have done so rank among the best and ablest lawyers in the country. Strange, yes, very strange, that the majority of the colored lawyers start for the [W]est and [S]outh. Why is it? Tell me, fellow members, is it because there is race prejudice in this state?" (quoted in B. Davis 1980, 15).

It was also impossible for professional blacks to secure office space in the downtown area. White building owners felt that blacks, even though professional, would not be acceptable to their white tenants (B. Davis 1980, 15–16). Blacks were thus restricted not only in the types of work they could perform and where they could live, but also in the areas of the city in which they could locate their own businesses.

## Education

Syracuse's public-school system was open to all regardless of race. The minister of Bethany Baptist Church, one of the leading black churches at that time, emphasized the role of education in gaining quality and equality. As a result of this emphasis, the black community regarded education highly. Daily attendance rates for black children (87.9 percent) were higher than those for white children (83.3 percent) in the lower-level grades. However, by high school, attendance for black students dropped significantly. No black students from the community attended Syracuse University during this time period (B. Davis 1980, 17). Although education was recognized and emphasized as a positive factor within the community, local white power groups' blockage of employment opportunities for blacks made education a fruitless endeavor. Young blacks, recognizing that the opportunity structure was closed for blacks with an education, saw no advantage in continuing school beyond the elementary level.

## Stratification and Social Life

Although there were few blacks in the city as a whole, the black community recognized the existence of a social class structure within itself for the first time during this era. A three-class structure consisted of the homeowners, the poor but respectable, and the "undesirables." The homeowners, at the top of the stratification system, were made up of blacks who worked for wealthy families, local hotels, and the New York Central Railroad. They owned relatively nice homes, stressed education and child rearing, and maintained respectable lives. The middle group, the poor but respectable, lacked education and did domestic work in the homes of white families of lower status. This group also maintained families, but were renters rather than homeowners. The criteria separating these two classes were ownership of property and the status of the family of employment. This form of conferred status from white families to black families was recognized as a symbol of prestige within the black community in some northern communities and throughout much of the South until the late 1950s. Lowest on the status hierarchy, the "undesirables" were the unemployed and those associated with illegitimate activities, such as prostitutes, pimps, gamblers, the homeless, and like kind (Schuyler 1967, 24–25).

To understand fully the social life in the black community, one has to appreciate Syracuse's central location in upstate New York and the influence of the Erie Canal and the railroad on the local environment. As urbanization moved inland, first by way of the canal system and later through a system of railroads, it had a tremendous impact on the movement of people and goods. Immigrant groups (Irish, German, Jewish, Italian, and Polish) moved along the canals and the railroads to the inland cities of Albany, Syracuse, and Buffalo in upstate New York (Palen 2005, 56–57). With this influx of new arrivals, Syracuse became a wide-open city, one in which vice prospered. As the city became wide open, so did the black community (Schuyler 1967). Not only did the undesirable class expand, but it provided a certain dimension to the social life of both the local population and the large transient population.

Employment groups established social clubs, such as the Hotel Burns Waiters Club; the WLTL Club, made up of waiters from the Globe Hotel; the Lodge of Colored Free Masons; the Colored Odd Fellows; the Colored Young Men's Social Club; and the Colored Knights of Pythias. These clubs provided many of the more desirable social activities (B. Davis 1980, 16). Barbara Davis states that "cakewalks" were popular and drew large crowds of both blacks and whites (1980, 16). Other kinds of social activities included balls, picnics, receptions, house parties, and socials, many of which were held at the St. Marks, a black hotel established in 1899 (B. Davis 1980, 15), and were geared toward both local and transient blacks.

*Political Activity*

As one would expect during an era labeled as exploitative, the Syracuse black community was virtually powerless politically. This state of affairs existed despite the strong support for black suffrage that emanated from the city. Passage of the Fifteenth Amendment in 1870 was reason for celebration (B.

Davis 1980, 12). However, there seems to have been a distinction between civil rights on a national level and how Syracuse itself viewed the rights of its local black citizens. Of course, it should be remembered that Syracuse had received national acclaim for its antislavery activities and therefore had a national reputation to maintain. Unfortunately, this reputation had little effect on local political activity. Local blacks were extremely weak politically throughout this period. Despite this relative powerlessness, however, they were vocal and active in several political organizations. The Colored Democrats, the Colored Republicans, and the Colored Citizens League made up the three most visible black political organizations in Syracuse (B. Davis 1980, 17). Following the Civil War, Syracuse blacks, along with blacks throughout the nation, basically voted Republican (Lincoln's party).

During this era, discrimination and segregation were widespread. Organizations such as the Colored Citizens League and the Touissant L'Ouverture Protective League led the fight for greater equality. Despite little power, they made some gains for the community, such as black delegates to the New York State Republican Convention, the first black inspector of elections in New York State, the first black juror in the city in the 1880s, and a black postman (Syracuse was the second city in the nation to hire one) (B. Davis 1980, 17). Appealing to the white power structure made these gains possible, for, in reality, the black vote, although sought, was not large enough to make white politicians cater to blacks. Although ethnic communities could call on the "boss" of the local political machine for favors and other needs, the black community was without channels to public policymakers (see Palen 2005, 62–68, for a discussion of the "political boss" system). Its lone avenue for change was to make vocal pronouncements through local black political and social organizations.

*Religion*

Three black churches dominated this era: the People's African Methodist Episcopal (AME) Zion, Bethany Baptist, and St. Philips Episcopal. When free and runaway slaves first came to Syracuse, they attended white churches. However, as the black population increased, blacks felt a need for their own church. With the assistance of whites, the People's AME Zion Church was established in 1848, becoming the first black church in the city. As the number of black Baptists increased in the community, a second church with a Baptist affiliation was established in 1887 (Brown 1943, 175). The Union Baptist Church later became known by its present name, Bethany Baptist Church (B. Davis 1980, 16). Families from both AME Zion and Bethany Baptist churches were instrumental in organizing St. Philips Episcopal Church in 1897 (Brown 1943, 175).

Along with employment, religion played an important role in the black community. Church membership helped to distinguish the three classes because church attendance became a major characteristic of the "poor but respectable" class.

A close analysis of the impact of community churches within this era and in the period of segregation suggest that they played both a functional role and a dysfunctional role. They stressed the need for education and the importance of the family, and they served the traditional role of outlet for the stresses and tensions associated with discrimination and segregation. But they also indoctrinated community members to their subservient status. The pulpit was used as a forum for spelling out the Christian virtues of tolerance for trials and tribulations and for suffering the indignities of discrimination and segregation, emphasizing that one's reward would come in heaven. It was not until the period of protest, with the teachings of Martin Luther King Jr., that some Syracuse black community churches, along with other black churches nationally, recognized the Christian virtue of defiance of un-Christian actions and behavior.

*Race Relations*

Bartie has described racial contact in the period of exploitation as being "semifluid" (1970, 2). Blacks were able to move within the white community because their movement was related to their low-status employment. Because blacks were constricted to low-status employment, their social relationships with whites were in keeping with their status. In other words, blacks were not treated as social equals, but as individuals whose main responsibility was to provide domestic and hard labor. White employers developed paternalistic relationships with their black employees. Through these relationships, whites quite often were very knowledgeable about the black employees' family and community and were thus able to keep close tabs on the black community's activities and mood.

Some contact with whites existed on a level outside of employer-employee relations, primarily among those few blacks who owned homes in white areas. Also, whites often attended black social functions such as cakewalks; however, they did so for the entertainment of observing the behavior of blacks (B. Davis 1980).

*Summary*

Overall, the period of exploitation saw the white power structure's use of the black community both economically and politically. Not only did the economic exploitation keep blacks in low-paying and low-status positions, but its effects on the educational commitment of black youth set the stage for the lack of economic viability within the black community for many years to come. This period also served as a transition between the period of defiance, when fugitive and freed slaves lived side by side with whites and had greater status within the Syracuse community, and the period of segregation, when blacks were virtually cut off from the white community. During this transition period, new definitions of status arose for blacks, and de facto segregation emerged as the social order of the community.

**Period of Segregation, 1910–1960**

As noted, during the exploitation period, a social order was established that virtually rendered a segregated existence for blacks. An identifiable black community that emerged during this period became solidified during the period of segregation. The Syracuse white power structure established informal norms of segregation regarding the community and its residents. In many ways, the de facto segregation of Syracuse, in outcome, was no different from the de jure segregation of the South.

Although the black population steadily increased during the exploitation period, the greater increase in the white population at the same time caused the percentage of blacks in the total Syracuse population to decrease. After

1920, one can discern a small increase that gets larger as one moves toward the end of this era.

Table 2.3 indicates that by 1960, the black population was 5.2 percent of the total population of the city. It further reveals that the black percentage of the total city population in 1960 resulted from a 144.4 percent increase in the overall population from 1950 to 1960. Alan Campbell compares the black population growth pattern in Syracuse with that of the rest of the nation (1964, 3). The black population in Syracuse increased at a slower rate than it did in central cities in the rest of the nation between 1900 and 1920. However, during the decade 1920 to 1930, the Syracuse growth pattern was approximately the same as the rest of the nation. The decade 1930 to 1940 saw the black population growth rate of Syracuse decrease to less than that of the nation, but the decades 1940–50 and 1950–60 revealed overall population percentage increases of 120.3 and 144.4, respectively. The 1940–50 black population increase in Syracuse doubled that of the nation, and the 1950–60 increase almost tripled that of the nation. Certain social factors occurring within the United States, among them the "push-pull" element, can account for these fluctuations of the in-migration of blacks to Syracuse. Push factors were those negative conditions that caused an individual or family to migrate to another geographical area. Pull factors were those positive conditions that attracted individuals or families to a particular geographic area (Schaefer 1988, 31). Both push and pull factors, along with technological advances, influenced the

**Table 2.3**
**Black Population of Syracuse, 1910–1960**

| Year | Blacks | Male | Female | Total Population All Races | % of Population Black |
|------|--------|------|--------|---------------------------|-----------------------|
| 1910 | 1,124 | 579 | 545 | 137,249 | 0.8 |
| 1920 | 1,260 | 677 | 583 | 171,717 | 0.7 |
| 1930 | 1,899 | 987 | 912 | 209,326 | 0.9 |
| 1940 | 2,082 | 997 | 1,035 | 205,967 | 1.0 |
| 1950 | 5,058 | 2,533 | 2,525 | 220,583 | 2.3 |
| 1960 | 11,210 | — | — | 216,038 | 5.2 |

*Sources:* U.S. Bureau of the Census 1910, 1920, 1930, 1940, 1950, and 1960.

out-migration of blacks from the South and the in-migration of blacks into the urban Northeast and Midwest.

World War I heavily influenced the post-1910 migration, and World War II heavily influenced the major migration between 1940 and 1960. Once significant numbers of blacks had migrated to Syracuse, they utilized advances in communication to influence kin and friends to migrate to an area where job opportunities were available. As with the European immigrants before them, Syracuse blacks were able to provide informal systems of support for the new arrivals from the South.

Reports indicate that blacks migrated to Syracuse from many different states, most of which were southern states, including Georgia, Alabama, Florida, Mississippi, Louisiana, South Carolina, North Carolina, Tennessee, Oklahoma, Missouri, West Virginia, Virginia, and Kentucky. Blacks also migrated from Washington, D.C., and from northern and central states such as Minnesota, Kansas, Illinois, Michigan, Ohio, Massachusetts, Pennsylvania, and New Jersey (Brown 1943, 24).

European immigrant labor was curtailed during World War I, creating a need for additional human resources in northern industries. Labor recruiters from the North advanced on the South to entice black workers to the "promised land" and even provided one-way tickets north for many of these black workers (Palen 2005, 184). Based on Brown's 1943 random sample of residents in Syracuse, it is estimated that slightly more than 63 percent of the black population had been born in the South, the majority in North and South Carolina. The preponderance of those who migrated to Syracuse had either been born in or lived in urban areas. However, Syracuse did receive a significant number of rural blacks, in particular migrant agricultural workers who made up the northeastern migrant stream during the harvest season and then remained in Syracuse. The farm laborer migration system was a typical form of migration for the upstate New York cities Rochester, Buffalo, and Albany, as well as for many smaller northern urban areas.

*Geographic Area*

By this period in time, the black community was restricted to two census tracts within Syracuse: the Ninth Ward, or "Washington-Water Strip," as the poorer area was referred to, and the Fifteenth Ward, known at that time as "Jewtown." The Washington-Water Strip was made up of nine blocks, with most of the black population concentrated within a five-block radius (Darby 1937, 9). It was into this area that the migrant farm laborers moved. They closely fit E. Franklin Frazier's (1939) characterization of the southern rural black migrant. Frazier saw urbanization as exacerbating family disintegration and disorganization of rural blacks. Because of a lack of education, working skills, and urban coping mechanisms, these migrants had difficulty adjusting to urban ways of life.

Italians, Irish, Poles, Indians, and Native Americans also inhabited Jewtown, which had gotten its name from the large Jewish population living in the area (J. Williams 1966a, 2). Jews, like blacks, were restricted in where they could live in Syracuse. Between the central business district and Syracuse University and on the lower east side of the city, the Fifteenth Ward, with its combination of residential areas, light industry, and different racial and ethnic groups, served as a "zone of transition."

In 1935, the "city fathers," in an attempt to eliminate slum housing in the Washington-Water Strip area (Ninth Ward), began a program of housing demolition. The resulting loss of housing in this area forced many of the poorer or migrant blacks to move into the Fifteenth Ward. With them, they brought many of the problems of the Ninth Ward: unemployment, marital instability, vice, and crime (Darby 1937, 9). Darby states, "Since then, the problem [of vice, crime, and so on] has grown constantly in intensity, and 'Jewtown' has now been brought down to the par of the Washington-Water strip by virtue of the forced shift of population" (9). As the Fifteenth Ward became encumbered with increasing problems and an increasing black population, Jews and other groups began to relocate within the city. Jews moved farther east, beyond Syracuse University. Italians, Irish, and other ethnic groups relocated into ethnic enclaves throughout the city. By the end of the period of segregation, there were major changes in the geographical location of Syracuse's black population. Some evidence of population dispersal could be seen as the poor black population began to move to the south side of the city and middle-income blacks began to move east, as Jews had before them.

*The Dunbar Center*

If one attempted to identify the one institution within the Syracuse black community that had the greatest influence on its citizens, that institution would be the Dunbar Center. From its inception, this center provided a variety of services to blacks. Throughout its history, it expressed its purpose as "[t]he improvement of conditions under which [blacks] work, live and spend their leisure time" (Darby 1937, 35).

Dunbar's beginning provides a good glimpse of the interrelationships between internal forces within the black community and external forces from the larger community. It is important to bear in mind the limited powers and resources within the black community and to recognize that internal influences in some cases, even when they were in operation, were dependent to some degree on external forces to achieve the hoped-for final goal. Such an arrangement was not unique to the black community in Syracuse; it was an almost universal phenomenon in black-white relationships throughout the country during the period of segregation. One only has to look at the history of black colleges and universities to see how various societies, religious groups, and philanthropic organizations assisted in the creation and continued existence of these institutions (Myrdal 1944; Frazier 1957). In only a few large cities, especially in the South, where large populations of blacks were located, were internal influences able to establish black institutions without external assistance.

James P. La Grin, a black exconvict who operated a barbershop in the black community, conceived the idea of some type of recreational program for black youths in 1918. Although the schools were integrated at that time, black youths were not allowed to utilize public or private recreational facilities. Mr. La Grin was concerned that many of the black youths who frequented pool rooms and dance halls in the "red light district" of the community would end up in trouble with the law, as he had, and so he felt that something had to be done to provide these youths with more wholesome recreational outlets. His efforts to organize blacks to create a recreational program for black youths proved unfruitful, or, at most, proposed projects would not materialize in the near future (Brown 1943, 30–31). One of the major stumbling blocks was the community's inability to generate the finances necessary for such an under-taking. La Grin was successful in creating interest, however, and in making the black community see the need for such a program. Blacks had already been pressuring the local power structure to do something to improve the quality of life within their community.

It was not until a Mrs. Hazzard and her sister, Mrs. Burlingame, both local white philanthropists, took up the cause and provided financial back-ing that something concrete was done. Even then, however, the project al-most failed because the black churches, attempting to maintain control over the program, made a sustained effort to kill the entire movement (Brown 1943, 34). Working in favor of the program, though, was the fact that the National Recreation Association in Washington, D.C., had already begun a national drive to promote recreational programs in large cities. As a result of Mrs. Hazzard and Mrs. Burlingame's work, Syracuse established a recreation board. One member of this newly organized board, Mrs. Lucia Knowles, became interested in the development of a recreational program for blacks. Using their membership in the Commonweal Club, a prominent organiza-tion for professional women, the three women were able to secure financial assistance so that in 1920 Rubinstein's Hall, owned by a Jewish organization, could be leased "twice a week for dances, socials, and club gatherings" for blacks (Brown 1943, 36). As the twice weekly program grew in popularity, it was decided the program would be called the Dunbar Center, named after black poet Paul Lawrence Dunbar (1872–1906). With increasing popularity, the program began to expand its services to the black community beyond mere recreation. These new developments in service meant that larger facili-ties and additional funding were needed. After repeated efforts by the Com-monweal Club, in 1928 the Dunbar Center became an agency funded by the Syracuse Community Chest and Council (Darby 1937, 35).

As one might imagine, during the segregation period the Dunbar Center became an all-purpose agency that dealt with myriad problems facing the black community. For example, during World War I, the federal government required birth certificates for all individuals employed in industries that had government contracts. Because most blacks migrating to Syracuse did not have birth certificates, the Dunbar Center assisted them in obtaining birth certificates or certification of citizenship (Brown 1943, 10). It also assumed

2.2. Dunbar Center, rear of building in winter, 1952. Courtesy of Onondaga County Public Library, Beauchamp Branch.

the role of a leadership organization as it questioned the absence of black teachers, city employees, and police and fire personnel in Syracuse (Cleaveland 1982, B6).

By the end of the segregation period, the Dunbar Center had expanded its services far beyond providing recreation to black youth. It had become a vital institution within the community. It served as an important link to the larger Syracuse community by promoting interracial cooperation, by helping to adjudicate cases of racial discrimination, and by assisting in the alleviation of employment barriers (Darby 1937; B. Davis 1980). Included among its many other services were job training, social services, a library, adult classes, a nursery school, housing, and a general meeting place.

*Economic Status*

The economy generated within the Syracuse black community during this period can best be seen by looking at black employment, income, and businesses.

Subcommunities, in particular black subcommunities, have traditionally been dependent on the larger community of which they are a part for employment and income. Black businesses, in contrast, have traditionally depended almost exclusively on a black clientele. The lack of this economic interplay between the black and white communities has resulted in a rather low and insecure economic structure within the black community. The black community was able to do very little to change this tradition at this time.

During the early part of the twentieth century, blacks in Syracuse were restricted in employment to manual labor, messenger service, and various forms of domestic work. No blacks were employed in professional or clerical positions (Schuyler 1967). Even industries located in the Ninth and Fifteenth Wards, where blacks were concentrated, such as the Continental Can Company and the Smith Typewriter Company, refused to provide employment to blacks (Kelly 1982, C3). The only times during this era when employment opportunities for blacks extended beyond the labor/domestic levels were during World War I and World War II. With a decrease in the white male labor population, both white women and blacks enjoyed temporary improvements in employment. If we look back at black in-migration trends to Syracuse, we can see that these periods of improved employment opportunities caused increases in the number of black migrants as Syracuse blacks informed friends and kin "back home" of the new opportunities.

However, for the era of segregation as a whole, the relationship of race to employment can best be characterized by a statement from Theodore Brown: "The [black] in [Syracuse] is confronted by employment problems, not unlike those confronting anyone else, but most of them are complicated by the further fact that he is a [black] and as such finds attitudes toward his employment that constitute peculiar and almost inseparable difficulties" (1943, 62). These difficulties increased as more blacks migrated to Syracuse. Barbara Davis quotes from the August 17, 1917, *Marcellus Observer,* a suburban weekly, which stated that "[t]he influx of southern [blacks] is becoming serious in [Syracuse]. While many of them have gone to the larger cities, at least 150 and probably more located in that city within the last two months. They are looking for work and although laborers are needed, many people will not employ the . . . [blacks] because their white laborers quit rather than work with them" (1980, 18). This quote depicts white laborers' general attitude toward working with blacks. And, more important, it acknowledges the importance that the white power structure attached to white laborers' attitudes.

Davis also relates a story written in a 1915 newspaper, the *Syracuse Post-Standard,* about an incident of overt racial discrimination in employment of a black female medical intern. "[W]hen the young doctor reported for her duties, the superintendent . . . , who had formed certain ideas as to the place of brown and black people in America, at once telephoned to the chief consulting surgeon, without even extending to the new intern the courtesy of a handshake. The authorities forthwith canceled her contract and with the greatest reluctance gave her two nights' lodging in a city that used to be the haven of the fugitive slave" (1980, 18). During the early 1900s, a general attitude of racial inferiority was thus fostered toward blacks, both laborers and professionals. This attitude was to persist throughout this era.

Table 2.4 shows the employment status of Syracuse blacks for the years 1920 and 1930, revealing some changes in black employment status from the turn of the century. Whereas laborers and domestics still made up a disproportionately high number of those employed, some blacks had moved into clerical and professional positions. Granted, the numbers were small: 1.9 percent of Syracuse blacks were professionals in 1920 and 4.1 percent in 1930. In addition, 1.3 percent were clerical workers in 1920, but only 0.8 percent served that function in 1930. Before 1920, there were no indications that any professional or clerical blacks resided within the city, so it was clear some progress had been made.

Changes in the occupational structure within the black community took place not because of any change in attitudes on the part of Syracuse's whites, but as a result of internal community processes. Black clerical workers and black professionals served only their community. Improvements in income and employment occurred despite negative action on the part of the white community, such as charging higher rents for black businesspersons than for their white counterparts for locations within the same general area. And the only locations available to blacks were among the worst in the city because the more desirable locations were reserved for whites. Black store and shop owners had to depend exclusively on a black clientele; to state that their only support came from the black community is to state an undeniable fact (Darby 1937, 13). A similar situation prevailed for black wage laborers because their

**Table 2.4**
**Employment Status of Syracuse Blacks Ten Years and Older, 1920 and 1930**

| | 1920 | | | | | | 1930 | | | | | |
| | Total | | Male | | Female | | Total | | Male | | Female | |
| | N | % | N | % | N | % | N | % | N | % | N | % |
|---|---|---|---|---|---|---|---|---|---|---|---|---|
| Population | 1,124 | 100.0 | 607 | 54.0 | 517 | 46.0 | 1,569 | 100.0 | 844 | 53.8 | 725 | 46.2 |
| Employed | 739 | 65.7 | 593 | 88.8 | 200 | 38.7 | 950 | 60.5 | 691 | 81.9 | 259 | 35.7 |
| Not Employed | 385 | 34.3 | 68 | 11.2 | 317 | 61.3 | 619 | 39.5 | 153 | 18.1 | 466 | 64.3 |
| Employed in | | | | | | | | | | | | |
| Manufacturing | 248 | 33.6 | 231 | 42.9 | 17 | 8.5 | 272 | 28.6 | 267 | 38.6 | 5 | 1.9 |
| Transportation | 81 | 11.0 | 81 | 15.0 | — | — | 14 | 1.5 | 136 | 19.7 | — | — |
| Trade | 63 | 8.5 | 54 | 10.0 | 9 | 4.5 | 59 | 6.2 | 55 | 8.0 | 4 | 1.5 |
| Public Service | 17 | 2.3 | 17 | 3.1 | — | — | 37 | 3.9 | 37 | 5.4 | — | — |
| Domestic/Personal | | | | | | | | | | | | |
| Service | 298 | 40.3 | 131 | 24.3 | 167 | 83.5 | 396 | 41.7 | 153 | 22.1 | 243 | 93.8 |
| Clerical | 10 | 1.3 | 7 | 1.3 | 3 | 1.5 | 8 | 0.8 | 6 | 0.9 | 2 | 0.8 |
| Professions | 14 | 1.9 | 10 | 1.9 | 4 | 2.0 | 39 | 4.1 | 34 | 4.9 | 5 | 1.9 |
| Others | 8 | 1.1 | 8 | 1.5 | — | — | 3 | 0.3 | 3 | 0.4 | — | — |

*Sources*: U.S. Bureau of the Census 1920, 1930. Occupation characteristics taken from Brown 1943, 70.

employment was restricted to the bottom of the occupational status structure. Even at this level, black workers were not in competition with white workers for the same jobs. For example, all the Syracuse garbage collectors during this period were black, for whites looked upon garbage collecting as a nonwhite job.

From the 1920s to the 1940s, statistics reveal a decrease in the employment level within the black community. Approximately 89 percent of all black males were employed in 1920. By 1930, this percentage had decreased to 81.9, and in 1940 only 47.3 percent of black males were employed (Brown 1943, 75). Of course, the population within the black community had increased from 1,260 to 2,082. The only conclusion to be made from these statistics is disturbing: as the black population of Syracuse increased, the proportion of blacks employed decreased.

In a 1942 survey of hiring practices by Syracuse companies, Brown found that of eighty-four companies with more than fifty workers, only eighteen employed blacks. He also found that of the thirty smallest companies (fifty to one hundred workers) surveyed, only two hired black workers, and these two had a combined total of only three black workers (1943, 77). These data, as well as data presented earlier, support the findings of other studies that as the number of blacks increased, discriminatory economic and social practices also increased. Furthermore, based on this information and the data presented in table 2.5, it is reasonable to assume that the jobs made available for blacks were of a menial type.

In table 2.5, it can be seen that 76.4 percent of black workers employed in Syracuse in 1941 were in unskilled positions. Only 2.8 percent were employed as professional workers. Brown further reveals that in 1941 only seventeen blacks had their own businesses (1943, 82). Of this number, one owned a small grocery store; a few owned "dime lot" coal and ice places; a few owned restaurants, newsstands, and pool halls; and one or two ran hairdressing parlors in the home.

Around 1941, the estimated aggregate worth of all black businesses in the Syracuse black community was around $50,000 to $65,000. These subsistence-level "mom and pop" businesses were undercapitalized and had a high rate of failure. The economic status of the black community up through 1941 could best be described as bleak. Salaries for black women averaged $6.00 per

## Table 2.5
## Employment Status of Blacks in Syracuse, 1941

| Employment Status | Number of Blacks (284) | % of Total Blacks (100.0) |
|---|---|---|
| *Professional and Managerial* | *(N = 8)* | *(2.8)* |
| Medical Doctors | 1 | 0.3 |
| Dentists | 1 | 0.3 |
| Social Workers | 5 | 1.8 |
| Chain Store Managers | 1 | 0.4 |
| *Clerical and Service* | *(N = 44)* | *(15.5)* |
| Labor Inspectors | 1 | 0.3 |
| Interviewers | 1 | 0.3 |
| Welfare Inspectors | 2 | 0.7 |
| Ministers | 9 | 3.2 |
| Mail Clerks | 2 | 0.7 |
| Attendants | 2 | 0.7 |
| Musicians and Entertainers | 26 | 9.2 |
| Radio Technicians | 1 | 0.3 |
| *Semiskilled* | *(N = 15)* | *(5.3)* |
| Mechanics | 11 | 3.9 |
| Plumbers | 1 | 0.3 |
| Stone Masons | 3 | 1.1 |
| *Unskilled* | *(N = 217)* | *(76.4)* |
| Porters, Janitors, etc. | 116 | 40.8 |
| Elevator Operators | 3 | 1.1 |
| Pressers | 6 | 2.1 |
| Cooks | 9 | 3.2 |
| Foundry Workers | 60 | 21.1 |
| Chauffeurs | 11 | 3.9 |
| Truck Drivers | 12 | 4.2 |

*Source:* From data presented in Brown 1943, 78.

week and for black men $16.00 per week. The lone exceptions, other than the few professional and clerical workers, were the garbage and ash collectors, who averaged $27.50 per week (Brown 1943, 85). Other sources of income for the black community were derived from illegitimate pursuits (e.g., numbers games, gambling, prostitution, and other forms of vice). Even illegal activities resulted in limited income because vice drew its clientele primarily from the already poor black community. They just served to recycle some of the already limited incomes within the community.

Although the economic status of the Syracuse black community can be explained to a large degree by the discriminatory practices fostered by the white community, other circumstances contributed as well. As stated earlier, many black residents were recent migrants from the South who arrived with limited work skills and few urban coping mechanisms. Were it not for the Dunbar Center activities, many would have gone homeless and without any means of subsistence. Lack of education played a crucial role in the blacks' inability to rise economically. Also, some developed an indifference to work after years of not making it in the workforce. However, one cannot overlook the impact of the discriminatory hiring practices of the Syracuse power structure on the black community's economic plight. Three factors, among others, highlight the discrimination suffered in employment and its impact (Brown 1943, 89–92). First, during World War II, many blacks successfully filled jobs that had previously been reserved for whites based on the rationale that blacks were incapable of carrying out the tasks. Second, blacks with equal training to that of whites were denied access to jobs comparable to those provided to whites. Many blacks were discouraged from preparing for certain occupations (nursing and teaching, for example) because of the manufactured inability to place them. Syracuse did not hire its first black teacher until 1950, yet within the black community were graduates from Wilberforce, Fisk, Fordham, and other universities. Most of these individuals were thus engaged in menial tasks. Third, blacks were quite often kept in skill-training programs twice as long as whites—not because of their performance, but because of the difficulty in placing them.

In one way or another, these factors had a deleterious affect on the black community's economic status. In some respects, the impact could be seen directly; in others, it was indirect but just as damaging—for example, the availability to blacks of only dead-end jobs requiring no skills and little education and offering no opportunity for advancement. This condition caused many blacks to reject education as an avenue for advancement. Others lost their work orientation after repeated attempts to move forward. They saw whites with comparable skills and training start out with better jobs and then advance, whereas they themselves, after years of satisfactory performance, were still relegated to the same low status and the same low-paying jobs.

However, some positive gains were made by blacks economically during this era. As noted, the first black public-school teacher was hired in 1950, followed by a second. This era also witnessed the first black police officer, firefighter, court clerk, and social worker. In addition, Syracuse University hired its first black faculty member. Most interesting is that as early as 1937 (Darby 1937), blacks were calling for the establishment of a black economic base so that they would not have to depend on the white community to provide accessibility to its system. Such an assertion has been made time and time again all the way through to the present, when virtually the same economic relationship exists.

*Education*

The trend of high enrollment among black students in the lower grades but low enrollment in higher grades that prevailed during the period of exploitation seems to have continued throughout the segregation period.

Table 2.6 reveals that for ages six through fourteen for 1930 and ages six through thirteen for 1940, black attendance was slightly higher than white attendance in public schools. However, after ages thirteen and fourteen, white school attendance increased compared to black school attendance for the years 1930 and 1940. Also significant for 1940, black school attendance decreased below the 1930 percentages for the sixteen-to-nineteen age groups. Just the opposite was true for white students. Factors that contributed to the decline in school attendance for students in the older age groups were: (1) the lack of a reward structure for blacks who had finished high school and even college but were unable to get jobs comparable to their education; and (2) an economic situation in the black community that was so bleak that all able-bodied persons within the family were encouraged to work. Another related factor centered on Syracuse's integrated school system. Black parents, because of their lower economic status, were unable to dress their children in the same manner as most white parents dressed their children. As a result, many of the black school children felt inferior to their white classmates. These feelings of inferiority were often expressed as resentment against school, generally because school provided the contact in which black children became aware of

**Table 2.6**

**School Attendance in Syracuse by Age and Race, 1930 and 1940**

| Age | % of Total Attending School | |
|---|---|---|
| | Black | White |
| *1930* | | |
| All Ages 5–24 Years | 56.7 | 66.1 |
| 5 Years | 57.9 | 62.3 |
| 6 Years | 87.0 | 86.5 |
| 7–9 | 100.0 | 96.6 |
| 10–13 Years | 99.1 | 98.9 |
| 14 Years | 100.0 | 98.0 |
| 15 Years | 83.3 | 92.5 |
| 16–17 Years | 63.0 | 70.8 |
| 18–19 Years | 18.2 | 34.9 |
| 20 Years | 32.0 | 21.9 |
| 21–24 Years | 3.8 | 10.5 |
| *1940* | | |
| All Ages 5–24 Years | 60.4 | 63.3 |
| 5 Years | 65.7 | 69.8 |
| 6 Years | 92.9 | 92.0 |
| 7–9 Years | 97.3 | 97.0 |
| 10–13 Years | 97.7 | 97.4 |
| 14 Years | 90.4 | 96.8 |
| 15 Years | 94.2 | 95.7 |
| 16–17 Years | 61.7 | 82.1 |
| 18–19 Years | 11.8 | 37.5 |
| 20 Years | 2.9 | 19.5 |
| 21–24 Years | 1.5 | 8.1 |

*Source:* From data presented in Brown 1943, 124.

differences in dress. Because of these feelings and the resulting resentment, many black children dropped out of school when given the least cause. Black parents did not object because dropping out meant earlier entrance into the workforce and thus income for the family (Darby 1937, 22).

Of those black students who graduated from high school, many were unable to get into college even as late as the 1950s because they had not been enrolled in college preparatory courses. Although integrated, Syracuse schools were very close to being segregated into tracks. Black and poor white students were placed in vocational tracks in disproportionately large numbers, whereas middle- and upper-class white children took college preparatory courses. Those few blacks who were enrolled in college preparatory courses were more likely to attend college away from Syracuse, a somewhat ironic choice given the financial status of blacks and the fact that Syracuse was the home of a well-established eastern private university. In 1934, Ellsworth E. Hasbrouck, who later became a distinguished Chicago surgeon, became the first black born in Syracuse to graduate with a baccalaureate degree from Syracuse University (Minority Manuscript 1985, 2–3). Before 1950, most black students who went to college did so at predominantly black colleges and universities in the South and bordering states. Those few who chose New York State teachers' colleges, particularly colleges located in upstate New York, often faced problems. Syracuse's first black public-school teacher provides an example of the conditions faced by black students when she tells of her arrival at an upstate teachers' college where most students lived off campus with local families. She had to stay at the dean's house for the first couple of days because local white families (no blacks lived in the town) were not receptive to her staying with them. Finally, a room was secured for her in the house of a local sorority, into which she eventually gained membership.

The absence of local black students at Syracuse University seems rather odd because this institution had traditionally been one of the northern universities where black students from the South matriculated because southern institutions were segregated. However, Syracuse University was beyond the economic capability of most black students.

More significant than the economic barrier, however, was the fact that Syracuse University discouraged black student attendance in general through its exclusionary rules regarding dormitory life. Black students could enroll in classes at the university, but could not obtain a room in school dormitories. Although the Dunbar Center protested this policy of racial discrimination on numerous occasions, its protest fell on deaf ears (Darby 1937, 23). Southern black students, of course, faced the greater issue of total exclusion by southern colleges and universities, so they were able to cross the lower barrier presented by the Syracuse University housing situation. Syracuse University was not unique in its discriminatory housing policies; many other northern institutions had similar policies at that time. It just seemed to local black students, regardless of conditions in Syracuse, that the local university's housing discrimination implied that the university really did not want black students. Many southern middle-income families, however, intent on providing the best possible education for their children, set up apartments in northern cities where colleges and universities with exclusionary housing policies but open admittance policies were located. The mother or some other adult female relative would inhabit these apartments during the academic year so that their children could attend the institution and be provided with care and supervision.

Syracuse University has long employed the talents of black athletes, even one Wilmeth Sidat-Singh, a black student athlete who attempted to pass as being from India (J. Williams 1966a). Despite his attempt, he was not allowed to compete in some instances—not because restrictions were imposed by Syracuse University, but because the athletic teams competed against southern universities, which at that time refused to engage in competition against black athletes. However, Syracuse University indirectly played a crucial role in the black community. Many of the individuals who worked at the Dunbar Center were black students from the university. Various faculty members lent assistance at various times to projects fostered by the black community.

Overall, the relationship between employment and education served as a self-fulfilling prophecy. With limited employment prospects, blacks increasingly abandoned education as an avenue for upward mobility. As education ceased to be a primary objective, employment prospects dimmed.

*Housing*

Brown, in discussing the problem of housing in the black community in the early 1940s, states, "In approaching the housing problem of the . . . [black in Syracuse], one is strongly tempted to throw up [one's] hands in despair and merely exclaim, 'The [black] housing situation is bad, unspeakably bad, hopelessly bad!' and let it go at that" (1943, 98). The problem resulted in part from the restrictive residential patterns imposed on the community. In many cases, decent and hardworking black families with children were forced to live next door to houses of prostitution and other types of vice. Such conditions lent themselves to a general aura of degeneration and blight (Darby 1937, 27).

Like any urban area, Syracuse had its share of poor housing. However, areas of extremely poor housing were almost exclusively filled by blacks. Segregation played a major role, both racial and economic, in this situation. With few exceptions, blacks were restricted to the Ninth and Fifteenth Wards. Although blacks shared these areas with poor whites, they were relegated to the worse housing in an area characterized by poor housing. In these sections of the city, many of structures were more than one hundred years old.

According to Brown, in 1937 the Syracuse Housing Authority conducted an extensive survey of the housing in these older, rundown sections of the city. It identified the areas as I (the poorest), II (next poorest), and III (least poor). As shown in table 2.7, the larger number of black households (296) was located in blighted area II, "next-poorest" area studied. These data show that although fewer blacks actually lived in the poorest area as compared with the next-poorest area, black households were concentrated in two of the poorest areas in the city. Less than 20 percent of black households in 1937 existed outside the study area (Brown 1943, 101). And most of those households were adjacent to blighted areas II and III in a new low-cost housing project that had been constructed in 1935. Only through the efforts of the Dunbar Center were blacks allowed to live in this project, called Pioneer Homes. Even then, black households constituted only 7.2 percent of all households in Pioneer Homes (B. Davis 1980, 25). A few other black families lived in houses that were in better condition, but these houses were located east of Syracuse University, away from the large concentration of black households.

The typical house occupied by blacks during this time period was a rental in which gas and electricity were lacking. Roofs often leaked, and floors, walls, and stair steps suffered from dry rot. When indoor plumbing existed, which was not often, it was in the form of a postage-stamp-size toilet off the

**Table 2.7**

**Race and Households in Three Blighted Areas, Syracuse, 1937**

|  | Area I | | Area II | | Area III | |
|---|---|---|---|---|---|---|
|  | *N* | *%* | *N* | *%* | *N* | *%* |
| White | 258 | 75 | 1,392 | 82 | 379 | 100 |
| Black | 85 | 25 | 296 | 17 | 0 | 0 |
| Other | 0 | 0 | 16 | 1 | 0 | 0 |
| Total All Races | 343 | 100 | 1,704 | 100 | 379 | 100 |

*Source:* From data presented in Brown 1943, 99.

back porch and a water faucet in the hall that served from four to five families. Ventilation was poor, with very little sunlight or fresh air in the house. Because gas and electricity were often lacking, space heaters and grates were used for heat. One does not have to strain the imagination to realize that with poor ventilation, the space heaters and grates posed major health and fire hazards (Brown 1943, 101).

The housing conditions tolerated by the black community stemmed from many causes. Housing discrimination immediately comes to mind as the major cause, but is too simplistic to be presented alone. Two other factors have to be taken into consideration. First, there was the economic status of Syracuse blacks. Even on rare occasions when adequate housing was available, the higher rent discouraged black families because they either could not afford the better housing or would have to crowd in with two families or with roomers to make the rent payments. Overcrowding of apartments or houses often resulted in adequate housing soon becoming substandard housing. A side effect was that such occurrences helped to reinforce the feelings of whites that blacks didn't need better housing because their occupancy would only lead to deterioration of the neighborhood or slum housing. Second, many black migrant workers from the South were willing to accept housing conditions that other blacks might not because Syracuse's poor housing, although bad, was often an improvement over the dwellings they were accustomed to inhabiting. Their acceptance of substandard housing helped to create and maintain a viable market for poor housing (Brown 1943, 110–12). However, as stated earlier, discrimination was the major cause of housing conditions in the black community. Evidence supporting this position can be gleaned from what happened to the few blacks who were financially able to afford better housing: in brief, they were often refused in their efforts to purchase or rent homes. Even in the few cases where they bought, their buying resulted from subterfuge on their part and that of liberal-minded whites. Brown provides the following scenario: "In the few instances where [black] purchases have 'broken through the line,' it will be found in investigation that the [black] purchased the property through some friendly white person who would purchase for the [black]. . . . In such cases, the [black] purchaser, and certainly [the spouse] will not have seen the property before the purchase except by casually driving by in a car" (1943, 112).

All legal mechanisms were used to prevent the sale of housing in all-white areas to blacks, such as restrictive covenants and other types of less-formalized agreements. Those who controlled the housing market saw blacks as undesirable tenants and made sure this perception was maintained within the white community by keeping blacks in substandard housing. With substandard housing and low incomes, those who controlled the housing market could support their claims of "undesirability" by pointing to the conditions under which blacks lived.

During the segregation period, even as late as the 1950s, Syracuse revealed little evidence of city planning related to housing. Within the black community, it would be safe to say planning was almost nonexistent. The only evidence of planning was the demolition of housing in the Ninth Ward and the construction of Pioneer Homes in 1935. Even then, Pioneer Homes was not planned for blacks, but for low-income whites. As has already been mentioned, only through the efforts of the Dunbar Center were some blacks able to gain access to these projects.

*Social Stratification*

The period of segregation was one in which the social life within the black community slowed because of an all-consuming emphasis on economic welfare (B. Davis 1980, 18). The three-class structure perceived during the exploitation period collapsed into a two-class structure that was based primarily on length of residence in Syracuse. Homeowners, poor but respectable individuals, and those who were regarded as undesirable were still present within the community, but distinctions previously made between those who owned homes and those who rented but were hard working became blurred as the community expanded in population. Many of the newcomers became associated with the lower class or the undesirables. During the exploitation period, the undesirables had consisted primarily of single males who were without family ties or attachments. By the segregation period, however, with the wave of southern migrants that poured into Syracuse during World Wars I and II, this group had expanded to include recently arrived families who were unable to cope with the economic demands of the area as well as single males and females who entered into common-law relationships to help cope with their economic instability and perhaps because a legal spouse had been left behind in the South. Because common-law relationships were looked down upon and economic instability was accorded less status, a two-class structure emerged.

Residential restrictions still existed for blacks, so these class distinctions did not manifest themselves in terms of residential location to any degree. Of course, blacks who were able to purchase homes outside of restricted areas were looked upon as having higher status. However, their numbers were not significant enough to be recognized as another class. Therefore, at the top of the two-class structure was the working class, made up of old residents of the black community who had achieved economic stability and some of whom owned their homes. At the bottom was the lower class, made up of new arrivals from the South and longtime residents previously referred to as "undesirables." The distinction made between the working class and the lower class, although based primarily on economics, was also moral. Working-class households, with their strong work ethic and family orientation, became concerned about their residential proximity to lower-class households. Not only did working-class families look down on common-law ties and unstable family relationships, but their concern was also focused on the lower-class residents' predilictions toward vice and various forms of rowdy behavior (Darby 1937, 28).

*Leisure and Social Life*

Social activities within the black community served both manifest and latent functions (Merton 1957). Blacks' utilization of various forms of recreation and leisure activities to interact with each other socially served as a manifest function. These activities provided relief from their day-to-day activities associated with jobs and making ends meet. The latent function of these activities was to replace all job-related activities. Many lower-class blacks, because of the many problems associated with trying to obtain employment, gave up their quest for jobs and focused their energies on social activities (Darby 1937, 30).

A 1946 study of a random sample of two hundred Syracuse black community residents revealed that the types of leisure activities participated in the most frequently were lounging at home (33.5 percent), going to the movies (33 percent), and reading (22.5 percent). According to the author of the study, lounging at home included doing nothing, listening to the radio, and working around the house. Of those who attended the movies, 48 percent stated they attended at least once a week and in some cases more frequently (Hamilton 1946, 27). At first glance, it might appear surprising that reading was one of the more frequent types of leisure activities, given the low educational level of black residents. Hamilton's data reveal, however, that, as would be expected, those who read books generally came from the small professional and clerical status groups (1946, 33). The magazines read the most frequently included *Life*, *Ebony*, *Negro Digest*, *Reader's Digest*, *Our World*, and *True Story*. Of the two hundred respondents studied by Hamilton, 13 percent indicated they did not read books or magazines as leisure. The majority of this group was made up of unskilled and domestic workers who had migrated from the rural South (1946, 35). Although the types of newspapers read ranged from the *New York Times* to the radical *Daily Worker*, the most frequently read newspapers were the two local white daily papers, the *Syracuse Herald-Journal* and the *Syracuse Post-Standard;* a local black newspaper, the *Syracuse Progressive Herald;* and two black national newspapers, the *Pittsburgh Courier* and the *Chicago Defender* (36). It seems from these data that blacks were concerned with the affairs of blacks nationally in that their reading material was geared in high numbers toward black publications.

Discrimination in social and recreational activities was both economic and racial. Commercial recreational facilities such as movie theaters, fight halls, and ball parks did not bar blacks. However, with the exception of movie theaters, the low economic status thrust on Syracuse blacks often kept them from participating in these activities. Hotels, nightclubs, bars, and restaurants did bar blacks because of race. Thus, for economic and racial reasons, blacks were dependent on their own resources for social activities. Card playing, dancing, and talking generally took place in private homes. Churches also provided social activities by organizing plays, debates, and speakers on a weekly basis. The Dunbar Center provided physical facilities where many recreational and social events took place. As a matter of fact, Dunbar was called the Dunbar Social Center at the time (Darby 1937, 32).

Black community boys had better recreational outlets than did the girls. The Syracuse Boys Club permitted membership of blacks, although the YMCA did not. Girls, on a limited basis, could use the facilities of the YWCA and the Huntington Club. However, blacks were not invited to social activities sponsored by these organizations.

Because of the discriminatory policies of the overall Syracuse community, blacks were constantly starting new clubs, many of which had a short life span. The Syracuse Lodge of Elks probably served the black community the most socially. Black membership in lodges was rather large, but lodges contributed little to the black community other than in a social way (Darby 1937, 33).

*Political Activity*

Political activity seemed to decline during this period, as did social activities (B. Davis 1980, 18). However, local Republican political dominance had a tremendous impact on the lifestyle of the black community. John Williams states, "Corruption [in the Fifteenth Ward] seemed to go hand in hand with the long time dominance of the Republican Party" (1966b, 5). Corruption flourished openly for more than twenty-five years in the black community, and it was supported by the police department (Williams 1966b, 5). Prostitution, gambling, and other forms of vice prospered despite several investigations that verified their existence. The lack of action on the part of local police stemmed from the fact that these forms of vice were backed, if not enjoyed by, "vested interests with political influence in the city" (Darby 1937, 27).

Therefore, the political structure within Syracuse was heavily tied into police corruption and vice. "Houses [of prostitution] catering to white men [were] taxed heavily for the privilege of running, and this provide[d] . . . considerable income which [those] interests [were] anxious to protect" (Darby 1937, 27). In turn for being allowed to operate, prostitutes were rounded up and told how to vote at election time. Because their income was based on a lack of enforcement of laws against prostitution, the girls and other members of the illegal opportunity structure supported the Republican machine. The black community was well aware that the problem did not center on the illegal establishments themselves, but on the external political powers that allowed the establishments to flourish in the community (Darby 1937, 27). Without power, the community was unable to put pressure on the political leadership of Syracuse to rectify this situation. During the period of segregation, the type of leadership that was to come later through organizations and churches was totally lacking. According to Darby, the only type of leadership available was that of black individuals whom the white political establishment had handpicked and who were dysfunctional to the community's overall needs (1937, 27).

The two major events that did have some political impact on the community were the establishment of the Dunbar Center, which acted as an advocate for blacks in the area of employment, housing, and social services, and the emergence of a small professional class. As this group grew in numbers, it provided the nucleus for the leadership that was to come.

*Religion*

Religious services in the black community can be characterized as being of two types: (1) formalized churches connected to more traditional denominations, such as Baptist, Methodist, and Episcopal, and (2) less-formalized storefront churches. As pointed out earlier, churches in the community traditionally played and continue to play both functional and dysfunctional roles. Because of the depressing economic and social conditions within the community, many residents sought solace through some form of religion.

Churches, both traditional and storefront, attempted to fill this need. As the community grew in size, traditional churches began to expand their functions beyond those directly related to salvation. Many provided social activities such as dinners, debates, plays, and speeches. In actuality, about 75 percent of these activities were secular in nature (Darby 1937, 25). However, the churches refused to provide recreational outlets for youth when these activities exceeded the boundaries of their belief system. For example, when the Dunbar Center first began, its activities were hosted by the People's AME Zion Church and, to a lesser degree, by Bethany Baptist Church. Conflict arose when the secular supporters of the center advocated dances for youth. To prevent this perceived sinful activity, ministers attempted to gain control of the Dunbar movement, which would have served two purposes: it would have aided churches in their efforts to broaden their functions, and they would have been able to outlaw activities such as dancing. Despite the ministers' failure to control the Dunbar movement, the major churches were able to expand their functions. Black churches, together with white churches, fostered meetings designed to bring about better understanding between the races (Brown 1943, 177).

By the 1930s, the black community was overwhelmingly Protestant; 86 percent of those with some form of religious affiliation belonged to the three aforementioned Protestant churches. The remaining church-affiliated blacks were divided between the Catholic Church and various storefront churches (Darby 1937, 25). As the community population continued to grow, and as southern migrants made up increasing proportions of the new residents, storefront churches became more and more visible.

In the two-class structure described earlier, a line of demarcation seemed to develop whereby the three traditional Protestant churches served primarily the older, more stable members of the black community and the storefront churches became the religious home for the southern migrant newcomers. The newcomers soon recognized distinctions in social status after their arrival. Once they perceived how the rest of the community looked upon them, they sought out a religious atmosphere in which they felt comfortable. Storefront churches, with their self-ordained minister or prophet, welcomed the newcomers with open arms. The minister or prophet also served as head of his or her religious organization and had no one else to answer to regarding policy or church behavior. Therefore, the church service often varied from traditional worship and worked toward generating an emotional release.

Many social scientists have looked upon storefront churches as purposeful to the psychological well-being of low-income black northern communities in which the residents have a southern heritage (Blackwell 1949; Harrison 1966). In fact, it has been shown that the storefront church follows the population, be it from one part of the city to another or from the South to the North (Blackwell 1949). Thus, according to Ira Harrison, "the storefront church may also be seen as an urban manifestation of the [black's] rural heritage" (1966, 161). In the performance of its activities, the storefront church provided its members with a state of sanctification that insulated them from hurt and disillusionment (Harrison 1966, 161). From this point of view, it can be looked upon as being functional.

From the perspective of the respectable members of the Syracuse black community, however, these local storefront churches were merely fly-by-night schemes to separate the poor from some of their already meager earnings. Although the emotionalism generated by the wide-open services had therapeutic value, this value was a secondary outcome. The primary outcome was to pass the collection plate while the members were at an emotional pitch, thereby increasing the amount given. Ministers and prophets often aligned themselves with God by stating that to give was to give to God, when in reality the giving only enlarged their own personal coffers.

Arguments can be presented pro and con as to the value of storefront churches or the positive effect of traditional churches within the community. However, there is no argument concerning the fact that religious institutions were an integral part of blacks' life. Next to the important task of making a living, attending religious service was an essential aspect of life, from both a secular and sacred point of view.

*Race Relations*

Objectively analyzing urban northern and southern communities in terms of race relations during this era entails a look at the impact of de facto segregation versus the impact of de jure segregation. In reality, both regions segregated blacks from whites. Whereas the South used a legal system to separate the races, the North used an informal system of segregation buttressed by economic repression.

Race relations in Syracuse in this period can best be described as being very poor. Blacks commingled with whites, but on whites' terms. Syracuse schools were integrated, but blacks were relegated to vocational courses in disproportionately high numbers. Formal laws restricting the sale of housing to blacks were absent, but through a system of economic repression and informal agreements not to sell to them, blacks were for the most part restrained within certain sections of the city. Informal laws also restricted blacks from eating in certain restaurants, staying in certain hotels, and attending certain social functions. Exceptions did exist, however, because restrictions were not applied uniformly. Syracuse's first black teacher, who also grew up in the community, tells of going to restaurants, drug store soda fountains, and other commercial establishments with her white friends without being refused service (Carter 2003). The vast majority of blacks did not enjoy such liberty, however. An upper-middle-class black mother and her husband, who were among the first black professionals living in Syracuse, tell a story that indicates how race norms circumscribed behavior among white liberals. Their son took college preparatory courses with white students and became very friendly with a female white student. The two young people studied together, walked home together, and generally were inseparable. Although the white parents knew of their daughter's friendship and tacitly approved, when the black student asked the daughter to be his date at the senior prom and she accepted, the white parents stepped in and refused to let her attend with him. The black mother recounts how distraught her son was at the rejection. It was his first personal confrontation with racism and not an easy experience to overcome. In essence, this incident reveals the boundaries placed on black/white relationships even in liberal settings.[2]

During the period of segregation, black-white social relationships basically occurred in two ways: white men frequented the "vice district" that existed in the black community, with some houses of prostitution in the district actually restricting their clientele to whites; and those few middle-class

2. We heard this story when we lived in Syracuse in from 1977 to 1982. Such accounts were topics of conversation at parties and other informal gatherings.

blacks who were able to live in integrated middle-income neighborhoods socialized with their more liberal white neighbors and friends. Blacks were in general restricted in their social relationships with whites, however. As the black population grew, whites became more repressive economically toward blacks, and race relations took on a more strained quality. Black churches and social organizations, such as the Dunbar Center, worked with white churches and other organizations to improve race relations within the city. Although these efforts were sincere, appreciable changes were not forthcoming during this era. One might conclude, however, that the state of race relations at the end of the segregation period laid the foundation for the protest movement that followed in the next era.

*Summary*

Race relations during the period of segregation served as an impetus to the black community in its fight for change. More specifically, the following elements can be said to be of some importance as the community began its quest for change: population increases that allowed it to grow into a more formidable group; black southern migrants' expectations of a better life in the North; economic repression of blacks by the white community; the beginning of a black professional class that could provide leadership; the emergence of leadership organizations such as the Dunbar Center; police corruption and graft that allowed vice to thrive openly in the community; and the general poor quality of life for black citizens.

These factors all converged at a time when the rest of black society in the nation, particularly in the South, was beginning to defy the status quo. One would have to conclude that these factors caused the Syracuse black community's defiance and its willingness to bring about changes in discrimination and segregation. National trends that occurred in the form of the civil rights movement had an impact on local conditions and helped to activate the Syracuse community to fight for change. However, the aforementioned conditions served as rallying points around which local blacks joined other blacks throughout the nation in an attempt to break down segregation and to improve the quality of life in black communities.

# 3

# The Syracuse Black Community in Transition

CHAPTER 2 CATALOGED the emergence of the black community in Syracuse, starting with the first two runaway slaves who were miners of salt and extending through the beginning of the 1950s. It showed how northern involvement against the system of slavery, especially by way of the Underground Railroad, influenced the early stages of growth within the community. Despite a reputation for being antislavery, however, Syracuse was revealed as having a vocal pro-slavery contingent. The debate between the anti- and pro-slavery camps did much to determine the tone of black-white relationships until after the end of slavery. The chapter also revealed how the end of slavery seemed to relieve Syracuse whites from their self-appointed and morally generated need to help local blacks in their plight. The exploitation of black labor that ensued was a major factor affecting the growth and development of the black community. Finally, the chapter showed how the norms guiding black-white relations that arose during the period of exploitation became a way of life during the period of segregation as blacks were segregated in housing and discriminated against in employment. These influences, although external to the community, charted the course of its growth and development. Because of the community's somewhat powerless position, internal factors had few influences on its growth and development. One exception was the influence local blacks had on their southern kin and friends to migrate north, for circumstances in the South were still perceived as worse than those of the North.

All of these factors in the first three eras in which the Syracuse black community existed had a cumulative effect on the things to come in race relations within the city. This chapter is labeled "The Syracuse Black Community in Transition," but in reality the analysis is much broader, for as the black community changed, so did Syracuse. Following World War II, the country as a whole changed. Hundreds of thousands of war veterans returned home with new aspirations and intent on making up for time lost during the war years. The federal, state, and local governments were prepared to repay the veterans, their families, and other sacrificing Americans, excluding blacks, by making home ownership a realizable dream for many who otherwise would never have been able to own a home (Abrams 1965, 61). These various levels of government were intent on rebuilding infrastructures that had deteriorated drastically during the war years.

Although these local, regional, and national aspirations seemed noble, worthwhile, and unrelated to the state of race relations, their initiation, coupled with black veterans' new attitudes and aspirations, helped to set the stage for the protest that was to come. It must be remembered that although the Federal Housing Administration (FHA) provided and encouraged home loans for veterans, they supported restrictive covenants used to exclude blacks from new suburban homes (Abrams 1965, 61). In Syracuse, as well as in other parts of the country, the protest movement grew when years of festering resentment and frustrations finally came to a head in the 1960s.

### Setting the Stage for Protest

The beginning of the protest movement can accurately be documented nationally and locally. However, the civil rights movement, as it came to be known, did not just start one day out of the blue. Certain attitudes, decisions, actions, and outcomes led to collective action on the part of a group that, up until that time, had been relatively docile. The events that led up to the civil rights movement and to the Black Power movement that followed can easily be described as representing the total history of people of African descent in America from slavery until the Montgomery bus boycott (officially recognized as the beginning of the civil rights movement) (Lomax 1962; Pinkney 1975).

Similarly, the civil rights movement in Syracuse was the culmination of the relationship between blacks and whites from the arrival of the first slave runaways until the beginning of the urban renewal project. Many of the attitudes, decisions, actions, and outcomes described in the previous chapter

were contributing factors. However, three important elements can be identified directly as causal factors in the initiation of protest: (1) changes in the
Syracuse power structure, (2) economic and housing conditions within the
black community in the early 1960s, and (3) federal programs.

*The Power Structure in Syracuse*

By the 1950s, one could recognize a dominant and pervasive power structure
in Syracuse and profile its membership. Just as the city had grown from a
small village to a medium-size urban community, the local power structure
had developed in size and power. It went through a transitional period that
began in the early 1940s and continued throughout the 1960s, so that one can
divide the history of the city power structure into two periods, dominated
first by the "old" power structure, or the Establishment (1900–1961), and
then by the "new" power structure (post-1961).[1]

Two leading figures stand out as controlling forces in the Establishment:
Rolland Marvin and Stewart F. Hancock. It has often been said that one man,
Stewart F. Hancock (after whom the local Hancock Airport is named), controlled the affairs of Syracuse in this period. He has even been referred to as
"Mr. Syracuse" (Freeman 1960). Despite these perceptions of power shared
by those knowledgeable about the Syracuse power structure, it is doubtful
that Hancock wielded the power held by his predecessor, Rolland Marvin.
Marvin's power (1929–41) was derived jointly from his positions as chairper-
son of the Republican County Committee and mayor of Syracuse. From these
positions, Marvin was able to muster something close to monolithic control.
By the time Hancock succeeded Marvin as leader, a transition in Syracuse
politics and power had begun, however modest (Martin et al. 1961, 305–7).
There was no question as to Hancock's power, but by this time power within
the Establishment was vested in more than one person. An earlier study
(Hodges 1958) shows that local businesspersons and industrialists dominated the power structure during the Hancock years. Of course, Hancock

1. John Williams used the name "Establishment" to refer to the old power structure
within Syracuse in an unpublished manuscript, "Portrait of a City: Syracuse, the Old Home
Town," written in 1966.

was a member, but holders of public office and local government officials also played supporting roles. Freeman, in a 1960 study on Syracuse, viewed three types of leaders: (1) "institutional" leaders, or those who headed the largest and most influential business, industrial, educational, labor, religious, and professional organizations and made the major decisions behind the scenes; (2) "effectors," or those who were employed by institutional leaders and who basically carried out company policy and saw to it that community decisions did not have a negative impact on the company; and (3) "activists," or those who were not associated with an institution, but were active in community affairs through volunteerism.

The Establishment during the Hancock years was made up of men who were mostly of northeastern European descent, espoused Protestant religious beliefs and, most important, belonged to the Republican Party. Being born in Syracuse, like their fathers, was a prerequisite for membership in the Establishment, but Republicanism was an ascribed rather than an achieved status. Graduating from college was a must, and income levels were in excess of $20,000 a year (Freeman 1960). The location of Syracuse University in the local community had to be a factor in the high level of educational attainment achieved by the Syracuse leadership. Compounding the dilemma of leadership was the fact that many other well-qualified and well-educated persons of leadership capability existed within the community. But without the proper background and the right connections, these individuals were excluded from the Establishment. Needless to say, members of the black community were completely excluded from all levels of leadership. The Establishment was a closed system, one resembling Robert Michels's oligarchy, whereby a small group of privileged and elite individuals control an organization by replacing themselves with their offspring (1949, 401). In many respects, the inbreeding of Establishment members proved dysfunctional in that the sons were quite often not as effective as their fathers in maintaining control (J. Williams 1966a, 10). One can possibly consider this weakness one of the many factors that led to transitions in the power structure.

Given the varied population that Syracuse has traditionally been noted for, it is somewhat surprising that the Establishment was not more ethnically diverse. Being of the wrong ethnic or racial background—Jewish, Italian, or black—automatically excluded one from membership. Only in the case of the

Irish was an exception made. Irish descendants became so politically power-ful that they could not be ignored. John Williams gives the following example of Irish political strength: "Once congregated in a region called Tipperary Hill, the Irish commanded so much power that they demanded and got the green light placed at the top of the traffic signal rather than in its customary position at the bottom" (1966a, 10).

As late as the early 1960s, leadership was inbred and paternalistic. Those not meeting the strict requirements for membership in the Establishment but demonstrating leadership capabilities were used in some small measure as ad-visors. Members of the black community, however, were excluded even from an advisory role. Rationalizing that this paternalistic mode of leadership was what Syracuse needed, the Establishment, in essence, epitomized what is often dys-functional about paternalistic urban power structures. Although these leaders viewed themselves as providing for the welfare of "their" people, in reality they were catering to their own self-interest to the detriment of others.

During its tenure, the Establishment managed to keep many outside industries from locating in Syracuse. Some were allowed to do so, but only after "gentlemen's agreements" had been made to keep local wages low (J. Williams 1966b, 7). These decisions were based on local industrialists and businesspersons' desire to control employment and wages within the city, and they had monumental consequences for the direction and growth of the black community. The point is that these decisions were not made merely to bring about economic oppression of blacks, but were economic decisions made by businesspersons to enhance their own profit. The fact that economic oppression of blacks was necessary to accomplish the goal of economic gain certainly did not bother the conscience of Establishment members.

The same can be said for the degree of vice and graft allowed to flourish in the black community. It was not permitted as an overt effort to punish blacks, but rather to keep such behavior geographically as far away from Es-tablishment neighborhoods as possible. Maintaining vice in the black com-munity served two functions: it provided a buffer zone between vice and Establishment neighborhoods, and it provided white workers with a sense of higher status than blacks.

Results of the decisions made by the Establishment helped to lay the foundation for protest, and the transition from the Establishment to a "new" power structure gave hope. As has been emphasized, wage control by the Establishment had encouraged, as an outcome, the economic oppression of blacks. By maintaining cheap labor and restricting competition from external industries, the Establishment was able to maximize profits. What is often the case and was certainly the case in Syracuse, white workers did not see the power structure, or in this case the Establishment, as a threat or barrier to their own ability to earn a better living through higher wages. They instead perceived black workers who were willing to work for lower wages as a threat to their own economic security. In essence, the institutional leaders, through the effectors, supported all forms of racial discrimination and prejudices because these actions and feelings fostered racial division among workers in Syracuse. By dividing workers along racial lines, the Establishment kept low-wage white workers in line by creating a lower-status working class among black workers and then by using the black lower-status working class as a threat against the white workers (W. Wilson 1978, 45).[2] Through economic oppression, the powerless black workers were virtually kept out of the labor market, and when they entered, it was in the lowest-paid and often temporary positions. Yet in the likelihood of a white worker revolt, black workers stood in abeyance as a threat.

The result of these tactics, contrary to the Establishment's purpose, was that the black community, after years of being denied access to a decent livelihood, was ripe for protest. Exacerbating the situation was an earlier expectation that the industrial North would provide better opportunities than had the agricultural South. The white community's attitudes and behavior patterns, buttressed by the decisions and actions of the power structure, rendered black migrants' expectations unmeetable. When the status quo began to be challenged in other parts of the country, in particular the South, protest came to be viewed as an action that could change the economic and social

---

2. This position is that of the orthodox Marxist. Capitalists, in an attempt to maximize profits, weakened the bargaining power of the working class by initiating divisions within their ranks along racial lines. They supported all kinds of racial discrimination to create a marginal black working class. With the creation of this marginal class, white workers perceived themselves as being in a privileged position. To protect this positions, they supported discrimination and directed their energies toward blacks rather than toward the capitalists.

constraints imposed on the black community. Both economic factors and a change in the Syracuse power structure from the Republican-dominated Establishment to the "new" power structure with its broader-based support were instrumental in impelling blacks to protest. Before this time period, all efforts blacks made to have their issues addressed fell on deaf ears. For example, in the late 1950s, black leaders such as Frank Wood, the director of the local Dunbar Center, and Lester Granger, executive secretary of the National Urban League, tried to get "city fathers" to sponsor a local affiliate of the Urban League. They were not successful in their efforts (Scruggs 1984, 9).

An earlier study of power and leadership in Syracuse (Martin et al. 1961) warned of the threat to the Republican Party's power posed by the rising Democratic Party. In the end, three major factors led to the diminishing power of the old Republican Party: (1) their steadfast refusal to address issues arising in the black community, which had traditionally supported them in local elections; (2) the increasing political activity of unions and their working-class constituents; and, most important, (3) a state probe that revealed the vice and graft present in city administrative offices, especially the police force (J. Williams 1966a, 5; 1966b, 9–10). Democrats, putting together a coalition of blacks, liberal whites, and union members and their ethnic blocks, were able to push the old-guard Republicans out of power. The "new" power structure was pluralistic in makeup. Both Republicans and Democrats were represented, as were the business, educational, religious, and governmental sectors. The new mayor in the early 1950s was Republican, but he had been head of the New York State Commission Against Discrimination, so the black community viewed him more favorably than they had his predecessors.

These changes, plus blacks' newfound political (voting) power, caused them to perceive a shift in the balance of power within Syracuse. Whereas the Establishment had not listened to their concerns, the "new" power structure was somewhat beholden to them politically. The time for protest was now right in Syracuse.

*Conditions in the Black Community*

By the beginning of the 1960s, conditions relating to employment, income, education, and housing for blacks in Syracuse had not improved. If anything, they had gotten worse. With a continued increase in the black population and continued discriminatory housing practices, the housing situation had certainly gotten worse. Overcrowded conditions, lack of money for repairs, and an unwillingness on the part of absentee white owners to improve rental structures exacerbated the already degraded situation. Similarly, employment and income opportunities had not improved. The community's poor economic condition was having an adverse effect on its residents and on the family unit as the number of female-headed households increased. These problems, in turn, had negative effects on schooling, rates of delinquency, and other urban social problems. These problems became so acute that it is necessary to look at some of them individually.

### Characteristics of the Black Population, 1960

As mentioned in chapter 1, between 1950 and 1960 the black population of Syracuse grew by 144.4 percent (Sacks and Andrew 1974, 20). That increase was greater than the combined growth rate (50.3 percent) for all central cities in the United States as well as for other north-central cities (57.3 percent) (Campbell 1964, 3). During the 1960s, growth of the black population continued to increase, but at a lower rate (90.7). Within a period of twenty years, the black population more than quadrupled. Although the 1960 black population made up only 5.2 percent of the total population of Syracuse (see table 2.3) and the 1970 blacks only 10.8 percent (see table 5.8 in chapter 5), these figures take on monumental significance considering blacks were restricted in where they could live. Newcomers to the black community were not able to find decent housing in other parts of the city or in suburban communities and so were packed into an already overcrowded black area. This should not be surprising given that discrimination in housing was encouraged by the FHA (Abrams 1965, 61).

Comparing 1950 and 1960 census data, one can see that the in-migration of blacks was not spread throughout the city, but concentrated in an area of contiguous census tracts located near the central business district. Table 3.1 indicates that in 1950, the black population was located primarily in census tracts 32, 33, 34, and 42. By 1960, with the black population more than doubled, the proportions of blacks increased tremendously in each of these

Table 3.1

**Syracuse Census Tracts and the Percentage of Blacks, 1950 and 1960**

| Census Tract | % Black | | % Increase | Actual Increase |
|---|---|---|---|---|
| | *1950* | *1960* | *1950–1960* | *1950–1960* |
| 32 | 39.9 | 73.2 | 88.2 | 352 |
| 33 | 26.4 | 57.0 | 115.9 | 1,038 |
| 34 | 6.5 | 24.5 | 276.9 | 598 |
| 42 | 11.6 | 61.0 | 425.9 | 2,389 |
| 35 | 0.2 | 6.0 | 2,900.0 | 220 |
| 41 | 0.9 | 17.4 | 1,833.3 | 446 |
| 53 | 0.4 | 7.5 | 1,755.0 | 314 |
| 30 | 0.0 | 5.5 | | 220 |

*Source:* Campbell 1964, 29, which cites U.S. Bureau of the Census 1960.

census tracts. More revealing is the fact that in actual numbers, 4,377 additional blacks had moved into these four census tracts during this time, although another 1,200 blacks had located in adjacent census tracts. It can be concluded from these data that the black population in Syracuse was concentrated within a limited area in 1950 and that the residential pattern had not changed appreciably by 1960, ten years later.

One can imagine the impact of a massive number of new people moving into an area in which housing is already deteriorating from overcrowding. Considering that 15 percent of the recently arrived blacks in 1960 were from out of state and that many of them were from the South, the impact of the new arrivals cannot be underestimated. Campbell states that in-migration of this magnitude was bound to cause instability within a community, even when the newcomers were of the same racial group and with similar backgrounds (1964, 5).

In 1960, the black community, with a median age of 22.8 years for males and of 21.5 years for females, was considerably younger than the white community, with median ages of 27.8 for males and 31.8 for females. The relatively low median age for blacks was probably owing to the recent migration of blacks to the city (Campbell 1964, 7). Young people are more likely to migrate than are older people (Blackwell 1975, 19–22). And it is important to note that a young population, in particular a poor young black population, has a high fertility rate. As Sowell states, "High fertility directly lowers the standard of living of a group by spreading a given income more thinly among family members" (1981, 7). Therefore, the young age and the large families present within the Syracuse black community proved to be dysfunctional from an economic standpoint. Also of importance is the relationship between age, occupation, and income. Regardless of race, those groups with the youngest median age tend to occupy the lowest-status occupations, and even when they occupy high-status occupations, they are at the lower entry levels, both of which, in turn, translate into low incomes (Sowell 1981, 5–8). When race is included as a variable, it compounds the issue.

Table 3.2 presents the annual individual incomes of Syracuse wage earners by race in 1959. Excluding the lowest income category ($1.00 to $999.00), blacks had a higher percentage of individuals in all of the lower-income categories ($1,000–1,999 to $4,000–4,999). Campbell attributes the large percentage of whites in the $1.00 to $999 income category to the large number of elderly whites in Syracuse (1964, 11). In the higher-income categories (all those more than $5,000), whites were represented in much higher proportions than were blacks.

**Table 3.2**
**Annual Income Distribution for Whites and Blacks, Syracuse, 1959**

| Income Categories | Individual Income Earners | |
|---|---|---|
| | *White (%)* | *Black (%)* |
| $1–999 | 23.1 | 21.60 |
| $1,000–1,999 | 12.6 | 18.00 |
| $2,000–2,999 | 10.7 | 18.30 |
| $3,000–3,999 | 11.5 | 19.30 |
| $4,000–4,999 | 12.2 | 13.70 |
| $5,000–5,999 | 10.5 | 6.30 |
| $6,000–6,999 | 6.9 | 1.00 |
| $7,000–7,999 | 7.9 | 1.60 |
| More than $10,000 | 4.6 | 0.05 |

*Source:* Campbell 1964, 11, which cites U.S. Bureau of the Census 1960.

Income differentials between races are explained when occupational differences are examined. Table 3.3 reveals differences in occupational status for blacks and whites according to sex in 1960. White males were represented in high-status occupations to a much greater degree than were black male workers.

Black male workers, in contrast, had higher percentages in the low-status occupations. These differences were especially true for so-called black jobs, such as service work and labor. Sex differences are noticeable particularly among white workers. However, comparing white females with black females reveals major racial differences. In high-status occupations, particularly professional

**Table 3.3**

**Occupational Status for Blacks and Whites in the Syracuse Metropolitan Area by Sex, 1960**

| Occupational Status | White | | Black | |
|---|---|---|---|---|
| | Male (%)* | Female (%) | Male (%) | Female (%) |
| Professional, Technical, etc. | 14.2 | 16.2 | 2.2 | 1.8 |
| Farmers and Farm Managers | 3.0 | 0.2 | 0.0 | 0.0 |
| Managers, Officials, and Proprietors | 10.8 | 3.2 | 0.8 | 1.6 |
| Clerical | 7.8 | 35.2 | 4.9 | 7.4 |
| Sales | 8.2 | 8.3 | 1.0 | 1.6 |
| Craftspersons, Forepersons, etc. | 22.2 | 1.5 | 15.0 | 1.0 |
| Operatives | 20.8 | 15.9 | 33.0 | 28.2 |
| Private Households | 1.5 | 5.0 | 1.2 | 16.9 |
| Service (Excluding Private Households) | 6.0 | 13.5 | 19.7 | 38.3 |
| Farm Laborers | 1.5 | 0.4 | 0.4 | 0.0 |
| Laborers (Excluding Farm) | 5.3 | 0.5 | 21.6 | 2.5 |

*Source:* Campbell 1964, which cites U.S. Bureau of the Census 1960.

*All percentages are out of the total labor force.

and clerical positions, white females are represented in higher proportions than black females. Among low-status occupations, such as service, black females are represented in higher proportions. As was true among black and white males, black females have much higher percentages than white females in the so-called black jobs, private households and service.

Table 3.4 indicates the scarcity of blacks in selected occupations in 1960. All occupations shown in this table reflect relatively good salaries or wages. Of the fifteen occupations selected for males, blacks were present in only two: mail carriers and carpenters. More revealing, is that out of 2,623 males employed in all of these occupations, only 9 were black, or less than 0.5 percent. Black females occupied 28 out of 1,498 occupational positions, or 1.9 percent. More specifically, based on these data, we can see that there were no black male teachers, social workers, police officers, firefighters, electricians, or plumbers in 1960. Syracuse's four black female teachers were appointed that year, 1960, and the social workers were also recent occupants in that field. Even the largest category of female employees, "sales/clerks," were employed primarily in small "mom and pop" stores in the black community. In 1960, there were no black salespersons in central business district stores.

Finally, a look at unemployment figures for this time period helps to highlight the problem of employment and income for Syracuse blacks. In 1960, the Syracuse unemployment rate for blacks was more than twice the rate for whites (Campbell 1964, 17). More important, the unemployment rate for young blacks, a group this analysis has focused on, was even greater. For example, based on figures provided by Campbell (1964, 17), the New York State unemployment rate for black males ages fourteen to nineteen was 120 percent greater than for white males of all ages. Given that the unemployment rate in Syracuse was higher in 1960 than that of New York State, it is reasonable to assume that the unemployment rate for young blacks in Syracuse was also greater than the rate for young blacks in the state.

It should be remembered that the decade leading up to the 1960s resulted in a tremendous increase in the black population of Syracuse. Many new arrivals were from the South, and most were young. As noted, population increases exacerbated the already poor conditions in the black community. Housing problems increased because of restrictions on where blacks could live. Unemployment increased as competition accelerated for the few available so-called black jobs. Incomes were low for young blacks as a consequence of low-status employment and recent entry into the job market. Discrimination in housing and employment thus played a major role in creating the conditions that existed in the black community in the early 1960s. With a young population that had low-status jobs or no jobs and low incomes or no income, the probability of protest increased immensely. Young blacks had

**Table 3.4**

**Number of Blacks in Selected Occupations in the Syracuse Metropolitan Area by Sex, 1960**

| Occupations | Male | Female |
|---|---|---|
| Accountants and Auditors | 0 | 0 |
| Authors, Editors, and Reporters | 0 | 0 |
| Chemists | 0 | 0 |
| Dietitians and Nutritionists | 0 | 0 |
| Librarians | 0 | 0 |
| Nurses | 0 | 0 |
| Social and Recreational Workers | 0 | 4 |
| Teachers (Public Schools) | 0 | 4 |
| Technicians (Medical/Dental) | 0 | 0 |
| Insurance Agents/Brokers | 0 | 0 |
| Mail Carriers | 5 | 0 |
| Real Estate Agents/Brokers | 0 | 0 |
| Office Machine Operators | 0 | 0 |
| Stenographers | 0 | 0 |
| Salespersons, Clerks | 0 | 20 |
| Carpenters | 4 | 0 |
| Electricians | 0 | 0 |
| Plumbers, Pipe Fitters | 0 | 0 |
| Elevator Operators | 0 | 0 |
| Firefighters | 0 | 0 |
| Police/Sheriff Officers | 0 | 0 |
| Total People Employed in All Occupations | 2,623 | 1,498 |

*Source:* Campbell 1964, 29, which cites U.S. Bureau of the Census 1960.

the least to lose and were more likely than older and more stable individuals to be involved in a protest movement.

## Federal Programs

Earlier in this chapter, we dealt with local external factors in a discussion of the power structure in Syracuse. In this section, we discuss federal programs and local, state, and federal governments as external influences on the black community. We place primary emphasis on the federal government because urban renewal and the urban highway program originated with this body. However, its presence in the local community required initiation by local and state governments. We analyze the roles that these programs played in changing the black community and in impacting its readiness to protest.

### Urban Renewal

One can trace urban renewal back to the Housing Act of 1937, which provided for a slum-clearance program.[3] Waylaid during World War II, the Housing Act of 1934 was replaced after the war with the Housing Act of 1949 (Palen 2005, 240–41). Crucial to this analysis is that the 1949 act included both a public-housing section and an urban development section. The latter section played a major role in what was to happen in the black community. Allowed under this section was the use of federal monies to purchase and remove slum housing, upgrade urban land, and then sell the land to private developers at about 30 percent of the cost to the government (Palen 2005, 242). Because one of the primary purposes of this program was to change land-use patterns in such a way that the city would benefit, local businesspersons' objective was to replace low-income slum housing with commercial enterprises as well as middle- and upper-income residential units. Areas designated for clearance that did not qualify for urban renewal under the Housing Act of 1949 or its

3. According to Palen, the 1934 Housing Act was successful in that cleared land was replaced with public-housing projects (as in the case of Pioneer Homes and the clearance of the Ninth Ward) rather than with commercial enterprises (2005, 240). These units were constructed (basically four stories high) in such a manner that a family atmosphere was created.

1954 revision were cleared by utilizing the federal highway program.[4] Leaders within central-city power structures across the country were concerned with the massive move of their residents to suburbia that followed World War II. Given the cheap vacant land available outside of central cities and the policies of the FHA and the Veterans Administration (VA) that encouraged suburban development, leaders within central-city power structures set a high priority on making central cities and their central business districts attractive to middle- and upper-income residents and consumers (Palen 2005).

National concerns with central-city revitalization characterize the local concerns of Syracuse's power structure at this time. The old Fifteenth Ward, originally known as Jewtown, where approximately 80 percent of all blacks lived in virtual segregation after Jews and other ethnic groups relocated to other parts of the city, was one of the main areas of concern in that it abutted the central business district. Given the low economic status of blacks and local housing restrictions that caused overcrowding, the Fifteenth Ward was a slum. Therefore, this area and the adjacent Sixteenth Ward, where black spillover was present, became primary targets for urban renewal. Despite the transition from the Establishment to the "new" power structure, leadership and power were still dominated by business and industrial interests. The "new" power structure sought out a plan that would: *(a)* create an urban highway system to bring suburban populations back into the city to work, shop, and recreate; *(b)* provide available new land to attract new businesses and financial institutions and hence to maintain old enterprises; *(c)* rid expensive downtown land of low tax revenue housing; *(d)* rid the area of crime as the slums were cleared and thus decrease suburban populations' fear of crime within the central business district; and *(e)* make the city a more attractive place for upper- and upper-middle-income families to live (Martin et al. 1961; Williams 1966a, 1966b).

Such a concern was not new to the Syracuse power structure. As early as 1943, a seventy-seven-member commission had been set up to begin planning a postwar effort to revitalize the central business district. It took from 1943 until the Metropolitan Development Association was established in 1959 for

4. The Federal Highways Act of 1944 called for state-federal cooperation in establishing and maintaining a national interstate highway system that would connect major urban areas throughout the country.

3.1. Harrison Street between McBride and Almond, "the heart of the Fifteenth Ward." Shown are Frank Mitchell and Barbara Washington, ca. 1950. Courtesy of Onondaga County Public Library, Beauchamp Branch.

comprehensive planning to come to fruition (Fleischman 1980). One of the first steps in attempting to revitalize the central business district was to clear the slums. Therefore, in the late 1950s, a slum-clearance effort was begun with funds from the federal Urban Renewal Program.

*Urban Highway Program*

The urban highway program involved the construction of Interstates 81 and 690. Interstate 81 runs north and south, and Interstate 690 runs east and west, virtually breaking the city into four quadrants. The two interstates intersect in the central business district, helping to explain their role in urban clearance. Although plans for the urban highway system were part of the effort to revitalize the central business district, it was not until the late 1950s that the actual routes were agreed upon and approval was received from state and federal governments.

Although urban renewal was already taking place in the general area, the start of the urban highway system is what really spurred the clearance of land and the removal of people in the Fifteenth and Sixteenth Wards. In the end, 103 acres of land were cleared. The July 15, 1957, issue of the *Syracuse Herald-American* stated that the routes of Interstates 81 and 690 had been selected in such a way that minimum population damage would occur. Such a claim was made despite the fact that more than 80 percent of the black population would eventually be affected by the clearance project. Of course, the reasons for selecting the final routes were the need to complete land clearance around the central business district begun by urban renewal, the lower cost associated with obtaining the right-of-way, and the black community's virtually powerless position.

Important to this situation is the role played by the local, state, and federal governments in devising and approving the plans. The local government, in selecting routes and developing the plan, and the state and federal governments, in approving the final plans and in providing the funding, were all a party to this massive clearance of urban land.

Because the final plans for construction of the urban highway system had been brought before the citizens of Syracuse without objections before its final approval, one might argue that the black community had its chance to object. It did not do so at that time, however, because blacks lacked the organization to raise meaningful objections and the outcomes associated with mass removal were unknown to them.

As stated earlier, signs of unrest really appeared with the initiation of the urban renewal project in the late 1950s, but serious unrest began in 1960 with the massive removal of people associated with the clearance of land to construct Interstates 81 and 690. Discriminatory housing practices increased the frustration experienced by displaced families in their attempt to find reasonably priced housing of adequate size and in sound structural condition.

**Relocation of the Black Community**

Campbell provides partial data on the actual number of families displaced at this time (1964, 31). According to his study, 748 families had already been removed by the time the data were collected. Although the data do not provide a complete picture, they do provide some suggestion as to the magnitude of the project. Of the 575 families removed in Syracuse, 63.7 percent were black and 36.3 percent were white. It has been estimated by blacks involved in the removal process that by the time urban renewal was completed, approximately 80 percent of the city's black population had been dislocated. Land was cleared in four contiguous census tracts, all of which were predominantly black and poor. Although both blacks and whites were dislocated, there were racial differences in the pattern of relocation. For the most part, blacks relocated close to their area of displacement, whereas whites were more likely to relocate throughout the city (Campbell 1964, 31). Among blacks, relocation helped to begin a rather distinctive pattern of class stratification based on residential housing patterns that was established, to some degree, by the 1980s. As a result of the city's purchasing their houses, some blacks were able to buy houses on the east side. Included in this number were the few professional blacks who lived in Syracuse and members of the old economically stable black families. In other words, middle-income blacks relocated to the east side of the city. Many of the blacks who rented were placed in the south end of town. Renting blacks included lower-income black families and those who had in-migrated recently from the South.

Blacks who bought homes in the east side were following the Jewish families who had left the old Fifteenth Ward two decades earlier. One might assume that blacks followed Jewish families because Jews had traditionally been more willing to have blacks live in their neighborhoods. Jews, like blacks, had suffered from housing discrimination in Syracuse. Support for the assumption that Jews were more tolerant toward black home buyers than were other groups comes from the fact that even though the old Fifteenth Ward had been inhabited by other ethnic groups (Italians, Germans, Irish, and so on) as well as Jews, the blacks who were being uprooted had the least difficulty purchasing homes in Jewish neighborhoods (Campbell 1964, 34–35).

With rental property, the situation was somewhat different although still discriminatory. Some of the rentals that blacks were seeking included public housing that fell under revised federal guidelines outlawing discrimination in public housing. But public housing was in limited supply, and earlier federal guidelines that encouraged segregation in public housing had established a trend that continued to exist despite changes in federal policy. Also, by 1963, President Lyndon Johnson had issued an Executive Order on Equal Opportunity in Housing that barred the use of federal funds where housing discrimination existed based on race, color, creed, or national origin. Johnson's order was issued in the face of overwhelming evidence nationally that blacks carried a heavy proportion of the burden of those displaced by urban renewal. However, the difficulties that blacks faced in relocating stemmed mainly from the shortage of public housing and the discrimination in private housing, and, as a result, during relocation they were often segregated into the least desirable housing. This pattern, of course, was a causal factor in the creation of new slums (Campbell 1964, 34).

Although further support against discrimination in housing was provided by New York State in the form of the Baker-Metcalf Act and sections 18A–18E of the state civil rights law, redress through both of these state statutes was unfortunately dependent on a complaining party. In the case of the Baker-Metcalf Act, the aggrieved party could seek cease-and-desist orders through the state Commission for Human Rights. If the order by the commission was ignored, then final relief could be obtained through the courts. Similarly, violation of the civil rights law could be brought directly before the court (Campbell 1964, 35–36). During the early period of relocation, before organized protest, blacks seldom used these state laws in fighting discrimination. As Campbell points out, blacks did not use state laws against discrimination because many did not know or understand their rights. In addition, the lack of organization within the black community to assist in these issues only compounded the problem. Housing discrimination was handled strictly on an individual basis. Individuals were not informed as to what action they could take.

Whatever problems there were with discrimination, the lack of enough public housing, and the difficulty of locating housing cheap enough for blacks to afford, many black people still had to move. To deal with this mass movement of people, the Dunbar Center organized the Eastside Cooperative Council. This group was made up of every agency that operated on the east side of Syracuse and that had anything to do with people: the Health Department, Syracuse University, the YMCA and YWCA, the Huntington Center, and the Dunbar Center. Regular meetings were held by the Eastside Cooperative Council and representatives of the Urban Renewal Program so the council members could be apprised of the plans for redevelopment. Council members would then discuss with their constituency what demolition would entail and when it would take place. In other words, they provided a timetable to local residents of the affected areas through their agencies. Through the council's efforts, the first attempt was made at planned relocation. Although the intent was noble, in actuality the informal system of transmitting the timetable for demolition was less than desirable.

One important factor in the relocation process was the establishment of a relocation office. This office had its genesis before the actual Urban Renewal Program. During 1954, attention was focused on the deplorable housing conditions in the black community. Robert Hale, sent to Syracuse by the Society of Friends (Quakers), conducted a six-month study to determine the housing situation for Syracuse blacks. Hale was thereafter appointed by then mayor Donald Mead to assist blacks in locating decent housing. Hale's appointment resulted not so much from his alarming findings, but from the tragic death by fire of two black youths from the Fifteenth Ward (Ganley 1963a, A1). With the onset of urban renewal, Hale was appointed as deputy commissioner of urban improvement. Through Hale's, the Dunbar Center's, and black leaders' efforts, the housing office originally manned by Hale was officially made the Relocation Office in 1959 to assist displaced black families in locating housing. William Childes, a black who had been with the county Welfare Department for twenty-six years, was appointed to head the office, becoming the first black man appointed to a city administrative position (Ganley 1963a, A13). Childes had vast experience and multiple qualifications for the job, but the task requested of him was monumental. To secure housing for blacks in a city where discrimination in housing was strongly embedded was no easy task. When the protest movement started in 1963, Childes was often placed between the black community he sought to help and the white community he was associated with as a result of his position. It was impossible for a one-person operation to acquire housing for a sizeable proportion of the city's blacks. He was often made the scapegoat for the entire housing dilemma faced by blacks (Ganley 1963, A13).

John Williams, in writing about his old hometown, gives some insight into the sad aftermath of urban renewal:

I paced around the battered streets of the 15th Ward, pausing at one boarded up house in which we once lived. It was one of the few remaining buildings still standing, but it was scheduled for destruction. What happened to everyone? Mrs. Levy's store was gone. . . . One store remained in that block, Guido's. From the front of Mrs. Guido's store, in every direction, some distance away, I could see new buildings going up. East, toward the University, the Upstate Medical Center. West, the new Public Safety Building. North, the new Medical Plaza. But toward the South, only the dull red brick of Pioneer Homes. It would not take long before the parade of glass and polished marble, of smooth-skinned modern monoliths marched inward toward the center of the old 15th Ward and erased it from memory. (1966b, 4)

Almost all of the black churches were located in the 103 acres scheduled for clearance. Whether or not a church was eligible for relocation depended on the federal government's definition of a church. All of the barbershops, restaurants, beauty shops, and other businesses were located in the urban renewal area. As the decisions were made regarding what to move, where to move it, and when to move it, major mistakes were made. In discussing what happened during the relocation of blacks, we found that there was a major problem concerning what to do about black churches. As we pointed out earlier, many of them were storefront churches. Because of the small number of people in their congregations, several did not meet the definition of a church as determined by the federal government; when a church did not meet that defnition, it was not eligible for relocation assistance. Therefore, many of these small storefont churches were unable to move with their members to the new location. Remember, the storefront churches were important to the large number of newcomers to the black community, so not qualifying for relocation assistance meant the breakup of an important entity within the community.

One particular parcel of land was designated in the urban renewal area (an area of land close to the central business district) for displaced black businesses. It was to be cleared, and all black businesses—any number of "mom and pop" stores, mostly grocery stores, beauty shops, barbershops, pool halls, and cafés—that did not have a relocation spot selected by the owners would be located there. Plans called for the owners of black businesses to be provided with land in the designated area and financial assistance to rebuild. Owners, frightened that they would be cut off from their customers, declined the offer to relocate their businesses together in an area close to the central business district. In retrospect in the late 1980s, many blacks felt that if black business owners had taken advantage of the federal government's offer to establish a black business district, major changes would have occurred in the black community's business structure. Establishing a black business district would have caused customers to gravitate toward one area to shop and secure certain services. However, one can only speculate as to the merits of centralization versus decentralization of marginal businesses, particularly when those businesses are not located within the area where their potential customers resided. In reality, what happened was that although some of the businesses that chose to follow their customers made out quite well financially, a majority did not. Because their black customers were dispersed throughout the south side of the city, these businesses were unable to recapture a clientele. Two years later, during the black protest movement, a group of blacks objected that blacks had not received any government subsidies to relocate their businesses on government-owned land. Unfortunately, this objection was not valid, and, more important, it came too late. Black businesses had by and large already relocated to spots of their own choosing.

Most of the black families who moved into the south side of the city received some form of public assistance and were renters. These blacks moved into the most dilapidated housing in the city. The white property owners were able to get large sums of money for their property so that they could move into other parts of the city and turn the south side over to poor blacks. The process essentially created another slum ghetto. Black renters paid relatively high rent with few conveniences. With the destruction of public housing in the urban renewal area that had accommodated large families, one of the major problems was finding affordable housing for those displaced families. In the end, many large families were forced into accommodations designed for smaller families, exacerbating an already bad situation. Of all the negative aspects of relocation cited thus far, probably the worst was urban renewal officials' decision to relocate the poorest black families together in one area. With the blacks who were capable of providing leadership relocating to another part of the city, the least-functioning black families were isolated, without any formal organization to guide them and without the ability to make an organized effort on their own behalf. These outcomes of relocation left a group already dispossessed of holdings and incapable of self-advocacy with little hope of a better life (see W. Wilson 1987).

Again and again one can see that a lack of organization and an absence of leadership within the black community had a detrimental effect on its growth and development. Discrimination and insensitivity on the part of whites were certainly a factor in the blacks' plight, but the lack of effective leadership and organization within the community itself cannot be dismissed as inconsequential. On the positive side, one can say that urban renewal, with assistance from the black protest movement, resulted in the eventual integration of residential areas within certain sections of the city. However, any time you forcibly uproot people, their homes, and their lifestyles, you get massive unrest. Most Syracuse blacks agree, in retrospect, that overt signs of unrest and discontent began with the initial announcement of the urban renewal project. Unrest and discontent emanating from urban renewal caused social upheaval within the black community that few other projects could have brought about. Black renewal—or "black removal," as the project came to be known—took place with little or no input from the community regarding its outcome. Although the relocation of blacks sparked the fire of protest in 1963, the fuel of unrest and discontent had already been spread in the period of exploitation. Urban renewal and the methods of relocation were merely the catalysts that got the local protest movement going.

## Search for Housing: The Case of Public Housing

Any attempt to understand fully the beginning of the protest movement in Syracuse has to be based on a clear understanding of the local housing situation for blacks. True, the relocation of approximately 80 percent of the population of one group would be cause for alarm. Syracuse's housing situation, although brought to the breaking point under relocation, was reason for concern regardless of relocation. Relocation simply made a terrible situation intolerable. We have already emphasized the amount of discrimination suffered in the quest for private housing and mentioned the difficulties blacks experienced in obtaining apartments when the first public-housing project, Pioneer Homes, was constructed in 1935. What we have not yet fully explained is the importance of public housing to blacks' drive for adequate housing and the problems they faced in dealing with administrators of public housing once they did get an apartment.

It should be realized that public housing represented some of the better housing available to blacks in Syracuse. Throughout the years in which public housing was available, blacks of all classes occupied rental units. Even ministers and other community leaders lived in public housing. Therefore, public housing was important to groups other than families living on welfare or some form of public assistance.

## Public Housing: Blacks and the Application Process

In attempting to secure units in public housing, prospective tenants had to meet not only the written criteria for eligibility, but also unwritten subjective criteria determined by the application officers and tacitly approved by the administrators. Because it was necessary to apply in person, the informal criteria were often invoked before the formal. The application officer used three informal criteria in determining "desirability," which, in itself, was an informal criterion: race, family makeup, and demeanor. Being black did not completely exclude a family, but quite often it did mean the family was relegated to certain public-housing projects—those located in black neighborhoods (Deutscher 1968). The rationales given for placement were, "That is where they really want to go and where they would be happier"; "It would create trouble if large numbers of [blacks] were assigned to projects in all white residential areas"; and, if the applicant family were white, "White people do not want to live in that part of town" (Deutscher 1968, 43–44). As one might guess, the result was that public-housing projects became basically segregated. Those projects located in black areas became almost all black, and those located in white areas became almost all white. The second informal criterion, "family makeup," as with race, was by law not a criterion for exclusion, yet the application officer would determine if a husband was present in the family and when the most recent child was born. The absence of a husband was viewed somewhat negatively, but illegitimacy resulted in the application being thrown away. The rationale was that divorced or separated women and especially unwed mothers were a source of potential trouble. They were likely to attract the attention of other married men living in the projects and the maintenance personnel as well. Last, "demeanor" represented an even more subjective criterion (Deutscher 1968, 46). How a person looked, spoke, dressed, or conducted himself or herself determined whether or not he or she was rated high or low on demeanor. Those applicants who best fit a middle-class model of acceptability were considered desirable and had the best chance of securing housing (Deutscher 1968, 45–46).

Needless to say, blacks had a more difficult time meeting the informal norms of desirability. Not only was race a factor, but female-headed households and illegitimacy were in higher proportion among blacks than whites. Finally, a black applicant, because of a lack of education, had a smaller chance of conforming to a middle-class model of appearance, speech, and deportment. This was certainly true for female-headed households and women with illegitimate children.

When the application officer perceived a family as desirable, even when formal criteria were not met, he or she offered suggestions to make them eligible. For instance, one main disqualifying criterion for acceptance was if the family already occupied suitable housing. If the application officer considered the family desirable, he or she suggested that the family move to unsuitable housing so they could be declared eligible (Deutscher 1968, 43).

This description of the relationship between prospective tenants and application officers illustrates the difficulties many blacks experienced in obtaining public housing. Race was a factor not only in whether an applicant could obtain public housing, but also in which housing projects blacks were placed. The oldest public-housing project was located in a black area, but the newest projects and those that could accommodate the largest families were located in white areas, adding to the discrimination blacks faced in public housing.

The issues that blacks had to deal with in public housing often centered on their relationship with housing managers and the Syracuse Housing Authority's administration. Granted, many of the complaints lodged by tenants against the Housing Authority stemmed from a lack of communication and inefficient information. However, even when negative perceptions held by blacks were untrue or not fully accurate, these perceptions added to their growing discontent regarding the housing situation.

William L. McGarry, then executive secretary of the Syracuse Housing Authority, stated in a letter to the editor of the *Syracuse Herald-Journal* (McGarry 1964) that the rules governing tenant occupancy were quite simple. All a tenant had to do to get along with the Housing Authority was to (1) see that the monthly rent was paid on time, (2) maintain adequate relations with one's neighbors, and (3) keep the apartment in good shape. However, tenants felt that they could not "get along with the Housing Authority." Their numerous complaints included: older projects being like prisons, lack of representation or voice in decision making, perceptions that bureaucrats and clerical staff were insensitive and nasty in their treatment of tenants, rents being adjusted to wipe out raises, inferior materials being used in construction and repair of units, yards and exterior areas giving the appearance of being dust bowls, inadequate information regarding electrical expenses that were assumed to be covered fully in the rent, lack of a mechanism for the resolution of grievances, and lack of privacy and protection against intrusion by Housing Authority personnel.[5] Therefore, long-running complaints by the tenants, based on a lack of communication, real problems, and inactivity by housing officials, made the housing situation in Syracuse a prime target for protest. A 1966 study by the Mayor's Commission on Human Rights identified the lack of communication between the Syracuse Housing Authority and its tenants as the main source of problems (Roth 1966, 1).

When the Syracuse Congress on Racial Equality (CORE) organized its first demonstrations to combat discrimination faced by displaced black families and the resegregation of blacks in newly created slums, black public-housing tenants were already riled up about their treatment. The problems of public housing became an integral part of the issue of housing in general. The whole problem of resegregation and relocation was closely tied to the policies and actions of the Syracuse Housing Authority. Granted, the problems faced by the Housing Authority in meeting federal guidelines that disallowed race as a criterion in qualifying for occupancy and the demand by CORE and other protestors that public housing remain integrated (at a ratio of 70 percent white and 30 percent black) meant that the Housing Authority had an almost

---

5. From a pamphlet put together by residents of public housing, along with an unnamed writer, in the authors' possession.

impossible task. Ironically, it had already informally adopted the 70 to 30 ratio as ideal. Sustaining this ratio was impossible, however, because, based on federal guidelines, displaced families were to be given high priority for placement in public housing. Also, discrimination was severe in the private-housing market. Based on these statements, it might seem that the Housing Authority was carrying out its activities in a way that supported the views of the demonstrators, but was being impeded by federal guidelines. However, a careful analysis of the Housing Authority's acts and policies, in particular its informal policies, sheds a different light on the circumstances. Although the goals of the demonstrators and of the Housing Authority coincided, the rationale accompanying each set of goals and the means for achieving them differed drastically.

It has already been demonstrated that informal policies relating to the "desirability" of occupants for public housing were discriminatory for blacks because the most desirable type of resident was one closely akin to a middle-class white family model. Blacks, because of lower educational attainment, separation and divorce, illegitimacy, and, in some cases, southern rural backgrounds, had more difficulty than whites in conforming to this model. Just as important and closely related were the views held by Housing Authority officials about potential black and white tenants' attitudes about their placement. Officials felt that blacks preferred to live in nonintegrated housing away from whites, where they would be more comfortable. They also felt that economically stable and law-abiding blacks, those whom they classified as "desirable," did not want to live or were afraid to live next to economically unstable and "irresponsible members of their own race" (Ganley 1963b, 25). They believed at the same time that whites would not live in housing projects if the balance tipped toward a black majority or if the project was located in a predominantly black area. Pioneer Homes, the oldest housing project and located in a predominantly black area, was 97 percent black, and Central Village, located close to the black area, had an occupancy rate close to a black majority. The three housing projects in predominantly white areas had the following racial breakdown in 1963: Eastwood Homes had ten black families out of two hundred (5 percent); Syracuse was 25 percent black; and James Geddes was 17 percent black (Ganley 1963b, 32).

All these factors, plus the discrimination imposed by the private-housing sector and the continued demolition of homes in the urban renewal sections of the city, compounded the relocation housing problems for blacks. Not only were they being removed from their homes because of urban renewal, but they were discriminated against in their quest for relocation. When housing was found, it was in low-income white areas adjacent to the old black areas, and the houses where they were expected to live barely met minimum standards. For these reasons, the protest movement focused on housing.

## The Protest Movement in Syracuse

The protest movement in Syracuse officially started in 1963. It centered on the relocation of blacks, but factors in black-white relations in the city that contributed to the movement had begun with the arrival of the first blacks in Syracuse. The national concern with civil rights that started in 1960 also certainly played an important role, but it was the housing problem in Syracuse, spurred by the relocation necessitated by urban renewal, that brought on the direct action. Before we provide a detailed analysis of the protest movement, we should clarify what the protest movement exactly was: a civil rights movement or a "black revolution," as referred to by the local white press?

### Civil Rights Movement or Black Revolution?

Black and white citizens of Syracuse had already identified with the civil rights movement that was sweeping the country, particularly in the South. Many participated in the 1963 March on Washington, which focused on jobs, and worked in whatever small way they could toward the passage of a civil rights act in Congress (Scruggs 1984, 7). So when the local protest movement was organized under CORE leadership, identification with the broad issues of civil rights was already a part of the commitment of those involved. Civil rights organizations such as the National Association for the Advancement of Colored People (NAACP), Friends of the National Urban League, International Union of Electrical Workers Civil Rights Organization, and later the Urban League of Onondaga County; human rights groups such as the Catholic Interracial Council, the Syracuse University Committee of Equality, the state Commission for Human Rights, and the Syracuse Interfaith Committee on Religion and Race; and antipoverty and related agencies such as the Urban

Renewal Citizens Advisory Committee, the Syracuse Community Development Association, and the Crusade for Opportunity—all worked toward the same overall goals (Scruggs 1984, 7).

However, many local entities—in particular the mass media, business leaders, and the top administration of Syracuse University—looked upon the protest movement as a singular movement confined to the local community. Either not seen or not understood or just ignored were the linkages of the local movement to the national civil rights movement. Hence, to these local entities and to many whites within the local community, the protest movement in Syracuse represented a "black revolution." This perception held to some degree because although the overall goals of the various protest organizations were similar, the manner in which they sought those goals varied drastically. To the white community, traditional civil rights groups, such as the NAACP, the Urban League, and the local Dunbar Center, represented the quest for civil rights; their tactics were not the direct action or confrontation employed by CORE and its followers. Scruggs, in his history of the local Urban League, points out that nationally nearly one-half of the affiliate chapters of the National Urban League were started as a consequence of the civil rights movement of the 1960s (1984, 9). Chapters all over the country, including the local Syracuse chapter, were started as the business community's response to the direct action methods used by more militant civil rights organizations. The Urban League represented how the local business community perceived civil rights should be sought and how it, by providing financial support, could exercise some control over activities and tactics (Willie 1965b, 19).

The mistake made by local leaders and by the white community in general was that they should have looked at the fight for human rights in various local communities across the country in terms of "standards set outside of the [local] community and the pressures that also originate outside the [local] community for conformance to these standards" (Willie 1965b, 15). One of the main standards established nationwide by the civil rights movement was that of forcing, through nonviolent but direct action, recognition that rights long due American blacks had to be immediately granted. This approach was the antithesis of many whites' general feeling that the gaining of rights should take place with deliberate speed. In Syracuse, many whites pointed out that things would eventually work out if everyone was patient and even that these changes would not come "in my lifetime and not in your lifetime, but in that of our children" (Willie 1965b, 14).

The protest movement in Syracuse was thus a part of the nationwide civil rights movement. Despite the fact that local initiatives might have seemed narrow in focus (housing and jobs), the overall thrust was to gain civil rights for the black community locally and for blacks nationally.

## Congress on Racial Equality

CORE quickly came to the forefront as *"the* organization" in the Syracuse protest movement. The Syracuse chapter of CORE was organized in 1960 during an early period in the national civil rights movement. Dr. George Wiley, a black assistant professor of chemistry at Syracuse University, was an early leader in the local CORE chapter. By the time the local civil rights movement began, the twenty or so original CORE members had grown to around one hundred, with an active membership of around eighty (Willie 1965b, 18). CORE's membership, which was predominantly white, drew heavily from professionals, college and university faculties, and college students. According to Willie, a CORE spokesperson stated that the "organization's basic operating premise [was] that by using direct, concrete, and cooperative efforts of social action, a minority group can effect constructive change in a community situation" (1965b, 18–19). Although the local CORE had some ties to the national CORE, it was basically an autonomous organization, which became more important as events unfolded.

## Formal Protest

Formal action began as early as June 1963, when Wiley and another CORE representative met with Syracuse's mayor William F. Walsh. Their concern, based on statistics from the Relocation Office, was that 97 percent of the blacks dislocated because of urban renewal had been relocated in areas adjacent to the slum clearance and many in substandard housing. They presented to the mayor a program that provided ways to improve the relocation process by combating discrimination and implementing neighborhood integration. A major ingredient in this program was a call for scattered-site public housing that would assist in achieving integration. If some positive steps were not taken, the representatives threatened direct action (CORE Information Committee 1963, 20).

During the prolonged discussions with Mayor Walsh, CORE turned to the private sector, hoping to get assistance in combating housing discrimination. An appeal to the Syracuse Real Estate Board and to individual real estate firms asking them to implement a program of nondiscrimination bore almost no results, however. Frustrated by the lack of response from the mayor and from the private sector, CORE led the first march of protest on August 26, 1963. Other organizations such as the NAACP, the Civil Rights Organization of the International Union of Electrical Workers, and the Women's International League for Peace and Freedom (WILPF) joined in the march in an attempt to gain public support (CORE Information Committee 1963, 20). Over the next few months, direct action took place in the form of marches; picket lines at urban clearance sites; disruption of demolition in renewal project areas; and numerous meetings between civil rights organizations, their supporters, and the local power structure. Numerous individuals were arrested and jailed during the 1963 demonstrations: black and white professionals, unemployed laborers, housewives, married couples, ministers, public officials, and university professors and students. Hundreds of others marched, picketed, raised money, staffed CORE's office, and made various contributions to the Syracuse movement (CORE Information Committee 1963, 1).

CORE's biggest accomplishment was the establishment of the Mayor's Commission on Human Rights in the fall of 1963. The mayor established the commission as a response to the demands made by the civil rights demonstrations (Willie 1965b, 24). However, demonstrations and pickets did not result in the commission's being provided with enforcement, subpoena, and injunctive powers, as CORE and the demonstrators had demanded (CORE Information Committee 1963, 3).

As CORE gained support and some success in the housing relocation issue, it began to expand its activities into the area of employment. Its confrontation with Niagara Mohawk, a local utility company, was significant when it leveled charges of discriminatory hiring practices against the company. Pickets and demonstrations occurred during the rather extensive negotiations that ensued.

*Local Reaction to Protest*

Local reactions to the protest movement can be organized into three response groups: those who supported the movement; those who recognized that change was needed, but supported peaceful negotiations and more deliberate change; and those who were against both change and the movement. Of course, on the surface, all groups gave the impression that they were supporters of equality for blacks. However, when the attitudes, policies, decisions, and actions of these response groups are closely analyzed, the true picture materializes.

The change in the power structure at this time played a significant role in the reactions to the protest movement. As the earlier discussion pointed out, the Syracuse power structure was undergoing change from almost monolithic control to pluralistic control. This move toward a more democratic process in decision making meant that various sectors (business, government, education, etc.) within the community had to be consulted and that they had to be mollified if the final decisions and actions ran counter to their interests (Willie 1965b, 8).[6] During such a process, the ability to make a quick decision became somewhat stifled, and, to some extent, control was weakened. Theoretically, the outcome of such a decision-making process is usually more acceptable to various groups with power in the community. Unfortunately, groups with less power are still outside of the decision-making process.

Such was the case in Syracuse. During the transition to a pluralistic power structure, represented by business, government, and education, strict control over the actions and activities of the masses were weakened. Hence, the intrusion of the protest movement in the transition already taking place in Syracuse was both rewarding and fortunate. It was rewarding in that change was put into motion within not only housing and employment, but also within other various sectors of the community. It was fortunate in that more disruptive and violent confrontations between protesters and officials did not take place. There can be little doubt that the old Establishment, controlled by Stewart Hancock, would have met the protestors with physical force. To

6. Expanding the power structure does not refer to mass consensus. Rather than one or two individuals making the decision, other powerful groups have to be involved.

Establishment leaders, the protest movement would have been more than an attempt to gain equal treatment in housing and employment for blacks; it would have been an attack on the Establishment's personal powers. Monolithic leaders have to protect themselves from any challenge, for fear of "open season" on their powers. A perceived threat to power plus a general attitude of disdain toward blacks would have set the stage for an explosive encounter. Attitudes toward blacks held by the Establishment can be gleaned from an interview John Williams had with Hancock: "Hancock pawed at his desk and peered curiously at me. Without warning and with thin lips trembling with indignation he said desperately, . . . 'The colored people write to their friends to come to [Syracuse] to get on relief, to get into the fine public housing we have here. We've been very kind to colored people in . . . [Syracuse]. Yes, we've been very kind'" (1966a, 8A). This statement reflects the attitude of a person who felt the city had done more than its share for blacks and that the city had been put upon as those who had reaped the benefits of its largess had brought their friends and kin to share in the bounty. However, such statements overlook the type of treatment blacks received in Syracuse at that time. Douglas Kerr, in an undated article titled "The Negro in Syracuse: A Perspective," provides the following description of this treatment:

> It was lunch time, and Edward was hungry. Since early morning he had swung a sledge hammer, breaking cement over a leaky water line. He walked away from the rest of his crew to a nearby restaurant-bar. It was a typical neighborhood bar: the kind that has two doors side by side, one for the thirsty, the other for the hungry. Edward chose the former. Three men sat at the counter eating. Edward couldn't help but hear them praise their lunch, meatloaf, a salad, beer. They were regular customers and the bartender-waiter had treated them by giving each an oversized helping of meatloaf. Edward couldn't help but notice the big chunks from two stools down. The man behind the counter moved in front of the construction worker without a word, but with an expression of, "Yeah, whata you have?" "One of those pieces of meatloaf," Edward said, sensing a request for his order. "We just sold out," the counterman said, his face expressionless. Edward spun off the stool and left. "That's the way to handle' em," the counterman said as he passed the trio on his way to the kitchen to slice more meatloaf for the lunch rush hour. Edward was a Negro.

Support for the protest movement came from many groups within the local community. As one would expect, the black community in general provided support, but to assume that the community in its entirety supported the movement would be wrong. There were those, how few or many is not really known, who for whatever reasons—including fear of job loss and fear of challenging the status quo—were not in favor of direct tactics in protest. It would be correct, however, to say that most members of the black community supported both the objectives and tactics used during the movement. Leadership in CORE, the NAACP, and other civil rights organizations came from a small but growing professional class of blacks. The 60 percent white membership in CORE, the Syracuse Protestant Ministers, the Catholic Interracial Council, the Syracuse branch of WILPF, and the numerous college professors, graduate and undergraduate students, housewives, church members, and citizens generally represent the support the protest movement had from the white community.

Those who recognized that change was needed but who advocated peaceful negotiations and more deliberate change did not support civil disobedience. Even some blacks supported more deliberate change. They felt that the leaders of the movement were wrong in their efforts to force city government and the business community to meet their demands. They were afraid of economic and violent reprisals from part of the white community.

City government, a large portion of the white business community, and the top administrators at Syracuse University shared this view. Enlightened members of the business community, spearheaded by the local chapter of the Chamber of Commerce, responded to the protest movement by setting up a chapter of the Urban League (as noted, an earlier attempt by blacks to gain support for a local affiliate chapter had failed). Individuals representing this group perceived that the civil rights struggle was reaching outside of their area of control. Establishing a chapter of the Urban League, which would depend heavily on the business community for leadership and financial support, was their attempt to gain control of issues of race and civil rights (Scruggs 1984, 8). In 1964, about a year after the local movement got started, the Urban League opened its doors in Syracuse. With the opening of a local affiliate, the business community hoped to shift the emphasis of the protest from CORE's civil disobedience tactics to the Urban League's corporate boardroom style. It is important to understand that CORE had assumed the leadership role previously held by the other major local civil rights organization, the NAACP. The black community had shifted its allegiance from the NAACP to CORE and looked to CORE for leadership, and the NAACP had joined in as CORE led the demonstrations against discrimination in housing—despite the fact that the NAACP had been in Syracuse since 1925 and had a black membership seven times that of white-dominated CORE (Willie 1965b, 11). In theory, the move by the business community to combat CORE with the Urban League was smart. The NAACP had lost support, but the Urban League, being new, did not suffer from an image problem in the local black community. Also, because the Urban League's main thrust was employment, which had always been a major problem for local blacks along with housing, it was reasonable to assume that the Urban League could replace CORE as the major civil rights organization. However, the business community overlooked or did not anticipate three important factors. First, in the national civil rights movement blacks were responding to the direct action, get-things-done-now orientation of the more militant organizations and were abandoning the less visible and slower methods of traditional organizations. Second, the establishment of a Syracuse affiliate chapter of the Urban League, with one staff member located in the Chamber of Commerce building, was too little too late. Being physically located in a building dominated by whites did little to attract confidence among blacks. Last, when CORE broadened its focus to include the employment practices of Niagara Mohawk, attention again focused on CORE and its direct action approach.

In some cases, the CORE–Niagara Mohawk confrontation caused bitterness among those in the business community who had helped start and fund the local Urban League office. In other cases, some members of the business community were grateful for the pressure from the local movement, the national civil rights movement, and the federal government. These pressures, which were external to the business community itself, were bringing to fruition what these businesses were already practicing or willing to practice: equal employment opportunities. This small group of businesspersons did not feel they could take the initiative for equal employment themselves because they feared economic, social, and political repercussions from the rest of the white community (Willie 1965b, 16).

Syracuse University responded to the protest movement in two quite different ways. A number of the faculty and students participated in the demonstrations and supported all phases of the movement. Other faculty, not necessarily exclusive of protesters, did what university scholars usually do: they wrote grants and studied the phenomenon. In contrast, the top administration, which was an integral part of the overall Syracuse power structure, reacted negatively to civil disobedience, although it publicly voiced support for equal treatment. Because of the different responses from top administrators, faculty, and students, internal conflicts arose on campus. A statement issued by then chancellor William P. Tolley represents the top administration's position:

> No civilized society can exist without respect for law. No free society can be strong without opportunities for citizens to protest against what they believe to be an unjust law or inequitable administration of a law. The right to assemble for purposes of reasoned discussion or peaceful demonstration within limits established for the reservation of order is guaranteed by both civic and academic authorities, in this city and on campus. To take laws in one's own hands is quite a different matter. For those whose conscience dictates a deliberate violation of law and order, the university may have compassion, but it cannot stand between them and the civil authorities or offer them institutional aid. Civil disobedience is a grave act fraught with serious consequences for the individual and for society. Those who feel or reason their way to this position must be willing to accept the penalties and consequences for themselves. Such penalties and consequences may entail extended imprisonment by civil authorities. For those associated with the university, the trustees and administrative officers must reserve the right to impose such penalty as individual action warrant. ("2 Professors Jailed" 1963a, 1)

Based on Chancellor Tolley's statement, students and faculty who engaged in civil disobedience ran the risk of encountering punitive action from the university. A noteworthy sidebar here is that Chancellor Tolley was photographed as he was about to hit a CORE demonstrator with his cane (J. Williams 1966b, 14).[7] This act speaks for toleration of only a certain brand of law and order: the

---

7. Williams further states that the photograph of Chancellor Tolley hitting a CORE demonstrator was limited in its distribution and squelched by the local media. This incident shows the close working relationship between the university and the power structure.

violent action of so-called law-abiding citizens against demonstrators. Chancellor Tolley requested that the dean of the chapel not allow a CORE demonstration—civil disobedience information meeting for faculty members and students to be held on campus. A Sunday speaker at the university's Hendrick Chapel who was to address the issues of protest was canceled. The rationale given for the cancellation was that the temper of students and faculty was not conducive to such activity being carried out on campus ("Chaplains Resist" 1963b, 1). The fact is that the university's top administration wished to disassociate itself from the protest movement. Student and faculty involvement in the demonstrations had come to be a source of embarrassment and threatened the close political alliance that had developed between the university and the city. Further exacerbating the threatened conflict was the general feeling within the business and governmental sectors of the city that the university was doing too much to further the advancement of blacks (Willie 1965b, 9). Syracuse University's Community Action Training Center (CATC), which focused on organizing the poor for power, was a case in point. Such activities, although funded by sources external to the university, indicated to some that the university was not playing ball with the power structure.

Because many of the activities that were viewed as dysfunctional to the status quo in race relations fell within the area of academic freedom and individual rights, the university had limited control. Therefore, the top administration had to focus its attention on those areas in which it did have control: nonacademic activities on campus and the violation of civil codes.

City government also responded positively toward equal treatment but resisted civil disobedience as a tactic. The general feeling was that the city had complied in its responsibility to blacks in the area of housing. Mayor Walsh made the following comment:

> The real remedy for the condition which these groups are complaining about, . . . lies not with the City. . . . Rather it lies within the heart and mind of the citizens of this community. . . . The residential dwellings which they [blacks] must have are owned by private citizens. It is they who have the power to rent or sell their properties to Negroes. It is they-will-not do this [*sic*], it then becomes incumbent upon the moral and spiritual leadership of [Syracuse] to undertake the steps necessary to create a climate of interracial

justice which will permit Negroes, full and ready access to adequate housing. (quoted in Clements 1963, A9).

Mayor Walsh was really saying that there was little the city could do other than morally support the right to equality and that it was the responsibility of the moral or spiritual leadership in Syracuse to bring around the rest of the community. Discrimination in housing occurred in the private-housing sector, he claimed, not in public housing; therefore, the city had no legal course of action. Of course, the mayor's opinion lacked validity on two counts. One, the protesters were concerned with the discriminatory practices of the Syracuse Housing Authority, which was under city government control. Two, for the mayor to assume there was little the city could legally do was to ignore a citywide open housing ordinance as an effective mechanism. Also, the mayor might have empowered his Commission on Human Rights with enforcement powers, as the demonstrators were demanding.

The Human Rights Commission was the mayor's response to the protesters' demand for city action in resolving the housing situation. Conflicts between the city and the demonstrators centered on the demand by CORE that the commission be given "subpoena, injunctive and enforcement powers" to combat discrimination effectively (CORE Information Committee 1963, 20). Failure to grant these powers to the commission (the city attorney felt the city could not legally grant these powers) sparked additional protests and civil disobedience. The mayor responded by calling the CORE actions "lawlessness" and by stating that he refused to bargain under such conditions.

Obviously, the city administration was desirous of a more deliberate method of change. In its negotiations with CORE and the Interfaith Committee on Religion and Race, it had to maintain a delicate balance between those protesting and the power structure to which public officials were beholden. One would have to assume that the city's response was tempered by the attitudes and opinions of members of the power structure. Yet it had to respond to the demonstrators, who included in their numbers responsible citizens from the city's education, religious, and labor sectors. Given these forces, the city administration attempted to find a middle position in which the demonstrators' demands would be satisfied and the power structure's resistance to these demands would be pacified.

Groups within the Syracuse community who opposed both change and the protest movement were well represented. The most vocal, however, were elements from the business community, remnants of the old Establishment, and the local news media. How the news surrounding the protest movement was printed and editorials were written reflected the general attitudes of those who opposed both the protest movement and change.

Articles and editorials centering around the protest movement carried four basic themes: (1) Syracuse had a record in the area of race and housing that matched any other city of comparable size; (2) blacks were really to blame for their housing status because of low finances, too large families, preferences for living among themselves, and the large influx of southern rural blacks; (3) dispersion of the black population throughout the city had occurred between 1950 and 1960 despite claims to the contrary; and (4) Communist influence was present in some of the tactics used and claims made by the protestors (Ganley 1963a, A1; A. Jones 1963, A22).

In the first theme, the major point stressed was that Syracuse was not antiblack. In comparison to northern cities of equal size, Syracuse had equaled their record in housing equity for blacks. Contrary to this claim in the news media, however, State Commissioner of Human Rights J. Edward Conway made the following statement, "Forty-one percent of all the housing complaints filed in upstate New York in 1962 came from [Syracuse]." Conway further asserted that the same trend was occurring in 1963 (CORE Information Committee 1963, 5). Syracuse's housing problems thus even exceeded those of other upstate New York cities such as Buffalo, Rochester, and Albany, as well as those of other northern cities, contrary to the newspapers' claim.

The second theme carried in the news media was a basic "blame the victim" argument (Ryan 1976). This argument exonerated the forces operating within the larger community by placing the blame on the blacks themselves. Blacks would really rather live together anyway, and accommodations for their large families were hard to locate in white areas. Blacks could not financially afford decent housing and because of their rural southern background could not adequately cope with urban lifestyles. The question raised with this form of reasoning is not the truth or falsity of these claims, but whether, given a different set of circumstances, blacks would still be barred from white neighborhoods. For example, would blacks from northern areas and with small families, good incomes, and a desire to live among whites have been able to obtain housing in white neighborhoods? The answer, of course, would have been no. All evidence presented thus far fully supports the proposition that blacks were generally denied housing based solely on race. For instance, a black physician in the armed forces filed a complaint with the state Commission for Human Rights against a prominent local attorney who refused him an apartment. During the hearing, the attorney admitted not renting the apartment to the physician because he was black ("Court Requires Attorney" 1963, 6).

The third theme, that "significant gains" in housing integration had been made between 1950 and 1960, was predicated on a gross misinterpretation of census data. Maps developed from census data used the categories "white" and "nonwhite." In an article written by Joseph V. Ganley, "black" and "non-white" were used interchangeably (1963a, A1); that was in error. What the census maps used in the Ganley article actually show was that between 1950 and 1960 the nonwhite population of Syracuse became increasingly dispersed throughout the city. Yet Ganley's article included a chart titled "The Negro Movement: 1950–1960" (A1), implying that the movement of nonwhites was actually the movement of blacks.

Theme number four, charging Communist influence on the protest movement, was by far the most insidious, for two reasons. First, it was promulgated by the executive editor of the *Syracuse Herald-Journal*, which provided it official credibility. Second, Syracuse had gone on a witch hunt for local Communists only two decades earlier (Williams 1966a, 15). Alexander Jones, the executive editor of the *Herald-Journal*, hinted in his editorials of Communist involvement in the local protest movement (see, e.g., A. Jones 1936). He did not go so far as to say that Communists controlled the movement, locally or nationally, but he intimated that Communist involvement took place on the fringes. Jones indicated he could "smell" Communists and that the disruptive tactics of civil disobedience were Communist inspired. With this wisdom, he relegated the Syracuse situation, in particular the charges of police brutality by two demonstrators who were arrested, as "old stuff" and indicated he knew who the Communist contact was in Syracuse. He further wrote that the mayor and the chief of police had demonstrated restraint in dealing with the demonstrators and applauded Chancellor Tolley's vow not to tolerate the breaking of the law by students or faculty.

Editorials such as those by Jones could have caused a major race war. There is no evidence that the editorials increased violence within the city, but, according to Williams, they served as food for the "conservative masses" (1966b, 12). The business community responded positively to the Jones editorials by increasing their advertisements in the *Herald-Journal*. Subscriptions increased as the masses responded favorably to Jones's claim that local protest was in some way connected to the thrust for communism in America.

## Conclusion

It is difficult to assess accurately the full extent of the protest movement's impact in generating the changes that took place in the areas of civil rights, housing, and employment in Syracuse. There is no doubt that the protests had a tremendous impact, but other external factors—such as state open housing laws, federal nondiscriminatory housing provisions, and federal affirmative action laws—all had an impact as well. There are two areas in which one can isolate the impact of the local protest movement to some degree: "norm formulation" through the mass media and decision making.

Groups of power have traditionally used the mass media to define, formulate, and disperse norms to the larger society. Also, they use the mass media to socialize those with less power in their own belief systems and behavioral patterns. Groups without power do not have these options in that they do not control the mass media (Quinney 1970). However, they can have some influence in determining norms and behaviors through the mass media when they enter into conflict-type situations. When conflict between a group that is powerless and one that has power is reported in the mass media, other powerless groups or even other groups with some power may support the powerless group in the conflict. Of course, the opposite may happen, and other powerless groups may support the powerful group, particularly if the powerless groups are of a different sex and race than the one that initially engaged in the conflict.

In Syracuse, there was strong evidence that the conflict between CORE, the less powerful group, and the power structure, as represented by the business community, the city government, and the top administration at Syracuse University, resulted in some other groups' joining with the power structure. This outcome is not surprising given that the conflict centered on better housing and employment for blacks, who constituted a subdominant group racially.

Conversely, only through conflict were those with less power, the blacks, able to air their concerns through the mass media. Even with unfair reporting by the news media, CORE and the demonstrators were able to introduce to the public new definitions and belief systems related to civil rights in Syracuse. There is also irrefutable evidence that other groups joined with CORE against the power structure in the fight for equality. Members of the religious, educational, labor, and even business communities joined in the fight to establish new norms of racial equity.

Input in decision making cannot be completely delineated from the establishment of new norms, but because of its importance, we discuss it separately. Through the protest movement, blacks, for the first time in the history of Syracuse, were able to sit at the bargaining table with whites in making decisions and formulating policy. True, the newfound outlet was restricted to issues of racial equity and was somewhat short-lived, but it did represent a new norm guiding race relations. Up until that time, blacks and whites had come together only in informal groups to discuss race relations generally.

As the power structure within Syracuse changed from monolithic control to pluralistic control, the emergence of the black community as a subdominant group to contend with was new. As Willie points out, although the power structure continued to control community resources and wealth, the black community had gained veto power (1965b, 9–10). In other words, it had the choice not to go along with the power structure. This choice represented power never before used by the community. CORE's refusal to acquiesce to the process of urban relocation and to the employment practices utilized by some industries is indicative of this new trend (Willie 1965b, 10).

As stated at the beginning of this discussion, it is hard to assess completely the impact of local protest because the emergence of the black community as a force to deal with was owing in part to factors external to the local community. That CORE could bring pressure on the city to intercede in the housing situation and on industries to change their hiring policies was in part the result of external factors. Federal guidelines associated with the use of urban renewal monies, state laws outlawing discrimination in housing, as well as newly enacted federal affirmative action laws made the pressure brought by CORE more effective. However, it is doubtful, based on the black community's past performance, that these external avenues would have been used or even been known about if the local protest movement had not emerged.

# 4

# The New Black Community in Syracuse

DURING THE 1960S, the Syracuse black community was transformed from a community dominated through segregation and discrimination by whites to a community in which leadership emerged and organization was attained. Its members began to have input into decisions that affected them. These new features of leadership, organization, and demands for input into decision making integrated the community into the Syracuse community more fully. These changes caused its members to realize that new opportunities could be obtained through group efforts. Therefore, we refer to the black community here as the "new" black community. The *new* designation does not mean that by the mid-1960s the black community became a proportionately equal partner with the white community. In reality, its position was far from equal. However, it could no longer be characterized as lacking in leadership, nor could it be characterized as being completely segregated and discriminated against. This chapter focuses on some of the factors, both internal and external to the community, that influenced its transition into the "new" black community.

### New Outlook on Community Participation

Up until the CORE-led protest movement, blacks had not been a very active part of the Syracuse community. They had depended, for the most part, on the white community for jobs other than the marginal occupations provided by the "mom and pop" stores, cafés, beauty and barber shops, and pool halls, and the illegitimate positions gained through prostitution and gambling.

Illegal activities were allowed by corrupt police as a result of payoffs and by white males' utilization of many of these services within the black community. Even so, those blacks involved in illegal activities walked a thin line. Take, for example, Percy Harris, a black gambler in the community who became involved in opposing racial segregation. Harris, who had been able to operate without police interference, was soon arrested and forced to leave town (Moore 1982). Voting was not a source of political power because many blacks, in particular those involved in illegal activities, voted the way they were expected to by those in power. Therefore, community participation by blacks had been marginal at best and certainly not in the best interest of their community.

Because of CORE and the protest movement, blacks recognized that through organized protest and togetherness, their concerns and needs could be brought to the attention of members of the power structure within Syracuse. Despite not being formal members of the decision-making structure, they had learned that they could bring those with power to the bargaining table. Furthermore, they had realized that they had, to some extent, "veto" power, particularly in areas where federal funding was involved (Willie 1965a). The new black community was bent on participation. In the beginning, such participation was rather narrow because blacks placed emphasis on exercising political and protest power in areas of concern that directly affected them. However, attempts were made to broaden participation into a full range of activities within the community.

Blacks' push for community participation was met with resistance by white decision makers. Many whites felt blacks were pushing too hard, too fast, and that they needed to recognize that social change did not evolve overnight. Many also felt that blacks were not qualified to serve on boards or to make decisions. Some whites just felt uncomfortable sitting on the board with individuals who looked different and oftentimes spoke and dressed differently (Willie 1965a). Although whites perceived these factors as important in denying blacks participation, the overriding factor in the denial was that those in power were not willing to share that power with groups that had less power. By controlling boards of private corporations, public agencies, and voluntary associations, members of power groups were able to make decisions that benefited themselves. Charles V. Willie, in describing the funding practices of the Syracuse United Community Chest and Council, concluded that most of this organization's funding was directed toward community agencies that served middle-class (white) populations (1965b, 11). In fact, its board members were often unaware of problems faced by the poor because they were so far removed from the daily lives of poor blacks and whites in Syracuse. They were also unable to see that the local protest movement was tied in many respects to the poverty issue. They neatly characterized the protestors as agitators whose behavior was dysfunctional to the general welfare of the city.

Members of more powerful groups tend to ignore the fact that the sophistication, ability, and smooth methods of negotiation needed to serve on public boards come about after years of practice and experience. They also overlook the reality that poor minority groups often do not have access to training grounds so that they can come to the board table with the requisite skills and experiences. The result in Syracuse was that the only decision-influencing mechanisms known to poor minorities were often seemingly crude, harsh, and insulting. It can certainly be said that these mechanisms did not conform to proper boardroom etiquette (Willie 1965a).

As a result of white-dominated boards' reluctance to utilize blacks, a means of communication was lost. Throughout this analysis, it has been very evident that communication between blacks and whites in Syracuse was lacking. Of course, when groups do not enjoy equipotent positions, communication suffers. Blacks, in their quest for inclusion in community affairs, found themselves virtually locked out by whites who were not willing to tolerate different types of individuals and were not willing to share their power. Many in the white community felt more comfortable with a conflictual relationship with blacks than they did with a cooperative relationship (Willie 1965b, 13).

## Newfound Political Power

By the 1960s, the black community recognized the importance of political power and sought full participation in community affairs. As blacks became active politically in national elections because of the federal Voting Rights Act, national, state, and local politicians and political parties heeded the importance of the black vote. Blacks, in turn, began to organize, run their own candidates, and support candidates whose platforms addressed black needs and issues. Syracuse was not any different. The traditionally strong Republican Party was losing power, and the Democratic Party, if it were going to gain control of the city administration, needed the black vote. Blacks found themselves with new political power. Not only could they utilize the power of protest, but they could also make political candidates more accountable to them in return for their vote.

Another national trend that had an influence on black political power in Syracuse was the rising call for "black power." Throughout the nation, many blacks had grown tired of the tactics of nonviolence and direct action. For many, particularly the poor, the civil rights movement had done little except to raise expectations. In 1964, the federal Anti-Poverty Act was passed. Its emphasis was on the local communities with grassroots control. As a result, it was expected that the fortunes of the poor would change. But, paradoxically, the antipoverty programs that followed did little to alleviate poor blacks' frustrations exacerbated by the lack of substantial changes in their economic condition (Meier and Rudwick 1970, 17). In northern urban communities such as Syracuse, blacks were faced with a bleak future. Many were transplants from the rural South with little education; consequently, they had almost no chance for employment in an environment where the number of unskilled jobs had decreased. Slogans such as "black power" thus had an appeal within the black community. Los Angeles, Detroit, and other urban centers had witnessed riots that had destroyed entire neighborhoods within black communities. Syracuse's riots were far less destructive, but the feelings of powerlessness, alienation, and frustration were nevertheless present. The national call for black power was thus translated in Syracuse into a quest for black political power.

*Black Organizational Leadership*

As has been pointed out, CORE replaced the NAACP as the leadership organization with the inception of the local protest movement. White liberals and intellectuals, however, largely controlled CORE. As the focus shifted to black power and to blacks doing for themselves and determining their own destiny, blacks moved to gain control of CORE. Whites were dropped from membership, and blacks assumed the task of formulating policies, designing programs, and determining tactics to be followed. Many Syracuse whites who had worked hard and fiercely in the struggle for black equality felt betrayed and hurt by this move. However, blacks believed that the only way they were going to gain their total freedom was through self-help and self-determination. Local blacks saw strength in racial identity. The feeling was that blacks needed to attain effectiveness within their community as the local ethnic groups had before them. Although this feeling was not shared throughout the entire black community, many argued that if blacks were to make progress, they had to get rid of "do-gooders" and others who thought they knew what was best for blacks. For instance, leaders within the black community would have to come from the black masses. Paradoxically, although this group of blacks called for self-help and self-determination, they also called upon the white community to provide jobs. Their quest for black power was limited to a call for political power because they did not yet see economic power as an attainable goal considering that blacks had little or no control over businesses within Syracuse.

Along with CORE, which began to lose its leadership position as direct actions diminished, the NAACP and the more recently established Urban League were seen as the main leadership organizations in the black community. The NAACP, with more than seven hundred Syracuse members in 1965, continued as a leadership organization. Approximately 25 percent of its membership was white, but blacks maintained control over its administration and its board. True to tradition, most of its officers and a majority of its membership came from the middle class. During this period in time, NAACP programs focused on housing, employment, and school integration. Its local initiatives, like those of the Urban League, closely followed those set down by the national office. Whereas CORE captured the black community during the protest movement with immediate issues of housing relocation, job discrimination, and school integration, the NAACP was still looked upon as the vehicle to resolve long-term issues (Willie 1965b, 18).

By the late 1960s, the Urban League had gained more respect within the community. Scruggs maintains that the physical relocation of the chapter offices closer to the black community aided in the Urban League's gaining acceptance (1984, 14–15). Scruggs also points out that the Urban League responded to the local call for "black power" by establishing programs within the community that assisted and informed the black masses: the Modified Street-Academy to assist students on the verge of dropping out of school, the Voter Education and Registration Program, and the television program *Black on Black*, which featured a variety of local blacks discussing black issues. As the local Urban League grew in size, its staff consisted of a racially integrated group. Its appeal to black power and its racially integrated staff and board allowed it to maintain a delicate balance between the black and white communities and to continue its viability within the total community (Scruggs 1984, 15).

CORE, the NAACP, and the Urban League developed a working relationship during this period that was both complementary and supportive. Although there were times when the groups disagreed on policy and methods of action, it was generally felt that they sought the same objectives. The NAACP stressed the legal aspect, CORE featured direct action, and the Urban League was geared toward research and information (Willie 1965b, 20).

Two other organizations should be discussed because they played a leadership role to some degree. The Dunbar Center cannot be completely overlooked; however, its role as a major organization decreased as the black community moved through the 1960s. Certainly, over the years, it had served as one of the community's leading organizations. As various civil rights organizations began to assume a leadership role, however, it began to play a lesser role. Once the Dunbar Center began receiving support from the United Community Chest and Council, it was in less of a position to play a militant role. However, as a community center/settlement house, its mission was too important to get sidetracked into areas that other organizations were designed to handle. In the areas of recreation and the amelioration of social problems, Dunbar continued to play a significant role in influencing both policy and change in the delivery of services.

The Organization of Organizations, established in the mid-1960s, also had an opportunity to play a leadership role within the black community. However, its effectiveness in carrying out its goals, which were not clearly defined, left some doubt as to its status. As best one can determine, the Organization of Organizations was established as an umbrella organization under which other organizations would operate. Broadly defined, its goal was to facilitate cooperation between organizations and to present a united front to the larger community in negotiating change (Mack 1966). It was generally believed that local and state governing bodies should feel the impact of not one organization in isolation, but of a total community when dealing with any portion of the black community.

One reason for the establishment of such an organization was the disappointment and frustration most blacks continued to suffer. Even with a proliferation of organizations dedicated to the betterment of local black life, few changes actually occurred. Blacks derived few benefits from the activity of the new organizations. Seemingly, the modus operandi within the black community at that time was to focus more on establishing organizations than on solving the problems faced by blacks. Three reasons seem to account for this state of affairs. First, having been historically denied the opportunity to meet and discuss their plight and welfare, blacks wanted to ensure that they got in on the act. Therefore, when established black organizations, with their leadership already in place, often denied newcomers access to meaningful participation, the newcomers simply established their own organizations. Second, the federal bureaucracy, in its attempt to assist low-income neighborhoods through President Johnson's Great Society programs, mandated community participation at the grassroots level. The result was a proliferation of neighborhood-level organizations. Third, the black masses saw what could be done through protest, as exemplified by the results of CORE's activities, so as new problems arose and old problems continued within the black community, their response was to establish new organizations to deal with them.

In principle, the Organization of Organizations should have been a functional solution to organizational proliferation and fragmented action. The activities of more traditional groups such as CORE, the NAACP, the Urban League, and the Dunbar Center, along with those of the new organizations, needed to be coordinated (Meadows 1966). The perceived need for the continued proliferation of new organizations would be lessened because both individuals and organizations could belong to the Organization of Organizations. Even nonblack organizations, agencies, and groups were welcomed as long as their goals were compatible with those of the Organization of Organizations (Meadows 1966). In principle, therefore, the idea of an umbrella organization was good, but in reality the Organization of Organizations caused major problems during its rather short existence. Failure to articulate clear goals was a major problem. After defining itself as a coordinating organization for other local organizations focusing on black issues, it failed to specify other goals and objectives. This failure, in turn, caused other problems, the primary one being feelings of boundary intrusion on the part of other local black-oriented organizations. Organizational boundary problems had arisen to some extent between the NAACP, CORE, and the Urban League, on the one hand, and the Dunbar Center and other local social-service organizations, on the other hand, because they all were competing for federal dollars and client populations (Meadows 1966). A similar occurrence took place among neighborhood protest organizations that were narrow in focus and often oriented around a single issue, but nevertheless competitive with established organizations. Without clearly articulating its goals and objectives, yet proclaiming that it was all-encompassing, the Organization of Organizations was quickly perceived as intruding on the boundaries of other organizations and agencies. This perception existed among the client populations being served as well (Meadows 1966). Many individuals within the black community had already become confused about which organization or agency to seek out when a problem manifested itself. Rather than adding clarity as a coordinating entity, the Organization of Organizations further confused the issue.

Self-preservation caused many of the agencies and organizations to reject the Organization of Organizations as a coordinating entity. They did not know what direction the Organization of Organizations was to take eventually. This issue was crucial because the era was prone to radicalism and oftentimes violence. Individuals and groups were often suspicious of others. Those with a more radical posture did not want their image tarnished by association with organizations perceived as conservative in their approach or dysfunctional to a radical stance. The same could be said for less radical groups, who felt that the more radical groups were dysfunctional and that their own association with these groups would hinder their ability to communicate and negotiate with the local power structure and with state and federal agencies. These factors, plus a lack of support and poor leadership, led to the early demise of the Organization of Organizations.

*Black Leaders*

From the time Martin Luther King Jr. emerged as a national heroic leader (Burns 1978, 243–48), blacks have measured leadership, or the lack thereof, by a charismatic model. The Syracuse black community was no different. Syracuse blacks were quick to proclaim, first, that the problem with the community was the lack of a leader, and, second, that it had never had a true leader. What they really meant by this statement was that it had never had a charismatic leader like Martin Luther King Jr. In actuality, few countries, let alone communities, have had charismatic leaders, and these few have had them infrequently throughout their history. It was apparent in Syracuse, however, that the black community, although not having a charismatic leader, had both leaders and leadership organizations.

Literature on black leaders, in particular the work deriving from community studies, has characterized leadership on a militancy continuum, from the nonmilitant "accommodationist" to the extremely militant "radical" (Smith 1982, 20–25). Although this type of categorization is useful in analyzing black leadership, it is difficult to place individual leaders along the continuum except at the extremes. Individual leaders who might be considered liberal or moderate, as opposed to the extremes of conservative or radical in a typology like that of Elaine Burgess (1964) for "Crescent City," are difficult to characterize. Suffice it to say that the Syracuse black community at different periods in time and even during the same period had leaders who exemplified the varied characteristics of conservatism, liberalism, moderation, and radicalism. In some cases, an individual leader might have exhibited a more conservative stance at one period in time and a more liberal stance during another. It would not be difficult to label Dr. George Wiley, the head of CORE during the protest era, as a radical leader; however, labeling other leaders is far more difficult. Given this dilemma, we look at black leaders in Syracuse from a structural perspective, based on community position. Four types of structural leaders can be seen according to this perspective: the organizational, the political, the social, and the informal.

Organizational leaders are those whose leadership position is a result of their status within an organization, be it civil rights, community service, educational, or religious. Political leaders are those individuals who have been appointed or elected to public office within the community or head a political group. Social leaders are those who head social clubs such as sororities or fraternities. Last, the informal leader is one who does not have a structural base within the community, but who is self-appointed or designated by the masses. The important criterion to be an informal leader is that he or she is recognized as such by the community. Jermain Wesley Loguen and Samuel Ringgold Ward, publishers of the abolitionist newspaper *The Impartial Citizen* and activists in the antislavery movement during the mid-1800s; Reverend George Stevens, pastor of Bethany Baptist Church in the late 1800s; Jimmy La Grin, founder of a recreational club that was the forerunner of the Dunbar Center during the 1920s ; and J. Luther Sylvahn, founder and publisher of the weekly *Syracuse Progressive Herald* in the mid-1900s serve as examples of individuals who assumed leadership positions as a result of their organizational or agency affiliation (B. Davis 1980). After 1950, other organizational, political, and informal leaders surfaced. The organizational leaders include Frank Wood, director of the Dunbar Center and later the first black to head a department in county government; Dr. George Wiley, who headed CORE during its years of confrontation; and Dennis Dowdell, the first executive director of the Urban League and later host of an informative television program called *News and View: Black Perspective.* Political leaders of this period included Benjamin Garland of Garland Brothers Funeral Home and the first black appointee to the County Board of Supervisors in 1961 and the Reverend Emery Proctor, who was elected to the board in 1966. Among the informal leaders were Dr. Henry Washington, the first successful black physician to practice in Syracuse and a strong advocate of equal rights for blacks, and "Stretch" Irons, a community activist during the protest movement. Peggy Wood served as both an organizational and a political leader in her role within the county and the state Republican Party and as head of a county social-service department.

Blacks who assumed leadership positions during the 1970s include political leaders such as Robert Warr, the first black elected to serve on the Syracuse Board of Education and later the first black elected to the city Common Council; Dr. Constance Timberlake, who served on the Syracuse Board of Education for several years; and Clarence Dunham, who was elected to the County Board of Supervisors in 1974 and was reelected up to the end of the

1980s. Sidney Johnson, who in 1976 became the first black superintendent of the Syracuse Public School System and in 1980 was elected to the Common Council, served as an organizational leader and then as a political leader. Louis Clark—the executive director of the Human Rights Commissions of Syracuse and Onondaga County, a political activist, and host of a weekly black television talk show—also served as an organizational leader. Shirley Davis, educator-administrator, board member of the Urban League, and active in social and community organizations, is an example of a social leader for this period. Dr. Charles V. Willie, educator-administrator at Syracuse University, was probably the most recognized professional informal leader within the black community. He was widely respected by all segments of the Syracuse community: blacks, whites, the power structure, and the masses.

Many unnamed others assumed leadership roles; however, no group within the black community assumed more of a leadership role among the black masses than religious leaders. Throughout the community's history, black ministers have been a major influence as they have led their congregations. Although some have been more adept than others, and some have had larger followings, such as the pastors of Bethany Baptist Church, People's AME Zion Church, and Hopps Memorial Christian Methodist Episcopal (CME) Church, they all have been and still are the major organizational leaders.

Those individuals named and many others not named have served in leadership roles at different periods in time. Each was instrumental in bringing about changes in the black community and in contributing to its growth and development. For example, Loguen and Ward, as publishers and antislavery activists, used their positions to bring runaway slaves to the community and help them maintain their freedom. In this sense, their work served as an internal influence on the growth and development of the black community. La Grin and others during his period helped the community by seeking out external support from the local white community. Although the idea of a recreational club, which affected the social and economic status of blacks for years to come, originated with La Grin, it was only through the financial assistance of Mrs. Knowles, Mrs. Hazzard, Mrs. Burlingame, and the influential Commonweal Club that what was to become the Dunbar Center was ever initiated and sustained (B. Davis 1980, 23). Frank Wood, Peggy Wood, Dennis Dowdell, and others played important leadership roles. Before the 1960s, as executive director of the Dunbar Center, Frank Wood probably assumed the role of black organizational leader more so than any other individual. Through his work at the Dunbar Center, he was engaged in providing social services, obtaining citizenship verification for southern blacks attempting to get jobs with companies that had government contracts, and breaking down discrimination by obtaining positions for blacks as police officers, teachers, firefighters, and clerks in downtown stores. During the 1960s, Frank Wood and Peggy Wood, Dennis Dowdell, Charles Willie, and others, specifically black ministers, served as mediators and provided input into decisions relating to urban renewal, better housing, employment, and education for blacks. After the protest movement and as the white power structure began to include blacks on boards and in local decision making, the Woods, Dowdell, Warr, Timberlake, Davis, Johnson, Willie, Dunham, Clark, and others became leaders in the Syracuse community at large. Those who ran for public office, although receiving support from the black community, also had substantial white support. Sidney Johnson, after resigning as superintendent of

4.1. Children assemble behind the Dunbar Center, ca. 1952. Frank Wood stands behind the group at center. Courtesy of Onondaga County Public Library, Beauchamp Branch.

schools and being elected to the Syracuse Common Council, had such wide support throughout the black and white communities that he was pushed as a mayoral candidate in the early 1980s.

Given the social structure that developed within the black community over the years, the lack of informal leaders or other types of leaders that represented all segments of the black community is understandable. Other than the black ministers, Frank Wood as head of the Dunbar Center, Peggy Wood as an Onondaga County social worker, Louis Clark as executive director of the Human Rights Commission of Syracuse and Onondaga County, and possibly Charles Willie, leaders did not truly represent the entire black community, particularly poor blacks. This is not to say black leaders were not concerned about the plight of the poor; it was just a situation whereby the black leader as a professional was basically cut off physically and socially from the poor. Although some black professionals had a general understanding and could empathize with the problems faced by poor blacks, they did not fully understand the day-to-day intricacies of being black and poor in Syracuse. In increasing degrees since the 1930s and especially after the early 1960s, class divisions developed in the black community along rather rigid lines. One of the negative aftermaths of housing integration was the exacerbation of class divisions between blacks. Professional blacks moved to the east side of Syracuse with Jews, and poor blacks relocated to the south with poor whites. Also of importance was the fact that most of the professional blacks were a recent addition to the black community. With a high degree of turnover within this group as their jobs brought them to and took them away from Syracuse, they often lacked knowledge of the problems that the local poor blacks continually faced. These conditions created a vacuum that did not lend itself to effective leadership for all segments of the black community.

## Grassroots Leadership: The Federal Way

An external influence designed to improve the status of blacks, other minorities, and the poor was provided by the War on Poverty initiated in 1964 by President Lyndon B. Johnson. Two conditions must be met in order for social change to take place among disadvantaged populations. First, a vision has to be communicated well enough to the disadvantaged population that it can see itself as being included in the vision. Second, social structures have to be available to the disadvantaged population that enable it to bring about change (Haggstrom 1968).

Johnson met the first condition as he extolled the virtues of his administration's War on Poverty. This description caused minorities and the poor to believe that their status within American society would be drastically upgraded. Plans called for minorities and the poor, through federal intervention, to develop institutions controlled by them. These institutions were seen as necessary for the attainment of economic and social power. Blacks, other minorities, and the poor were encouraged to assume leadership roles in designing and implementing programs that would serve as a mechanism for self-help among them (Levitan, Johnston, and Taggart 1975, 293). A candid assessment of community action programs that were essential aspects of the War on Poverty indicates that, although noble in intent, they failed both nationally and locally in Syracuse. Their failure can be attributed directly to the fact that the second condition was never met. If one considers the New Deal launched during the Roosevelt administration as the first attempt to wage war on poverty, one can see the differences between the successful New Deal and the unsuccessful War on Poverty (Gladwin 1967). The New Deal was buttressed by structural changes in the economic system that had broken down during the Depression of the 1930s. Little or no emphasis was placed on helping individuals because it was assumed that individuals had the skills and ability to make it once the system was put in order. Johnson's War on Poverty assumed just the opposite. Emphasis was not placed on structural changes in the economy, but rather on developing a grassroots leadership based more in theory than in action. Poverty was looked upon as a "disabling way of life," not as an "imbalanced income distribution" (Gladwin 1967, 34–35). Therefore, the emphasis was placed on individuals and on improving their skills and competences.

One of the major questions raised concerning the War on Poverty was, "War against whom?" Certainly the focus of the war was the amelioration of poverty, but who was the enemy in the fight? One could not assume that the power structure in Syracuse and other American cities had been targeted because the emphasis was not on bringing about structural changes in the economic and political systems. The evidence clearly shows that one of the major strategies employed by the federal government in administering the War on Poverty was conflict avoidance with business and industry. Antipoverty programs, in outcome, benefited most those who needed help the least. In order to lessen opposition to the programs, funds were made available in such a way that business, industry, and professional workers who assumed positions of high status and salary had a vested interest in the programs. Although in principle the idea was that these organizations and individuals would help the poor, oftentimes no concerted efforts were made in that direction. In Syracuse, large corporations were enlisted to operate Job Corps centers. Middle-class volunteers controlled many of the programs, and businesspeople and professionals attempted to control the boards of community action programs. Although the federal government attempted to appease local power structures by providing financial benefits, the Office of Economic Opportunity (OEO), which served as headquarters for the War on Poverty, developed strategies designed to circumvent traditional social agencies in the fight to ameliorate poverty. Understanding that the War on Poverty had embraced the social-structural approach to poverty is essential in comprehending its policies and decisions. The social-structural approach maintains that poverty is a condition neither created by nor solvable by those involved in it. The OEO reasoned that traditional social agencies had done a poor job over the years in fighting poverty; therefore, if progress was to be made, initiatives would have to come from elsewhere. Because the OEO assumed, rightfully so, that local power structures would resist any attempt to circumvent local social agencies that they controlled, it also assumed that only the federal government had the power and commitment to overcome this resistance. Gladwin states, "This concept of a federal-local confrontation was carried so far that some of the language in Title II of the Economic Opportunity Act seems almost to provide for federal support for organized insurrection against local authority" (1967, 37).

Many members of the black community talk about how the CATC of Syracuse University ran into resistance from the local community from the time it was initiated. Given CORE's direct action tactics in combating housing and educational segregation, an agency designed to help the poor develop autonomous and powerful groups that would become self-advocates for their own problems was bound to face difficulties.

The CATC, in its attempt to train the local black masses to become self-advocates, was looked upon as not cooperating with the local power structure. It should be kept in mind that the poor black masses in Syracuse had previously been virtually powerless in negotiating with the power structure. Even the newly arrived middle-class blacks often did not fully understand many of the problems and circumstances faced by blacks in general. Because CATC was associated with Syracuse University, the power structure put pressure on the university to curtail its activities. Limitations, however, were placed on how far the university could go in controlling CATC actions and programs for fear of violating the academic freedom of faculty members associated with the center.

The Crusade for Opportunity, another community action program that replaced the CATC, faced similar problems as the Syracuse business and civic community continued to ask whether the program should not be lodged in either a local governmental agency or within the local voluntary sector to give it legitimization and community support.[1] The Crusade, like its forerunner the CATC, obtained its funding directly from the federal government. Needless to say, such an arrangement caused conflicts and competition between the Crusade and the local government as well as local public and private agencies that had traditionally provided those services. However, legitimate questions were raised in Syracuse about whether traditional agencies, with their virtually all-white business and professional boards, were able or even willing to address themselves seriously to issues of black poverty in a meaningful manner (Willie, Notkin, and Rezak 1964; Willie 1965a, 1965b, 1970).

Blacks who were selected to serve on advisory committees for community action agencies in Syracuse were handpicked (Willie 1967). When local leaders arose out of the masses in the black community, they were often brought into the fold of the power structure by placing them on the payroll of city agencies or an antipoverty agency. In this way, the effectiveness of a grassroots movement was kept to a minimum and its viability threatened. Black professionals warned white community leaders against resisting black and poor groups in their quest for a redistribution of power. They pointed

1. The discussion of the Crusade for Opportunity was gleaned from notes taken at the community seminar held October 4, 1967 (Willie 1967).

out that a change in power relations must be expected if Syracuse wanted to avoid major racial violence (Willie 1967). As noted earlier, although racial violence did not hit Syracuse to the extent it did other American cities such as Los Angeles, Detroit, and even Buffalo, some violence did occur. The local power structure continued to resist efforts toward a redistribution of power, however. Community action programs, in particular the CATC and the Crusade for Opportunity, had very limited success, mainly because of the policies and strategies employed by the federal government. Although developing programs that represented revolutionary social intervention, the government adapted a policy of "conflict avoidance" with local power structures. This paradox made efforts fruitless on the whole. In the end, poor blacks' expectations were raised, but no outlets were provided to meet those expectations. Those persons within the Syracuse black community and within other black communities throughout America who profited from the War on Poverty were those with the educational qualifications and professional credentials that allowed them to gain positions in antipoverty agencies. Without full support and guidance from the federal level, neither a redistribution of power nor financial benefits trickled down to the masses. The War on Poverty represented an instance in the history of the black community when external influences designed to strengthen grassroots leadership and hence reduce poverty did little other than raise the level of frustration and despair.

### Jobs on the Horizon

It was pointed out earlier that the white power structure, in protecting the interests of local business, had utilized the black worker as part of a scheme to maintain low wages locally. Black workers, as a result, had been relegated to semiskilled and unskilled jobs paying the lowest wages. White workers, although paid low wages, were somewhat appeased in that they were not on the bottom of the wage scale, nor did they hold the lowest-status jobs. Also, the power structure used black workers as a threat to white workers in order to keep them in line and working for low wages.

By the mid-1960s, the Republican-led local power structure had weakened considerably through scandals and a strong coalition put together by local Democrats. By 1969, the first Democrat had been elected mayor. Coinciding with the decline in the Republican-led power structure's control was an influx of national corporations to the Syracuse metropolitan area. These factors, as well as the initiation of federal programs in the aftermath of the civil rights movement and in response to urban violence, created an atmosphere of rising economic expectations within the black community.

### Blacks' Occupational Status, 1965

Before we describe the changing occupational status within the Syracuse black community, it is necessary to provide an occupational picture of blacks before 1968, which most blacks consider to be a pivotal year. To imply that blacks made occupational progress only after 1968 would be false, just as it would be false to state that progress was made throughout the black community in 1968 and thereafter. By 1965, the first black teacher had been in the Syracuse school system fifteen years and the first vice principal had been appointed. Blacks held positions in the fire and police departments, and after years of negotiation black salespersons worked in downtown and suburban stores. In the service area and in heavy industry, blacks had held jobs for years. The most glaring areas of deficiencies in employment of blacks were the skilled and professional sectors (Wood 1965). Frank Wood states in his booklet on black employment in Syracuse that "the Negro is the 'last hired and first fired,' [and] this is more true now than it was in the past because the areas in which Negroes have usually been employed in, are the areas in which jobs are being lost to automation at the rate of 40,000 per week on a national scale" (1965, 2). The irony is that blacks were able to get industrial jobs only after the Republican power structure lost control and national companies located in Syracuse. The newly located companies were willing to hire blacks in unskilled and semiskilled industrial jobs, but by this time industries were becoming automated, and the newly hired blacks were losing their jobs in a transition to high technology more so than because of racism and discrimination. Wood further points out that approximately 86 percent of the black females and 88 percent of the black males in Syracuse were employed in these types of jobs. Whites, in contrast, were represented in much lower percentages: 32 percent of females and 54 percent males (1965, 2).

In 1965, the public sector, one of the leading sectors for black employment, had the following breakdown for employees. In a city with a workforce
of 4,798, a mere 5.2 percent were nonwhite. Onondaga County employed
2,350 persons, of whom 7 percent were nonwhite. New York State, with 3,916
persons employed in the Syracuse metropolitan area, employed approximately 25 to 30 nonwhites, or less than one percent. Finally, the federal government employed 5,827, of whom about 200 were nonwhite, or about 5.2
percent (Wood 1965, 3).[2] Although these data reflect an overall increase in
the employment of blacks in public-sector jobs, the increase was not in line
with the overall increase in the black population. It should be remembered
that the black population grew the fastest in the periods 1940–50 and 1950–
60, with increases of 120.3 percent and 144.4 percent, respectively.

Table 4.1 provides a list of the numbers of blacks in Syracuse employed in
positions that were relatively new for blacks within the community in 1965.
No claims are made that the list is entirely exhaustive, but it can be considered representative of the employment status of blacks at that time. It can
be seen that twenty-seven blacks were classified as owning their own businesses or managing places of business owned by others. Of the twenty-seven,
only two were managers, both of gasoline stations. Black-owned businesses
included numerous restaurants, two funeral homes, an auto-driving school,
a rug-cleaning establishment, two trucking companies, an electrical contrac-
tor, cleaners, and a demolition (wrecking) company, among others. Not included were more than twenty-five beauty and barber shops that existed in
1965 (Wood 1965, 2). Barbershops, beauty shops, and pool halls, along with
small cafés, had been the mainstay of black businesses for years.

Clerical workers constituted the largest category of black workers at this
time. These workers ranged from secretaries and typists to bank tellers. At
first sight, one should find it interesting that although there was only one den-
tist and one psychologist, nine physicians were present in the black community. However, of the nine physicians, only one was in private practice. That
was Dr. Henry Washington, the first successful black physician to practice in

2. It must be kept in mind that the category "nonwhite" was not exclusively made up of
American blacks, although we would estimate that in Syracuse about 95 percent were black.

**Table 4.1**

**Nontraditional Occupations Held by Syracuse Blacks, 1965**

| Occupational Category | Number | % of Total |
|---|---|---|
| Auditors | 3 | 1.1 |
| Black Business Owners/Managers | 27 | 9.9 |
| Chemists | 3 | 1.1 |
| Clerical Workers | 46 | 16.8 |
| Commercial Designers | 4 | 1.5 |
| Dentists | 1 | 0.4 |
| Dieticians | 1 | 0.4 |
| Employment/Personnel Workers | 4 | 1.5 |
| Engineers | 3 | 1.1 |
| Firefighters | 5 | 1.8 |
| Lawyers | 3 | 1.1 |
| Librarians | 3 | 1.1 |
| Ministers | 20 | 7.8 |
| Newspersons | 4 | 1.5 |
| Nurses (Registered) | 6 | 2.2 |
| Pharmacists | 2 | 0.7 |
| Physicians | 9 | 3.3 |
| Police Officers | 4 | 1.5 |
| Postal Workers | 1 | 0.4 |
| Psychologists | 1 | 0.4 |
| Recreation Workers/Administrators | 7 | 2.6 |
| Salespersons | 16 | 5.8 |
| Social/Welfare Workers | 27 | 9.9 |
| Teachers/Administrators/Professional Staff | 45 | 16.2 |
| Technicians | 14 | 5.1 |
| University Professors | 4 | 1.5 |
| Urban Workers/Administrators | 11 | 4.0 |
| Total | 274 | 100.7 |

*Source:* Developed from a list of what was referred to as "unusual positions" filled by Syracuse blacks in Wood 1965, 1–14.

Syracuse. Of the remaining eight physicians, one was on staff at St. Mary's Hospital, and the other seven were interns at St. Joseph's Hospital. The lack of black doctors and dentists in private practice in the black community was a trend that continued into the 1980s. Social-welfare workers fell into two categories, those with advanced degrees in social work (sixteen) and those with only baccalaureate degrees (the remaining eleven). Most of the social workers with an undergraduate degree served as caseworkers for the Syracuse Department of Social Welfare. Those with graduate degrees were in positions at the VA Hospital, Upstate Medical College, Syracuse Health Department, the state Commission for Human Rights, the Onondaga County Department of Social Welfare, the Huntington Family Center, the Syracuse Relocation Office, the Dunbar Center, and the Onondaga County Division of Research and Development. Included with public-school teachers was one vice principal. Considering it was not until 1950 that the first black teacher was hired, it is not surprising that out of a large city staff of teachers and other professionals, there was only one black vice principal and no principals. Black faculty at Syracuse University were represented in the home economics, special education, chemistry, social work, and sociology departments. Most of the professionals listed under "urban workers" were associated with either urban relocation or the Crusade for Opportunity, the federally funded antipoverty agency. The evidence here seems to indicate that by 1965 blacks had made some gains in jobs that were outside the traditionally held low-status positions. However, it was not until externally initiated programs, such as affirmative action, took hold that the black community saw significant changes in the occupational status of its members.

## Affirmative Action

External factors that have influenced the growth and development of the black community have been defined as those factors that occurred outside of the black community itself. External factors or influences can be derived from the local, state, national, or international level. In addition to the Syracuse Urban Renewal Program, the urban highway program, and antipoverty programs, another external program, initiated by the federal government, was established to change the job situation for blacks: affirmative action.

Affirmative action is very difficult to identify as a program or set of laws because what is known today as affirmative action evolved out of the Civil Rights Act of 1964 and a series of Executive Orders issued between 1965 and 1971 (Calvert 1979, 282). For the purposes of this analysis, it is not necessary to provide a detailed chronology of the laws and Executive Orders that make up affirmative action. The key statute is Public Law 88-352, which was passed July 2, 1964, as part of Title VII of the Civil Rights Act. In simplistic terms, this law forbids discrimination in employment based on race, sex, religion, color, or national origin (Calvert 1979, 282). In analyzing the effects of affirmative action on Syracuse, we utilize Larry Williams's four stages of affirmative action (1981, 4–5).

*Fair Employment Era*

According to Williams, the fair employment era existed from around 1945 until 1964. He characterizes this era as the "try not to discriminate period." In Syracuse, however, the "try not to discriminate period" minus any legal or enforcement powers did little to change blacks' employment status. As pointed out in chapter 3, during World War II blacks enjoyed employment opportunities beyond that of laborer and domestic, but this improvement was short-lived. As World War II ended and white veterans returned, eliminating the shortage of workers caused by the war, blacks and white females were again relegated to either the lowest-status jobs or no paid employment. The employment problem was exacerbated by the tremendous increases in the local black population identified in the 1950 and 1960 censuses. Therefore, as was the case in many other parts of the country, the fair employment era did little to improve the employment of blacks in Syracuse. It should be recognized, however, that this era set the stage for more aggressive action by the federal government, the courts, and society.

*Equal Opportunity Era*

Williams sees the equal opportunity era as extending from 1964 to 1970 and calls it the "don't discriminate era." This era began with the passage of the 1964 Civil Rights Act, which outlawed discrimination in employment. This act represented action taken by Congress in response to the massive nation-wide demonstrations staged by blacks to raise the social consciousness of American society to the social and economic plight of blacks. We have already presented data that show how by 1965 some progress had been made in gaining employment in education, fire and police protection, sales, social services, and clerical services. However, the Syracuse black community generally regarded the year 1968 as the beginning of a significant change in the employment of black professionals. National companies located in the Syracuse SMA, such as Bristol-Myers, Allied-Chemical, Anheuser-Busch, Crouse-Hinds, Carrier, Chrysler New Process Gear, General Electric, and General Motors, began making concerted efforts to hire blacks. Wood (1965), in his analysis of the occupations held by blacks in 1965, focuses on what he refers to as "unusual" positions. If the 1965 occupations Wood includes were considered unusual for Syracuse, then those made available to blacks after 1968 can be considered ultraunusual. Electrical and mechanical engineers, architects, chemists, microbiologists, accountants, and others were brought into the black community. Syracuse University began its faculty recruitment program during this period. Although very small in number, these incoming blacks were different in that they were professionals. Before their arrival, only a few professional families could be counted among Syracuse's 21,383 blacks in 1970.

*Affirmative Action Era*

Williams sees the affirmative action period, which extended from 1970 to 1976, as the "hire minorities and women era." It was quite evident that by the end of the 1960s more aggressive action was needed to improve the employment status of blacks nationally. The Equal Employment Opportunity Act of 1972 broadened coverage to include local and state agencies, all colleges and universities, state employment offices, and private companies and unions with at least fifteen employees or members (Calvert 1979, 290). Also, the powers of the Equal Opportunity Commission were strengthened in 1972. In Syracuse, nationally based companies and large local companies continued their quests for black workers. They were joined by local educational institutions, the City of Syracuse, and, to a lesser degree, Onondaga County.

Some blacks, however, viewed the election of Mayor Lee Alexander in 1969, who became the first Democratic mayor of Syracuse, as more important to the change in job status for blacks in the public sector than the strengthened affirmative action laws. It was felt that the improvement for blacks in public-sector jobs occurred primarily because of employment by the city, where Democrats had gained control with Alexander's election. County government, which was still controlled by Republicans, did not hire blacks on the same level as did the city. Under Alexander's leadership, an affirmative action ordinance was passed for city government to increase the percentage of blacks employed comparable to the percentage of blacks in the population of the city. No such ordinance was passed for the county, although the county did pass an ordinance that covered minority employment for those businesses that contracted to do business with the county.[3]

At any rate, in both the public and private sectors, the drive was toward hiring professional blacks. Industries looked for engineers, accountants, and others with college degrees. Educational institutions and public agencies were in search of blacks with degrees at the baccalaureate level and higher. Native blacks and those who migrated to Syracuse during the 1940s and the 1950s, for the most part, were unable to take advantage of the new opportunities because they lacked adequate skills and education. Therefore, the changes that took place in the occupational status of blacks did so as a result of the recruitment and relocation of blacks to Syracuse. This distinction is important, for the influx of blacks into Syracuse that continued into the 1980s was different from the influx before that time. Earlier black migrants had been unskilled and primarily from southern rural backgrounds. Blacks who came later were more urbane and much better educated. Professional blacks, although still small in numbers, had a tremendous impact on the black community's social, political, and economic outlook.

During the affirmative action era, blacks made strides in obtaining skilled jobs previously unavailable to them. This does not mean that discrimination had been eliminated, but that qualified blacks had better opportunities for employment in skilled jobs.

---

3. Telephone interview with Mr. Louis Clark, executive director of the Human Rights commission of Syracuse and Onondaga County (L. Clark 1985).

*Reverse Discrimination Era*

The reverse discrimination era denotes the period, according to Williams, when the concerns of white males began to crystallize into a countermovement against affirmative action. Beginning after 1976 and extending through to the 1980s, evidence of a shift in hiring practices can be seen in many areas within the Syracuse business, educational, and industrial community. Most notable was the decrease in black faculty at Syracuse University. Decreases in employment of blacks in the public sector were also noticeable; however, some of the decreases were because of cutbacks in federal funds made available for local social programs.

An employment analysis beyond the scope of this monograph would be necessary to determine the exact influence that affirmative action laws had on the changing employment picture for blacks in Syracuse. However, it is safe to assume that it had a positive influence. If the decade 1960 to 1970 is used as a measuring stick of its impact, one can see increases in higher-status occupations for blacks by looking at table 4.2.

**Table 4.2**
**Occupational Comparisons of Blacks in Syracuse, 1960–1970**

| Occupational Status | Males (%)* | | Females (%) | |
|---|---|---|---|---|
| | *1960* | *1970* | *1960* | *1970* |
| Professional and Technical | 5.8 | 8.4 | 2.6 | 9.4 |
| Managers, Officials, and Proprietors | 0.8 | 3.0 | 1.5 | 0.2 |
| Clerical and Kindred Workers | 4.5 | 7.0 | 8.1 | 23.5 |
| Salespersons | 1.2 | 1.4 | 1.6 | 3.0 |
| Craftspersons, Forepersons, etc. | 14.6 | 17.6 | 1.0 | 1.0 |
| Operatives, etc. | 31.5 | 32.0 | 28.8 | 21.8 |
| Private Household Workers | 0.8 | 0.2 | 15.4 | 6.1 |
| Service Workers | 18.6 | 18.3 | 38.5 | 32.2 |
| Farm Laborers | 0.2 | 0.2 | 0.0 | 0.5 |
| Laborers | 22.2 | 11.1 | 2.6 | 1.7 |

*Source:* U.S. Bureau of the Census 1970.
*Percentage of total number of workers within each occupation.

Most noticeable are the increases for both males and females between 1960 and 1970 in the professional, technical, and clerical occupations. Although there were slight increases for black males in managerial, official, and proprietor positions, the percentage of black females in these positions actually declined. Also worthy of note was the decline in the percentage of black male workers in the laborers category and of black female workers in the private household workers category. One can certainly assume affirmative action played an important role, particularly in the increases in higher-level occupations for blacks. However, it should be remembered that individuals filling these positions were recruited mainly from outside of the black community. Affirmative action had less of an impact on the local black family. Children of local black families who received baccalaureate degrees primarily attended colleges and universities away from Syracuse and did not return for employment. As noted, growth in the size of the professional class was clearly one of in-migration of educated blacks.

## Education and the Integration of Syracuse Schools

Mention has already been made of the impact that employment discrimination in Syracuse had on black youths' incentive to stay in school. It should be remembered that as early as the era of exploitation (1870–1910) black religious leaders had emphasized education. As such, daily attendance rates for black children in the lower grades was higher than for white children. However, by the time black youths reached high school, attendance rates dropped significantly. Despite religious leaders' praise of the virtues of education, black youths without the prospects of jobs dropped out of school. This trend was to continue throughout the history of the Syracuse black community. In actuality, the tendency to drop out was exacerbated by the influx of black southern migrant families and their tradition of nonschooling.

Also worthy of remembering is the fact that Syracuse schools were open to all, regardless of race, as early as the era of exploitation. As the black population increased and residential segregation became an institution, the de facto segregation of schools resulted.

The 1954 Supreme Court decision *Brown v. Board of Education of Topeka, Kansas,* which outlawed segregated schools, had little effect on segregated schools in Syracuse. Like many other northern communities, Syracuse did not have laws establishing segregated schools, as did southern communities, which had been ruled unconstitutional by the Supreme Court. Syracuse's segregation of schools had resulted from de facto residential segregation and thus was not affected by the Court's decision.

The move to eliminate segregated schools in Syracuse was closely tied to CORE's efforts to diminish the effect of discrimination in the relocation of black families during the urban renewal efforts in the inner city. In 1962, the Syracuse School Board proposed attendance boundaries that would have virtually excluded whites from attending Sumner Elementary School and would have created a black majority enrollment. Dr. George Wiley, head of CORE, protested the proposed plan, but to no avail. The school board refused to reconsider CORE's proposal or to draw up an integration plan. By the time the city schools were opened in September 1962, parents had organized a picket of the administrative offices of the school district and a one-day boycott of Washington Irving Elementary School (Cornwall 1986). These actions on the part of parents, most of whom were black, signaled the beginning of a fight for public-school integration in Syracuse that was to extend throughout the 1960s and the 1970s.

Although Zoe Cornwall (1986), in her history of the civil rights movement in Syracuse, views the Syracuse School District as not being insensitive to the poor academic achievements of black students in segregated schools, a quote from an interview with Walt Shepperd, a white teacher at the predominantly black Madison Junior High School, exemplifies the attitude some white teachers had about black students. He reported being interviewed for employment by the supervisor of the English department: "I had an interview with a wonderful lady who was the English supervisor, one of the old public school, white-glove people. She truly was a lovely lady, but she tried to explain to me, for my own good, that I had a lot of talent obviously and looked like I'd be a good teacher. Why would I waste my time at Madison when I could go teach some place real. The attitude was those [black] kids at Madison can't read, can't learn, aren't motivated, are all criminals, whatever" (quoted in Cornwall 1986, 80).

Although Shepperd's recollection of his interview with the English supervisor reflects the attitude of one person only, putting better teachers at schools with mostly white students who are better prepared and motivated seems to have been and to continue to be a rather common practice. Inexperienced and poor-quality teachers are usually placed at inner-city schools with the idea that poor and minority students can't learn anyway (Blackwell 1975, 109). This process serves as a self-fulfilling prophesy in that minority and poor children perceive that they are not expected to learn or to have an interest in school; therefore, they do not learn or show an interest in their studies (Zeul and Humphrey 1971, 492). Even though the Syracuse School District received in 1961 a Ford Foundation grant that focused on preparing black students from the Madison area for integration, students in inner-city schools received hand-me-down learning materials. Walt Shepperd stated, "We got hand-me-downs. I didn't have Johnny Tremain books. . . . I taught 9th grade and everyone in New York State reads Johnny Tremain in the 9th grade. I had to borrow . . . copies from another junior high school" (quoted in Cornwall 1986, 80–81).

This inconsistency in policy and resource allocation between inner-city schools and suburban schools was reason enough to justify black parents' demands for integrated schools. Although many within the black community saw integration as an end in itself, black parents were not blind to the educational advantages of integrated schools. This was particularly true for middle-class blacks, and their presence in the fight for integrated schools steadily increased over the years. Many policymakers and foes of integration voiced objections to what they perceived as the use of education as a means of social engineering. Although proponents for integration saw schools as a microcosm of society that should reflect society's moral ethos, real issues did exist that centered on the quality of education provided. In demanding that the school system be integrated, black parents in Syracuse were aware of two factors related to quality: one, school administrators had demonstrated through their past actions that the quality of education would be superior if middle-class white children were in attendance; and two, the power structure responded to the demands for better quality when these demands were made by middle-class whites rather than by blacks and the poor. Evidence to support this contention was readily available in the family incomes of students attending integrated inner-city schools. Of the few white students who attended these schools, almost all were from low-income homes.

The first pressure external to the black community for the integration of schools came in the form of a statewide mandate by state education commissioner James Allen in 1963. Allen operationally defined a school as being racially imbalanced if 50 percent or more of the student body was black. A breakdown of the student population in Syracuse at that time revealed that 16 percent of the elementary students and 9 percent of the high school students were nonwhite. On the elementary level, however, eight of the schools were all white, five were less than one percent black, and two inner-city schools (Croton and Washington-Irving) were 78 percent and 88 percent black, respectively. At the junior high level, six of the schools were all white, four had less than one percent black students, and one school (Madison) was 78 percent black (Cornwall 1986). Based on Commissioner Allen's definition, there were no racially imbalanced high schools, though.

In attempting to respond to Commissioner Allen's mandate, the Syracuse School Board approved a plan than would close Brighton, Washington-Irving, and Madison schools. The student bodies of the two predominantly black schools (Washington-Irving and Madison) were bused to other schools throughout the district (Scruggs 1984). White students from Brighton were assigned to nearby schools. In attempting to appease white parents and to conform to the state mandate, the school board attempted to integrate black students through busing and to maintain neighborhood schools for whites (Cornwall 1986). These efforts did little to diminish the concerns of parents whether they were for or against school integration. Black parents perceived that their children were bearing the burden of integration through busing. Black children were the ones who had to get up early in the morning and be bused out of their neighborhoods, whereas white children assumed a normal routine at neighborhood schools. The general feeling in the black community was that black parents and black children were being made the sacrificial lambs of integration. White parents, in contrast, felt that having their children in the same classroom with black children was a major sacrifice in itself. Many of them keyed in on the issue of "busing" to fight against their real concern, the integration of Syracuse schools ("Appraisal of the Croton School Boycott" 1966).

Black and white parents' attitudes became more overt in 1966, when the Syracuse School Board made a decision to close Croton Elementary School, one of the two predominantly black elementary schools. Black parents in the Croton attendance district, already seething over what they perceived as unfair busing decisions in the case of the Madison and Washington-Irving schools, came together to fight the decision to close Croton. Their plan was to keep Croton open as an integrated school ("Appraisal" 1966). Of course, this would have meant cross-busing, or the busing of both black and white children. The Croton Mothers Club was founded, and assistance was elicited from other local groups, such as the Committee for Integrated Schools (a group of black and white concerned citizens), Citizens of Pioneer Homes (an advocacy group from a low-income area), the NAACP, and groups associated with the Crusade for Opportunity. These concerned citizens came together, planned, and carried out a one-day boycott of Croton Elementary School. Freedom Schools were set up for students not attending public schools on that day.[4] The rationale for the boycott was to make the entire Syracuse community aware of the plight of black parents and children and to let the school board know that the parents were serious. These efforts were successful in that what started out as a protest of black parents from Croton spread to other sections of the city. Churches, both black and white, Protestant and Catholic, offered their facilities as Freedom Schools. Other white and black parents joined the Croton parents by supporting the boycott and sending their children to Freedom Schools rather than to their respective schools ("Appraisal" 1966a).

Certain events had taken place in Syracuse that caused this type of reaction on the part of black parents. As the new black community arose, blacks realized the value of collective action. With urban renewal still under way, the city had to show that it was dealing with issues of discrimination in order to obtain continued federal funding. On the other side of the issue was white parents' reaction to the possibility of their children being bused to Croton. Up to that point, white parents' arguments against cross-busing had centered on the "value of neighborhood schools" and the "dangers and disadvantages of busing"; now the arguments became overt racist sentiments. Some white

4. Parents set up and served as teachers in what were referred to as Freedom Schools. The idea was to provide some form of instruction for students during the boycott of Syracuse Public Schools.

4.2. Community mentoring program at Croton Elementary School (now Dr. King Magnet School), 1961. Shown at center is David Wilkins, owner of Record City Radio on Townsend Street. Courtesy of Onondaga County Public Library, Beauchamp Branch.

parents objected to their children's having to sit in a classroom next to black children. Other white parents made derogatory comments about black children, calling their intelligence "substandard." A white parent group submitted a questionnaire to white teachers asking their attitudes toward integration with questions like the following: "Would you like to teach dirty kids or clean kids?" ("Appraisal" 1966).

Blacks, realizing their newfound power and faced with such blatant racism, became more resolved in their attempt to integrate the Syracuse School District with busing across racial lines. They also realized that they could not depend on the school board to introduce cross-busing as a means of integration. The Syracuse School Board, elected mainly by a strong Republican Party, was beholden to the local power structure. Its members' general attitude, seemingly supported by the power structure, was that the school board could afford to wait out blacks' concerns rather than antagonize whites and have them relocate to the suburbs ("Appraisal" 1966). Yet the power structure could not afford to let racial conflict jeopardize the federal funding of their urban renewal projects. Racial conflict over school integration was particularly sensitive to federal urban renewal funding because segregated schools, under a system of neighborhood schools, reflected segregated housing within the city. Guidelines for urban renewal funding mandated that those families being displaced through urban renewal not be resegregated.

The exercise of "power" from within the black community, with help from some whites, resulted in success for the Croton parents. The Syracuse School Board replaced its decision to close Croton Elementary School with a plan that called for volunteer busing of white students to Croton and busing of an equal number of black students from Croton. This plan was a dismal failure, as might have been expected by the white parents' attitudes (Cornwall 1986, 90). This exercise of "power" by blacks also resulted in two changes in the Syracuse School District and changes in the student population at Croton. The changes in the school district included the revision of the social-studies curriculum throughout all grade levels to include black history. Also, a concerted effort was made to increase the number of black teachers and black administrators. Lowell Smith and Cornelius Sayles were hired as the first two black principals, and the district began to recruit teachers from predominantly black colleges and universities (Cornwall 1986, 90–91).

Two changes at Croton took place during the 1967–68 academic year. One program was designed to get white students to attend Croton. This program, called Unlimited Education Achievement, became a "school within a school" because students enrolled in this program did not attend classes with other Croton students. The program was set up so that academically bright students in grades four through six would participate in enriched classes. Another program, which began as Croton-on-Campus and was later renamed King-on-Campus, was a cooperative program between the Syracuse School District and Syracuse University. Three hundred students in grades four through six attended classes for half a day at Syracuse University. The idea was to improve their social and communication skills and to help them gain self-confidence (Cornwall 1986, 91). The King-on-Campus idea originated with a local black minister. With the help of Robert Warr, a black member of the Syracuse Common Council, the minister was able to get the university chancellor to agree to house such a program on campus (Cornwall 1986, 91).

Although representing a step forward at that time, changes at Croton were in reality dysfunctional to the general purpose of integration, which was to bring black and white students closer together and to provide an environment in which both could study and learn together. Within this environment, it was hoped that both groups would develop a better understanding of and appreciation for each other. However, the Unlimited Education Achievement program, with its academically bright students, was almost all white. The "school within a school" classes were segregated in that only the academically talented white students were transferred into the program. Black students, seeing only white students in enriched classes and segregated from their classes, had to feel low in self-esteem. Of course, they attended King-on-Campus to overcome this low self-esteem, but the point is that the Unlimited Education Achievement program exacerbated the very problems that King-on-Campus was designed to alleviate.

In Syracuse, as in other cities throughout the United States, efforts to achieve racially integrated schools proved to be an ongoing process. Combining intracity and intercity residential mobility with resistance on the part of some white parents and school officials, the process of racially balancing Syracuse schools extended well into the 1970s. With pressure from the office of the New York State commissioner of education, blacks were able to continue their efforts at desegregation.

*School Desegregation and the Urban League*

In the early 1970s, 82 percent of the public-school students in Syracuse attended racially imbalanced schools. By the 1974–75 school year, however, the percentage attending imbalanced schools had dropped to 52 percent. Contributing to this decrease was the opening of George W. Fowler Senior High School and the closing of Central Tech, which was located in the inner city. As a result of these changes, all four Syracuse high schools were integrated (Cornwall 1986, 94). The same could not be said for Syracuse junior high and elementary schools, however.

In 1975, the Urban League entered the school desegregation dispute, thirteen years after the original order to integrate was issued by Commissioner Allen. Scruggs states, "[The Urban League's entry] was a classic case of

applying pressure to change 'systems' in order 'to make them relate specifically to the needs of blacks and other minorities'" (1984, 18). In 1974, Shirley
Davis, a black elementary school principal and parent of a young son who was
scheduled to attend the school of which she was principal, requested that her
son be transferred to either George Washington or Ed Smith schools, which
were located within walking distance of her home.[5] Her reason was that she
did not want her son in the same school building where she was principal.
Mrs. Davis was informed by the Pupil Services Department of the Syracuse
Public School System that she would have to make a deal on her own with the
principal of either Ed Smith or George Washington because her son was not
in either attendance district. Both principals refused to accept the transfer, so
Mrs. Davis again requested a transfer through Pupil Services. She was given
the choice of Webster or Jefferson schools, which had low black enrollments
(see table 4.3). Mrs. Davis was not happy with these choices because her son
would likely have been the first child on the bus and the last off after an approximately fifty- to sixty-minute ride each way. The child certainly would
have been the only black child on the bus. With these concerns in mind, Mrs.
Davis decided not to transfer her child to either school and to put him in a
private school. Being a member of the Urban League's board of directors,
Mrs. Davis discussed the situation with Vivian Moore, its director of education, focusing especially on the fact that black parents did not have options
under the busing plan, although white parents did. They researched this issue
and the issue of imbalanced schools and confirmed that black parents did not
have options in determining where their children attended school.

It was also established that five elementary schools in the district still
maintained racially imbalanced enrollments according to New York State
guidelines. Table 4.3 shows that these schools were Danforth, Seymour, Dr.
King, Charles Andrews, and Sumner. It also indicates that two junior high
schools had imbalanced enrollments: Roosevelt and H. W. Smith. Research
by the Urban League further revealed that more black children were dropping out and thus not finishing high school at the same rate as white children.

5. A considerable portion of this section was taken from a taped interview with Shirley
Davis (1990). Many others, including Andrew Willis, who was executive director of the Urban
League at that time, confirmed this information through telephone interviews.

**Table 4.3**

**Percentages of Students by Race and Grade Level for Each Syracuse School, 1976**

| Elementary Schools | | | | | | Junior High Schools | | | Senior High Schools | | |
| Grades K–6 | W | M* | Grades P–6 | W | M | Grades 7–9 | W | M | Grades 10–12 | W | M |
|---|---|---|---|---|---|---|---|---|---|---|---|
| Danforth | 10.8 | 89.2 | Dr. King | 95.9 | 4.1 | Roosevelt | 31.9 | 68.1 | Nottingham | 54.9 | 45.1 |
| Edward Smith | 62.5 | 37.5 | Charles Andrews | 37.2 | 62.8 | H. W. Smith | 45.9 | 54.1 | Corcoran | 71.4 | 28.6 |
| Seymour | 39.8 | 60.2 | Sumner | 26.2 | 73.8 | Eastwood | 66.9 | 33.1 | Fowler | 72.9 | 27.1 |
| George Washington | 68.4 | 31.6 | McKinley Brighton | 50.4 | 49.6 | Grant | 72.1 | 27.9 | Henninger | 78.5 | 21.5 |
| Huntington | 86.5 | 13.5 | Belleview Heights | 70.7 | 29.3 | Levy | 57.1 | 42.9 | | | |
| Salina | 75.2 | 24.8 | Elmwood | 62.1 | 37.9 | Shea | 61.7 | 38.3 | | | |
| Roberts | 81.0 | 19.0 | Nichols | 60.8 | 39.2 | Clary | 73.4 | 26.6 | | | |
| Delaware | 73.4 | 26.6 | Porter | 78.3 | 21.7 | Blodgett | 65.9 | 34.1 | | | |
| Webster | 85.4 | 14.6 | Clinton | 61.0 | 39.0 | Lincoln | 82.1 | 17.9 | | | |
| Cleveland | 75.2 | 24.8 | Frazer | 69.7 | 30.3 | | | | | | |
| Meachum | 79.2 | 20.8 | Percy Hughes | 72.1 | 27.9 | | | | | | |
| Salem Hyde | 90.2 | 9.8 | Franklin | 91.5 | 8.5 | | | | | | |
| Lincoln | 92.5 | 7.5 | | | | | | | | | |
| Jefferson | 87.4 | 12.6 | | | | | | | | | |
| Total %** | 68.3 | 31.7 | | 56.8 | 43.2 | | 63.1 | 36.9 | | 70.7 | 29.3 |

*Source:* U.S. Department of Health, Education, and Welfare 1976–77, 976–77.

*W = white; M = minority.

**Total % all elementary schools: white = 62.4; minorities = 37.6.

Probably the most disturbing outcome of the Urban League's research was the general feeling that teachers located in schools with racially imbalanced enrollments were on the whole less qualified than teachers at suburban schools (S. Davis 1990).

With these data in hand, Davis and Moore brought the issues of options for black parents and imbalanced schools before the Urban League board of directors. Discussion continued for many meetings before the Urban League took action. Resistance to taking action was strong on the part of some white board members, particularly those who lived outside of the city. One board member, a white realtor, bitterly opposed taking action because school segregation also reflected housing segregation. In the end, a white executive with General Electric, who was from Georgia, pushed the board to approve the Urban League's taking legal action. Somebody had to file suit, though. Because Mrs. Davis, the black principal-mother, had placed her child in a private school, it was felt it would be inappropriate for her to file suit. Also, because she was employed by the school district, undue pressure could be brought against her. In the end, James Graves, a black member of the Urban League board who lived across the street from Charles Andrews School, which was racially imbalanced, agreed to file suit on behalf of his daughter. In many ways, the Graves child was perfect for the suit in that she was bright and involved in all kinds of activities. However, the idea was not to use her because of her academic progress, but because her civil rights were being violated. Graves's daughter did not have the options enjoyed by white children as a result of the volunteer busing plan. She had no choice but to attend Charles Andrews School. Also important was the fact that Graves worked for IBM and was not vulnerable to local economic pressures as the black principal-mother would have been (S. Davis 1990).

With the backing of the Urban League board and of Andrew Willis, the executive director of the Urban League, a decision was made that Graves would file a brief with the New York State commissioner of education, who had the power to order Syracuse schools integrated. The decision to file with the commissioner rather than with the federal courts was shrewd because court litigation would have taken years. Davis and Moore presented the Urban League's position forcefully: "Ideally, parents should be able to walk into any school in the district and find no appreciable difference in the quality of education being offered. However, reality indicates that those differences are there, and because of this, parents and community must become committed to change a system that does not provide quality education for all children" (quoted in Scruggs 1984, 19).

The action taken by Graves and the Urban League characterizes the new black community. After years of looking to external forces to bring about change within the black community, blacks themselves initiated change. Willis and the Urban League recognized that opposition to their plan developed not only from the white community, but from some blacks as well, so they developed a strategy to make the total community see the value of integrated education (Scruggs 1984, 19).

After the suit was filed, several individuals received threats, including Shirley Davis, who was told she would never advance further within the Syracuse system. Many black teachers were threatened with their jobs because of the suit. One person who came under tremendous pressure during this period was Constance Timberlake, a black civil rights activist who had been elected to the Syracuse School Board. As board vice president, Mrs. Timberlake and her family were the constant target of threats. Also, she and the other female board member, Janet Edison, suffered the indignities of trying to operate under an "old buddy system" maintained by the male-dominated board. Although the entire school board met privately before public meetings, it was often apparent that the male members had already gotten together and agreed upon the position the board would take. Such a process was particularly frustrating to Timberlake's efforts to represent the black community.

Pressure was also brought on the Syracuse United Way to cut off funding to the Urban League if it did not drop the suit. Pressure was so great and the feelings ran so high that in 1976 when Commissioner of Education Ewald B. Nyquist ruled that Syracuse schools must be integrated, the local state legislative delegation worked toward his dismissal (Cornwall 1987, 98). According to Commissioner Nyquist's ruling, elementary schools had to range between 15 and 45 percent minority (Scruggs 1984, 19).

*Syracuse Responds to Mandatory Integration*

The Syracuse School Board responded locally to Commissioner Nyquist's mandatory integration order by studying various plans, including quadrant concepts, modified quadrant plans, and triangle plans (Scruggs 1984, 19). Choosing the triangle plan, in which attendance groupings of three schools were balanced racially, students would spend the first three years in a neighborhood school and the last three bused to another schools. Rather than imposing this plan on the entire school district, a pilot group was selected. Parents had until July 1976 to submit voluntarily to the plan or busing would become mandatory in September 1976. The plans chosen by the school board called for the triangle plan to spread throughout the district the next year. Parents did not voluntarily agree to bus their children, though, so busing became mandatory for the first-year pilot group. Those parents affected by busing came together and formed Syracuse Citizens Rebelling Against Mandatory Busing (SCRAMB). When schools opened in the fall of 1976, SCRAMB organized and carried out a successful three-day boycott in which 1,300 students participated (Rice 1976a, A2).

During the time between the mandatory integration order and the SCRAMB-ordered boycott, the Syracuse School Board made a strategic move in its appointment of a superintendent. It chose Sidney Johnson, who had previously worked within the system, as its first black superintendent. Johnson, a conservative black Republican who was against mandatory busing, served a conciliatory function between the black and white communities. For blacks, Johnson was a source of pride in his being a black man in a position of power. For whites, Johnson's stand against busing made him palatable. At Johnson's behest, the school board requested an extension in the order to integrate until May 1977. Reasons for the request included the appointment of a new superintendent, the need for more time to implement a voluntary plan, and the opportunity to study the "magnet school" concept (Rice 1976a, A2). As Johnson and the school board awaited Nyquist's response to their request, SCRAMB continued their call for neighborhood schools. Their arguments centered on local rather than state control of schools, concern for the safety of children, the inappropriate use of schools for social engineering, and white flight from the city (Rice 1976b, A1). Blacks, led by Graves and the Urban League, questioned whether Johnson's plan would meet the intent of Nyquist's order. Finally, Nyquist approved the request for an extension and called for a detailed plan for integration by January 30, 1977. The new plan would go into effect in September 1977 (Cornwall 1986, 96). By 1977, Commissioner Nyquist had

been forced to resign and had been replaced by Gordon Ambach. Superintendent Johnson of the Syracuse Public School System, after much deliberation
and meetings with parents, devised a seemingly workable plan, which called
for approximately 4,000 students to be displaced, mostly as a consequence of
the closing of schools. However, the plan was drawn up so that only 350 additional students would require busing. All schools would be racially balanced
except three elementary schools (Bednarski 1977, 1). SCRAMB accepted the
newly approved integration plan, withdrew a lawsuit they had initiated, and
disbanded (Cornwall 1986, 97).

Although Graves and the Urban League still voiced opposition to the
integration plan, their suit had brought about major changes in the school
system. With the initiation of an open-enrollment policy for all elementary
students within the system, blacks had at least gained parity with whites. The
original complaint that black parents did not have options had been rectified.
With the eventual establishment of magnet programs in inner-city schools,
the school system was able to draw white students into the inner city.[6] Most
important, with the New York State commissioner of education keeping a
close watch on enrollment patterns, by the 1981–82 school year all Syracuse
schools were racially balanced (Cornwall 1986, 97). Considering that the
original mandate for racially balancing schools throughout New York State
had been made by Commissioner Allen many years earlier, in 1963, the Urban
League's intervention was pivotal to the integration process. An interesting
sidelight to the integration saga was that many of the dissident white parents
ended up becoming teachers in the Syracuse Public School System, which
could have had two possible results. One scenario was that these individuals
who were so opposed to their children's attending integrated schools would
be unlikely to view black children in a positive manner, so their becoming
teachers would be dysfunctional to the educational process. The second possible outcome relates to different characterizations of the dissident parents'
attitude. Perhaps they were not against integration per se, but were simply

6. The magnet school concept was designed to draw whites into inner-city schools by
providing features or programs not offered in suburban schools. The Syracuse magnet system
offered an extended-day program, special science and mathematics programs, a gifted program, and a computer program at different inner-city schools.

concerned about the quality of education offered in inner-city schools, as were black parents. Whereas black parents viewed integration as a mechanism for improving the quality of education available to their children, many white parents were unwilling to accept the integration of inner-city schools until a degree of quality was assured. One would hope that those dissident parents who became teachers resisted integration for this reason rather than because of racism. Of course, based on statements made at public meetings, some parents found integration itself unacceptable , so their becoming teachers could have had only a negative impact on students.

The fight for integration of schools in Syracuse had important historical significance for the growth and development of the black community. Along with housing integration and employment opportunities, school integration was initiated by blacks in their fight against the policymakers within the Syracuse community.

## Consequences of a New Era

The emergence of the new black community marked the beginning of a new era in black-white relationships in Syracuse. This era also signified an upsurge in competition among blacks as well, however. As blacks gained new jobs and higher status within the community, the physical separation of middle-income blacks from lower-income blacks became more evident. Along with physical separation came a certain degree of social and even psychological separation. By the beginning of the 1980s, middle-class blacks had developed a well-defined system of social clubs and organizations. Many blacks, of course, moved in integrated social climates, but the important point to remember here is that the social environment frequented by middle-class blacks excluded lower-class blacks.

As the social and economic environment of middle-income blacks expanded beyond the black community, a psychological withdrawal took place. Middle-income blacks became psychologically committed to maintaining their status within society and middle-class values and to ensuring that their children could sustain or even surpass their status. Education, travel, the right neighborhood, and the right associations became paramount for middle-income blacks. Many of these values were antithetical to those demonstrated by lower-income blacks. It was not that lower-income blacks were not interested in assuming a better lifestyle. Data presented in the preceding chapters strongly indicate that lower-income blacks for the most part wanted to improve themselves, just as did middle-class blacks. However, the stark realities of making it on a day-to-day basis caused them to disregard behavior demonstrative of middle-class values and to act in a manner that coincided with what has been called lower-class values (Hyman 1953; O. Lewis 1959; Clark 1965; Valentine 1968; Kriesberg 1970).

Many blacks saw this social and psychological separation as dysfunctional to the continued progress of blacks in Syracuse. When one analyzes the processes that had occurred and were still occurring in Syracuse during the 1980s, that such a disjunction would materialize seems inevitable. Integration and new opportunities did not mean change for everyone within the black community. Housing in middle-income integrated neighborhoods was available only for those who could afford the price. As economic barriers were lowered, those individuals with the education and training entered better and higher-paying jobs. These opportunities were not available to those with less education and skills. Although many colleges and universities opened their doors to black youths from lower-income families in the late 1960s and early 1970s, only those with the skills or who were willing to work hard and overcome almost insurmountable odds were successful and graduated. With the high dropout rate among Syracuse black youths, only a few were able to go to college.

As the new black community emerged and became more of an agent in determining its own destiny, what also came with it was a widening gap among blacks. On the one hand were those who were able to take advantage of new opportunities, but on the other were those unable to improve their lot. Although the two groups had things in common, their history and continuing racism, the differences between them were magnified by economic and social developments.

# 5

# Syracuse and Change
# in the 1980s

THE 1980S IN SYRACUSE marked a pivotal time in its association with the black community. Many blacks saw this decade as a period of stabilization, a time when black progress in the city leveled off or came to a virtual standstill. Recognizing that society is dynamic, not static, one would have to assume that "stabilizing" in this case meant that the progress made by the black community in the 1960s and the 1970s had slowed considerably. Other blacks saw the 1980s as a time when black progress actually began to erode. It should be kept in mind that changes in race relations in Syracuse tended to lag behind those occurring in many other parts of the country. The protest movement emerged in this city well after it had started in many other sections of the country, most notably the South. During the early 1970s, when blacks in many other sections of the country began to perceive signs of a change in the mood of American society, blacks in Syracuse were beginning to feel the emergence of power. Most important, that critical mass of professional blacks who started migrating to Syracuse in 1968 and continued to do so throughout most of the 1970s began to have some impact on the black community by the 1980s. Therefore, by the end of the 1970s, evidence pointed toward the black community's having gained power and being in a better position to influence its future growth and development.

## Changing Mood in American Society

Although changes had occurred in black-white relations in Syracuse that would indicate more internal power within the black community, countervailing

149

influences nationally caused many members of the community to question whether or not continued black progress was possible. Faustine Jones (1977), in a study of racial attitudes and white behavior between the years 1969 to 1975, surmises that the mood within American society was changing from liberalism to conservatism. This new conservative mood, according to Jones (77–78), was having a negative impact on blacks, other minorities, and the poor. Gerald Gill (1978), in a follow-up study to Jones, also claimed that the mood within American society had changed, for reasons varying from race relations to the economy, and for the period after 1980 we can add the election of Ronald Reagan as president.

One reason often mentioned for the changed mood was black activists' expulsion of whites from active participation in the protest movement as the movement's focus changed from integration to black power and blacks controlling their own destiny. It should be remembered that this happened in the mid-1960s in Syracuse, when CORE, a predominantly white organization at that time, expelled its white members. Whites felt betrayed and hurt by their repulsion, and it can be assumed that many reoriented their concerns and efforts away from black-related issues and became more conservative over time.[1] A second and somewhat related reason was an upsurge in apathy toward or even a backlash against state and federal programs geared toward minorities and the poor (Gill 1980, 2), the so-called liberal legislation passed during the 1960s such as affirmative action, busing to integrate public schools, and various social programs. A third purported cause of the shift in mood was the change in the American economy from prosperity to hard times. Spiraling inflation and a recession caused the economic pie to shrink, followed by perceptions that support of social programs for minorities and the poor were threatening middle-class lifestyles. Fourth, there was the development of what Christopher Lasch (1978) refers to as the culture of narcissism, or the "me generation." The crystallization of the "me generation" resulted in a shift away from issues of racism, poverty, sexism, and equity generally to a concern about one's own social and economic well-being. Obviously, each of

---

1. This statement should not be construed as an attempt to condemn blacks for their repulsion of whites from these organizations. We are merely listing events that likely influenced the changing mood in America.

the reasons associated with a changed mood in American society was inter-related with the others.

Concrete evidence of a shift in public policy that accompanied the changed mood can be seen by looking at Phase I of the Reagan administration's budget cuts in late 1981, which included: *(a)* a $3.8 billion cut from the Comprehensive Employment and Training Act (CETA) program and a loss of 314,000 jobs; *(b)* a $1.1 billion cut to Aid to Families with Dependent Children (AFDC), with an accompanying 401,000 families dropped and an additional 259,000 families receiving reduced benefits; *(c)* a $700 million cut in food stamps that caused 875,000 families to be dropped and 1.4 million families to receive reduced benefits; *(d)* a $2.2 million cut in unemployment benefits, a reduction in the duration of benefits, and eligibility restrictions for 1.4 million workers; *(e)* a $600 million cut in Medicaid with a minimum 3 percent cut in services for thousands of poor people; *(f)* a $560 million reduction in the school lunch program that resulted in 590,000 children being dropped from the program; and *(g)* a reduction in public-housing subsidies for 2.4 million low-income apartment renters ("Economic Perspectives" 1981, 43–44). Although these cuts occurred on a national level, their impact affected many poor Syracuse residents, a disproportionately high percentage of whom were black. Just as important were the Reagan administration's well-articulated policies geared toward rearranging national priorities away from social programs and toward defense. As Jack Meyer argues, Reagan did not change direction incrementally, but fully at once by jolting the system with dramatic and sweeping changes (1986, 70–71). These changes had an immediate impact on people's current status and their view of the future.

## Local Reactions to the Changed Mood

Needless to say, blacks and whites in Syracuse viewed Reaganism and the changed American mood differently. Just as Americans generally had moved toward a "me" focus and away from concern with social programs designed to aid the poor and minorities, it is safe to assume many Syracuse whites made a similar shift.

To get a better handle on how blacks and whites viewed their past and future progress, we examine data from the *Urban League Community Survey*

*1982* (Stamps 1982).[2] These data reflect how local blacks and whites perceived both the general situation in the United States and the local situation.

*Past Progress*

Respondents were asked in 1981 to indicate their perceptions regarding whether the general situation for blacks and whites in the United States had improved, remained the same, or gotten worse during the "past five years."

Table 5.1 provides racial differences in 1981 perceptions of how blacks faired generally over the "past five years." It is not surprising to find that a higher percentage of blacks (46.2) than whites (27.1) perceived that the general situation had actually gotten worse for blacks. Conversely, 44 percent of the whites but only 24.5 percent of the blacks perceived that things had improved for blacks. A higher percentage (41.2) of other minorities (Hispanics, Native Americans, Chinese Americans, and Japanese Americans) felt things had gotten worse for blacks, which closely resembles

**Table 5.1**

**Perceptions of Black Progress According to Race, 1981**

| Over the Past Five Years, the General Situation for Blacks Has: | Blacks (%) (N = 493) | White (%) (N = 207) | Other* (%) (N = 34) |
|---|---|---|---|
| Improved | 24.5 | 44.0 | 14.7 |
| Remained the Same | 26.2 | 24.2 | 20.6 |
| Gotten Worse | 46.2 | 27.1 | 41.2 |
| Don't Know | 3.0 | 4.8 | 23.5 |

*Source:* Stamps 1982, 59.

*Note:* $X^2$ = significant at .001 level with 6 degrees of freedom (df).

*"Other" includes Hispanics, Native Americans, Chinese Americans, and Japanese Americans.

2. Data presented in this chapter are derived from the *Urban League Community Survey* (Stamps 1982) unless otherwise noted.

blacks' own perception of their progress. Interestingly, 23.5 percent of the other minorities stated they did not know how blacks had fared over the past five years.

Just the opposite was found when the perceptions of white progress in "the past five years" were tabulated. Table 5.2 shows that a higher percentage (41.4) of blacks than of whites (24.6) in 1981 felt things had improved for whites. Actually, the highest percent (48.3) of whites felt that things had not changed for whites. Among other minorities, an equal percentage (34.4) either felt that things had generally remained the same for whites or did not know how whites had fared.

The 1979 National Urban League Black Pulse study revealed similar findings. Blacks nationwide perceived that black progress was worse than at earlier periods in time (National Urban League 1980b, 3). With the onset of the 1970s and the end of the protest movement, blacks in Syracuse and in the nation showed increased concern regarding black progress (Stamps 1982, 22). More specifically, by the 1970s, the percentage of blacks nationally who were satisfied with black progress had decreased by one-half. Even middle-income blacks, with incomes in excess of $20,000 a year, were dissatisfied with black progress (National Urban League 1980b, 3). This state of affairs was found in both the National Urban League Black Pulse study and the Syracuse study.

**Table 5.2**
**Perceptions of White Progress According to Race, 1981**

| Over the Past Five Years the General Situation for Whites Has: | Black (%) (N = 485) | White (%) (N = 207) | Other (%) (N = 32) |
| --- | --- | --- | --- |
| Improved | 41.4 | 24.6 | 28.1 |
| Remained the Same | 33.2 | 48.3 | 34.4 |
| Gotten Worse | 14.8 | 23.2 | 3.1 |
| Don't Know | 10.5 | 3.9 | 34.4 |

*Source:* Stamps 1982, 60.

*Note:* $X^2$ = significant at .001 level with 6 df.

*Future Progress*

Respondents to the 1981 Urban League survey were asked to look ahead to the next five years and indicate whether or not they expected the general situation for blacks and for whites to improve, remain the same, or get worse.

Table 5.3 indicates that 42.7 percent of blacks and 33.7 percent of whites perceived in 1981 that the situation would generally get worse for blacks over the next five years. Slightly more than 44 percent of the other minorities had similar perceptions. Approximately 38 percent of whites felt black progress would improve, although only 29.6 percent of the blacks shared this view. Of interest in table 5.3 is the relatively high percentage of each group (black, white, and other minorities) that indicated they did not know about the future progress of blacks. Keeping in mind that although these data were collected in 1981 in the early stages of the Reagan years, when indications for future black progress were not encouraging, it seems that some blacks, whites, and other minorities still held out hope that the trends of the 1960s and early 1970s would continue well into the 1980s.

Table 5.4 indicates that whites had a somewhat unclear picture in 1981 about white progress. Approximately 37 percent of whites perceived that the general situation would improve, but a relatively high percentage perceived that things would remain the same (26.8) or get worse (28.3). Among blacks, the highest percentage (42.8) perceived that things would improve for

**Table 5.3**

**Perceptions of Future Black Progress According to Race, 1981**

| Expect the General Situation for Blacks in the Next Five Years to: | Black (%) (N = 480) | White (%) (N = 205) | Other (%) (N = 34) |
|---|---|---|---|
| Improve | 29.6 | 37.6 | 23.5 |
| Remain the Same | 17.5 | 16.6 | 23.5 |
| Get Worse | 42.7 | 33.7 | 44.1 |
| Don't Know | 10.2 | 12.2 | 8.8 |

*Source:* Stamps 1982, 62.

*Note:* $X^2$ = not significant at the .05 level.

Table 5.4

**Perceptions of Future White Progress According to Race, 1981**

| Expect the General Situation for Whites in the Next Five Years to: | Black (%) (N = 477) | White (%) (N = 205) | Other (%) (N = 34) |
|---|---|---|---|
| Improve | 42.8 | 36.6 | 35.3 |
| Remain the Same | 26.0 | 26.8 | 44.1 |
| Get Worse | 18.9 | 28.3 | 11.8 |
| Don't Know | 12.4 | 8.3 | 8.8 |

*Source:* Stamps 1982, 63.

*Note:* $X^2$ = not significant at the .05 level.

whites, and among other minorities the highest percentage (44.1) perceived that things would remain the same. These findings indicate that although a segment of the Syracuse population had expectations that the general situation within American society and in Syracuse would improve, almost three-fourths of the city's population perceived that the general situation would remain the same or get worse through the mid-1980s.

The Black Pulse study concluded that the widespread concern among blacks regarding the lack of past progress and the doubt of future progress for blacks provided the ingredients for racial disorders. Incidents of disorder did occur in Miami and Tampa, Florida, in 1980 and 1986, respectively (National Urban League 1980b, 3). The Syracuse black community, however, had not erupted by the end of the 1980s. It should be reemphasized that with significant numbers of blacks perceiving that the future progress of blacks would get worse, the general feeling in the black community cannot be characterized as positive. Even under normal conditions, such general feelings of negativism would be counterproductive. In the case of a minority community striving toward greater equity with the dominant community, they would be devastating.

**Rankings of the Most Important Problems**

In order to ascertain a better picture of the general situation facing blacks and whites as perceived by blacks, whites, and other minorities in the early

1980s, the Urban League surveyors asked the respondents to provide, based on their own perceptions, the two most important problems facing blacks and whites. It was felt that identifying the most important problems each group faced would provide a better understanding of perceptions of black and white progress.

Perceptions of the most important problems faced by blacks and whites during the early 1980s reflected the general concerns of the nation as articulated by the communications media: unemployment, crime, and the high cost of living. Table 5.5 shows these perceptions.

There was a high degree of agreement between blacks and whites in identifying the most important problems faced by blacks, although the order varied somewhat. Only in the cases of lack of political power, listed by blacks and other minorities but not by whites, and family disorganization, listed by whites but not by the other two groups, did the lists disagree in terms of problem identification. Blacks and whites rank-ordered four out of the first five most important problems similarly, with the first two problems, "unemployment" and "crime," being ranked the same.

Blacks, whites, and other minorities ranked the same top three problems faced by whites (see table 5.6): the high cost of living, unemployment, and crime. Whereas there was a high degree of similarity between the three groups in ranking the ten most important problems faced by blacks, this was not true for their ranking of problems faced by whites. After the top three most important problems faced by whites, variations were found between the three groups in the kinds of problems identified and in their rank ordering.

If we key in on blacks, we can attempt to draw a clearer picture of the relationship between the changed American mood and how the Syracuse black community viewed black progress during the late 1970s and early 1980s. It has clearly been shown that based on these data, most (60 percent) of the black community was not optimistic about the future progress of blacks. Also evident was that the community had definite perceptions about the most important problems facing blacks. These findings were almost identical to those in the Black Pulse study, which was based on a national sample. The Black Pulse study findings showed that unemployment was ranked as the number one problem facing blacks (National Urban League 1980b, 10), and, in a similar vein, Blackwell and Hart found that the need for better economic

**Table 5.5**
**Ten Most Important Problems Faced by Blacks According to Race, 1981**

| According to Blacks | Rank | According to Whites | Rank | According to Other Minorities | Rank |
|---|---|---|---|---|---|
| Unemployment | 1 | Unemployment | 1 | Poverty | 1 |
| Crime | 2 | Crime | 2 | Unemployment | 2 |
| High Cost of Living | 3 | Inadequate Education | 3 | Racism/Discrimination | 3 |
| Racism/Discrimination | 4 | High Cost of Living | 4 | Crime | 4 |
| Police Brutality | 5 | Racism/Discrimination | 5 | Police Brutality | 4 |
| Poverty | 6 | Poverty | 6 | Low Wages | 4 |
| Inadequate Education | 7 | Inadequate Housing | 7 | Inadequate Education | 4 |
| Inadequate Housing | 8 | Family Disorganization | 8 | High Cost of Living | 4 |
| Low Wages | 9 | Low Wages | 9 | Lack of Political Power | 4 |
| Lack of Political Power | 10 | Police Brutality | 10 | — | — |

*Source:* Stamps 1982, 66.

**Table 5.6**
**Ten Most Important Problems Faced by Whites According to Race, 1981**

| According to Blacks | Rank | According to Whites | Rank | According to Other Minorities | Rank |
|---|---|---|---|---|---|
| High Cost of Living | 1 | High Cost of Living | 1 | High Cost of Living | 1 |
| Unemployment | 2 | Unemployment | 2 | Unemployment | 2 |
| Crime | 3 | Crime | 3 | Crime | 2 |
| Other, Unspecified | 4 | Family Disorganization | 4 | Inadequate Education | 3 |
| Racism/Discrimination | 5 | Racism/Discrimination | 5 | Lack of Ethnic Pride | 3 |
| Poor Mental Health | 6 | Other, Unspecified | 5 | Poor Mental Health | 6 |
| Low Wages | 7 | Inadequate Housing | 7 | Family Disorganization | 6 |
| Family Disorganization | 7 | Poor Male/Female Relations | 8 | Job Discrimination | 6 |
| Poor Physical Health | 9 | Low Wages | 9 | Other, Unspecified | 6 |
| Religious/Spiritual State | 9 | Police Brutality | 9 | — | — |

*Source:* Stamps 1982, 68.

conditions was the main problem facing the black community as perceived by blacks in five American cities (1982, 61–62).[3] Considering, as did Blackwell and Hart (1982, 52), that economic conditions included inadequate jobs, income, unemployment, and inflation, support for the Syracuse black community findings (Stamps 1982) seems stronger. Members of this community, in addition to ranking unemployment as number one, also ranked the following economic problems in the top ten: cost of living (3), poverty (6), and low wages (9) (see table 5.5). Of note, the findings of the Black Pulse study and of Blackwell and Hart's study refocused on what Gunnar Myrdal found in *An American Dilemma* in 1944. The major problem blacks faced nationally in 1944 was economic in nature, and almost four decades later the same conditions existed.

It should be emphasized that more than perceptions buttressed concerns about unemployment and related economic issues as the major problems faced by blacks during the 1980s. By late 1979, the black unemployment rate was three times that of the nation as a whole (National Urban League 1980a, 1–2). U.S. Labor Department statistics for the last part of 1981 reveal that the black unemployment rate was 15.5 percent and the rate for whites was 6.9 percent. Most alarming was the unemployment rate for black teenagers, officially set at 51 percent at that time (Blackwell and Hart 1982, 75). Unofficial estimates, such as those provided by the National Urban League, which included discouraged teenage workers, projected an even higher teenage unemployment rate during 1981.

How the black community viewed problems they identified as important is significant. In other words, what were the root causes of the problems facing the black community in the 1980s, as seen by blacks? In the sociological literature, one explanation of the causes of social problems is the social structure (Merton 1957). The survey data provide support for this social-structure explanation of the social problems faced by blacks in Syracuse. One might argue that some of the problems identified stem from group inadequacies (Ryan 1971). However, by looking at the problems identified in the surveys and how they were ranked, we can ascertain whether the black community

3. Blackwell and Hart (1982) sampled the following metropolitan areas: Atlanta, Boston, Cleveland, Houston, and Los Angeles.

saw structural problems as being most important. High ranks given unemployment, high cost of living, and racism/discrimination all pointed to structural inequities or problems over which the black community had little control. Similarly, problems such as police brutality, inadequate housing, and crime tend to be community-specific structural problems over which an individual community has little control (Blackwell and Hart 1982, 74–75). Only in the cases of inadequate education, low wages, and lack of political power did blacks identify problems over which their community had more control. Of course, the degree of control is related to whether the problem is associated with forces external or internal to the community itself. If the problems are internally created in the black community, then the community has only itself to blame. The survey findings show that blacks perceived external structural problems as the dominant issues faced by blacks and thus as the major impediments to their progress.

## Population Changes

Chapter 1 indicated that the Syracuse population peaked during the 1940s. As revealed by 1950 census data, Syracuse's population began to decrease; a trend that was continued into the 1980s. Census data for 1980 shows that the population of Syracuse as a proportion of the Onondaga County population decreased from a high in 1930 of approximately 72 percent to less than 37 percent in 1980 (U.S. Bureau of the Census 1980). Such a decrease can be attributed to the suburban movement that swept the country following World War II (Palen 2005). Many people migrated out of Syracuse and settled in surrounding suburban towns and communities. Individuals who in-migrated to the Syracuse SMA also settled in suburban communities in larger proportions than in the central city.

Table 5.7 reveals that the Syracuse population decreased from 197,208 in 1970 to 164,000 in 1984. The decade 1970 to 1980 saw a 3.6 percent decrease in the Syracuse population. For Onondaga County, of which Syracuse is the central city, a 1.9 percent decrease occurred between 1970 and 1980. However, from 1980 to 1984, the county's population seems to have stabilized. The fact that neither Syracuse nor the county population witnessed a growth is interesting in that the SMA saw slight increases over the same time period.

**Table 5.7**
**Population Statistics, 1970–1984**

| Year | Syracuse | Onondaga County | SMA |
|------|----------|-----------------|-----|
| 1970 | 197,208 | 472,746 | 636,507 |
| 1980 | 170,105 | 463,920 | 642,971 |
| 1984 | 164,000 | 464,000 | 631,000 |

*Source:* Sacks and Sacks 1987, 10.

For the SMA, a 1.0 percent increase occurred from 1970 to 1980 and a 1.2 percent increase from 1980 to 1984. These data indicate that population growth within the area took place away from the central city.

**Population Changes and the Black Community**

The black population in Syracuse has shown a steady increase since the first blacks appeared during the 1770s. The increase has been almost totally concentrated in the central city. The suburban movement of the 1950s that occurred in the area was primarily a white movement. As whites relocated to suburban communities surrounding Syracuse, causing a drop in the city's population, blacks continued to move into the central city. The result was an increase in the percentage of blacks in the central city population. This trend continued into the 1980s.

From the figures in table 5.8, it can be determined that the percentage increase from 1970 to 1980 in the Syracuse black population was 25.2, although there was a percentage decrease of 20.4 for whites for the same period. The table also reveals that whereas the portion of whites making up the Syracuse population decreased from 88 percent in 1970 to 81.3 percent in 1980, the percentage of blacks increased from 10.8 in 1970 to 15.7 in 1980. The same trend occurred for Onondaga County and the SMA: between 1970 and 1980, the percentage of the respective white populations declined, but the black populations increased. Decreases in the proportion of whites for the county and the SMA occurred because of declines in the white population. Also, the decrease in the overall county population can be attributed to the 21,184

Table 5.8

**Population Characteristics by Race, 1970 and 1980**

| Year | Race | SMA | Onondaga County | Syracuse |
|------|------|-----|-----------------|----------|
| 1970 | Total | 636,507 | 472,746 | 197,208 |
| | White | 608,618 | 445,970 | 173,611 |
| | Black | 23,398 | 22,718 | 21,383 |
| | % Black | 3.7 | 4.8 | 10.8 |
| 1980 | Total | 642,971 | 463,920 | 170,105 |
| | White | 601,625 | 424,786 | 138,223 |
| | Black | 31,023 | 30,117 | 26,767 |
| | % Black | 4.8 | 6.5 | 15.7 |

*Source:* U.S. Bureau of the Census 1970/1980.

reduction in the number of whites. Although the black population increased in the county, the increase was not large enough to offset the white decrease. For the SMA, the white population decreased by 6,993, and the black population increased by 7,625, which more than offset the white decrease. However, the overall increase noted in the SMA population occurred because of an increase in the number of other minorities.

A close scrutiny of these data pertaining to the black population reveals that it was more concentrated in Syracuse in 1970 than in 1980. For example, 91.4 percent of the black population in the SMA lived in Syracuse in 1970. By 1980, this percentage had dropped to 86.3. The identically same percentage (97.1) of the SMA's black population that resided inside the county in 1970 did so in 1980. The increase in the suburban black population that occurred between 1970 and 1980 happened because of an increase in middle-income blacks who migrated to the area. Many of these middle-income blacks chose to live outside of the central city, but within the confines of Onondaga County. The number of blacks living in the central city who relocated to suburban communities was small.

Because the focus of this study is Syracuse and not those living in suburban communities, it is necessary to refer back to our definition of the black community. We defined it in terms of identification and a sharing of a mutual

history and problems rather than in terms of geographical location. Therefore, based on this definition, suburban blacks who identified with the black
community would be considered part of it regardless of where they lived. As
pointed out, of those 4,000 plus blacks who lived in suburbia by 1980, a disproportionately high number were professionals. Their choosing suburban
communities as a place to live had at least two major impacts on the black
community. First, it can now be seen that although the black professional
population in Syracuse grew after 1968, it still remained relatively small in
the central city. One can assume that black suburbanization was partly responsible for the slow inner-city growth. The second impact is more complicated because it has to do with whether these professional blacks identified
with the black community and how their decision affected the growth and
development of the community.

Given our definition of the black community, suburban blacks who
identified with the community would be considered part of it regardless of
where they lived. Two different approaches to black community participation emerged in interviews and conversations with suburban blacks. One
group of suburban blacks seemed to view their relocation to the area as
temporary, a part of their career movement within their companies. This
group's commitment was more to their professions and their companies
than to Syracuse or its black community. These individuals lived within the
local area, but did not view themselves as being a part of the area. A second
group of suburban blacks, whose relocation was also tied to their company,
joined social clubs, fraternities, and sororities, worked as role models with
inner-city kids, attended central city churches, and generally identified with
the community. This group, although not included in the survey results
presented in this section, did have some impact on the community. In addition to the activities just mentioned, its members were also often partially
responsible for their company's sensitivity to issues affecting blacks and to
the sponsorship of inner-city programs. Both groups were less effective politically because neither could vote in city elections, but they were eligible to
vote in county elections.

Reasons for locating in the suburban area were basically the same for
both groups of black suburbanites. Professional blacks bought homes in areas that offered more house for less money and where the resale possibilities

were maximized. Of the areas in the central city where professional blacks lived or would have liked to live, housing prices and property taxes were high. Suburban communities often offered more house for less money. Many blacks stated that although they felt isolated living in neighborhoods where they were the only blacks or the few blacks present were scattered, they could not afford economically to live in the central city where housing resales were often much slower. The census data presented in chapter 1 indicating a decreasing white population within the city and an increasing white suburban population validate this claim.

## Summary

Black suburbanization was more pronounced during the 1970s than during previous decades. White suburbanization, in contrast, started during the 1950s and has been far more extensive. Black suburbanization tended to concentrate geographically closer to the central city than did white suburbanization (Palen 2005).

Although suburban blacks are not directly dealt with in this study, many identify with and contribute directly to the Syracuse black community. All suburban blacks, regardless of their community identification or lack thereof, contribute indirectly to the black community in that they affect black income and education statistics. Less tangible, but just as important, is the fact that professional suburban blacks influenced the black community by helping break down the stereotypical views of blacks often held by Syracuse whites. These views were holdovers from the 1950s and early 1960s, when black newcomers were often uneducated and unskilled migrants from the rural South.

Finally, as noted, the Syracuse black community increased its voice in influencing public policy owing in large part to external influences such as the federal government. Therefore, the changing mood in America, buttressed by the policies of a newly elected president in the early 1980s, caused the black community to adopt a mood that can only be described as frustration. Recognizing that a mood of frustration permeated the black community from its leaders down to the masses is important in understanding the direction for blacks in the 1980s. The main question becomes: did this mood cause the community to regroup and fight harder during the 1980s to overcome the changed priorities or to withdraw and drift in what many saw as a period of stability? Other questions arise: Was power shared, and did public policies benefit from black input? How did the community fare during the 1980s in terms of housing, employment, education, and the quality of life generally? We address some of these questions in the ensuing chapters as we look at the Syracuse black community as it was during the 1980s.

# 6

# Social Class, Housing, and Neighborhoods

THE PREVIOUS CHAPTER DEALT WITH how American society and the Syracuse community underwent a changed mood. The more liberal stance of the 1960s and early 1970s gave way to a more conservative stance that prevailed in the late 1970s and throughout the 1980s. What effects this changed mood had on the black community becomes the major question to be answered in the remainder of the book.

An analysis of blacks in Syracuse during the 1980s can be better understood if we describe the social-class structure and how this class structure related to housing, neighborhoods, and lifestyles in general. Social-class status played a major role in how members of the black community interacted with each other and in the intercommunity relationships between blacks and whites. Beginning in the late 1960s, when a major increase in the size of the black professional class occurred, relationships between whites and this new black class shifted to some extent from the somewhat dominant-subordinate mode that had traditionally prevailed in Syracuse. Although relatively small in size, the new black professional class brought with it resources that had the potential for bringing about further changes during the 1970s and 1980s.

Probably more important was how these new, better-skilled, better-educated, and more articulate blacks fit into the overall scheme of things in the black community. Were they able or willing to become contributing members of the community as it attempted to gain more power in influencing public policy? In other words, did this new professional class represent power that was available to the black masses? Did the power that blacks in

Syracuse fought for during the 1960s materialize by the 1980s? We addressed these questions briefly in chapter 5, but provide a more detailed analysis starting with this chapter.

## Early Class Structure in the Black Community

As described in chapters 2 and 3, the earliest known recognition of a class structure within the black community was around the turn of the twentieth century during the period of exploitation (1870–1910). It is fairly ironic that the first class structure had three distinct classes, whereas during the 1930s lines between the two top classes became blurred, eventually leaving only two recognizable classes. The earlier three classes consisted of the homeowners, the poor but respectable, and the undesirables. By the 1930s, the homeowners and the poor but respectable merged into what was referred to as the "old stable black families." This merging happened in part because of the increasing number of black southern rural migrants who came to Syracuse during World War I and World War II. Established members of the black community looked upon this new group with some disdain because of its unstable family life and tenuous economic status. As the homeowners and the poor but respectable began to distance themselves from the newcomers, they themselves were looked upon as one class.

As Syracuse's black population more than doubled from 1950 to 1960, so did its professional class. Although still small in number, these new higher-status blacks joined the handful of old professional black families to formulate a solid middle class. In 1959, when a group of black community women received a charter for a local chapter of Links, Incorporated, its members probably perceived their status as being at least upper middle class.[1] This group and their families represented the top of the black class structure at that time. In the aftermath of the civil rights movement and federal intervention in the job market in the form of affirmative action, the migration of professional blacks continued at an accelerated pace. By the 1980s, the overall growth of the black population had slowed, as had that of professional blacks.

---

1. Links, Incorporated, is a national organization of black women who are recognized within their communities as being of high social and professional status.

However, from the 1950s until the 1980s, the class structure within the black community expanded considerably.

## Black Social-Class Structure

Table 6.1 depicts the social-class structure that existed in the black community during the 1970s and 1980s. The sections that follow provide a description of each of the classes making up the structure.[2]

### The Upper Class

James Blackwell points out social scientists' assumption that an upper class does not exist within black communities (1985, 126). They see the top strata within the black community as consisting of a diversified middle class. Given the small size of the upper class in the black community (1.4 percent), one

**Table 6.1**

**Social-Class Structure of the Black Community, 1970s–1980s**

| | |
|---|---|
| Upper class | 1.4% |
| (nouveau riche) | |
| Upper middle class | 6.6% |
| (professionals, managers, and white-collar workers) | |
| Lower middle class | 28.5% |
| (skilled blue-collar and clerical workers) | |
| Working class | 35.9% |
| (working poor) | |
| Lower class | 27.6% |
| (underclass and poverty stricken) | |

*Source:* Blackwell (1985, 126) presented a similar class structure; the table here is configured using data from Stamps (1982).

2. Daniel W. Rossides (1976) presents a composite estimate of an American class structure for white communities (racial and ethnic minorities are excluded): the upper class (1–3 percent), upper middle class (10–15 percent), lower middle class (30–35 percent), working class (40–45 percent), and lower class (20–25 percent).

might indeed be inclined to view it as a subgroup within the middle class. The inclusion of an upper class in the community is not justified on the basis of size, however, but on how those individuals perceived themselves. For the most part, those individuals who were objectively placed (using the Hollingshead Scale) in the upper class based on education and occupation perceived themselves as being in the upper class or demonstrated an upper-class lifestyle.

As mentioned earlier, the upper class in the black community was in the 1980s a recent phenomenon. Before the 1960s, only a handful of blacks could be considered as resembling an upper class. This recently evolved stratum was too small to be broken up into substrata such as an old and a new upper class. Also, most of its members had only recently attained upper-class status. Even in the case of individuals who were from old upper-class families, as characterized by Blackwell, their current family status would be defined as "new" because both spouses did not come from upper-class backgrounds. An example of a new upper-class family would be a person from an old upper-class black family whose spouse was originally from a middle- or upper-middle-class background, but had now attained membership in the new upper class as a result of upward mobility owing to education, occupation, and income. A few blacks did come from recognized old upper-class families with roots in the South. The daughter of a former black college president is one example; she and her husband, both retired professionals and world travelers, were recognized as one of the early upper-class black families. Another early upper-class family was made up of a retired physician and his wife, now deceased. They had strong social and kinship ties with black society in Atlanta, Georgia. The female spouses in these two families were leaders in organizing the first upper-crust social organization in the black community, the Links.

The upper class of the 1980s was made up of professionals, some of whom had retired. Relative to incomes received by blacks in Syracuse in general, incomes of the upper class were high, but not necessarily the highest in the total population. Based on 1980 census data, 1.1 percent of the black families in Syracuse had an income of $50,000 or more yearly, and 4.5 percent had incomes between $35,000 and $49,999 (U.S. Bureau of the Census 1980, 352). Upper-class family incomes, excluding retirees, ranged from $35,000 to more than $100,000 a year. Upper-class families consisting of two earners, both of whom were professionally trained and pursuing professional careers, had the highest incomes.

Most upper-class black families lived intermixed with upper-middle-class whites, a disproportionately large number of whom were Jewish and Italian. These integrated neighborhoods were located in close proximity to Syracuse University. By occupation, this group was made up of physicians, surgeons, college professors and administrators, business executives, and public-service executives. Similar to Blackwell's findings (1985, 128), the upper class placed a premium on marital stability and education for their children, who attended either private elementary and secondary schools or, because of their residential location, the top public schools in the Syracuse School District. After finishing high school, these children attended top black colleges (e.g., Spelman, Howard, Morehouse, and Hampton) or prestigious white colleges (e.g., Harvard, Princeton, MIT, and University of Pennsylvania).

Through social organizations, political affiliations, fraternities, and sororities, as well as through kinship bonds and old-school ties, this group was intertwined in a national network of friends and acquaintances. Although the group's social contacts tended to be black communities nationally, its professional and political contacts, local and national, tended to be both black and white. Blackwell acknowledges that there might be some truth in the stereotype that all upper-class blacks know each other or at the very least have common friends and acquaintances (1985, 28). Upper- and upper-middle-class blacks in Syracuse often joked that there were only ten thousand professional blacks nationally; they just circulated from city to city, creating an illusion of being more numerous.

An interesting aspect of upper-class black lifestyle in Syracuse was the lack of emphasis on material possessions. Upper- and upper-middle-class blacks have traditionally been characterized as being conspicuous consumers (Frazier 1957). In Syracuse, however, automobiles, large and opulently furnished homes, furs, diamonds, and other material indicators of affluence were secondary to living in a respectable neighborhood, attending the right schools, having professional affiliations, and supporting local cultural activities. Of the upper-class blacks who attended church, most had formal affiliations with Baptist and Episcopal churches. However, based on the survey data used in this study, church attendance among upper-class households can best be described as sporadic regardless of church affiliation.

## The Upper Middle Class

In the Syracuse black community, the upper-middle-class group was larger than the upper class in the 1980s, but significantly smaller than the lower middle class. It made up about 6.6 percent of the black population. Some members of this strata felt they belonged in the upper class, and because of the rather blurred lines that existed between the two strata, it was difficult to deny their membership other than on objective criteria. Many individuals categorized as upper middle class participated in the same social activities and clubs as did those considered upper class. The top social clubs were made up of members from both the upper class and the upper middle class. Some individuals from the upper middle class and the lower middle class did not belong to the top social clubs, nor were they invited to attend activities given by these clubs or by upper-class families. These individuals and families often felt slighted because they were not included in upper-class membership and upper-class activities.

What added to these feelings was the fact that entrance into so-called high society in the black community was relatively easy and based on objective criteria. Entrance was not based on longevity in the community, as has been the case in many other black communities, particularly those in the South where family traditions have long been established. In cities such as Washington, D.C.; Richmond, Virginia; Durham, North Carolina; Charleston, South Carolina; Nashville, Tennessee; and Atlanta, Georgia, regardless of one's objective social status (occupation, education, and income), newcomers were not readily admitted into certain social circles. An invitation to join in top social functions other than fund-raisers materialized only after years of living within those communities. In the Syracuse black community, in contrast, objective social criteria went a long way toward establishing social position and acceptance. Newcomers who met these criteria—including place of residence, outgoing personality, a semblance of decorum, and a wish to belong—were often readily accepted into upper- and upper-middle-class activities. One of the main reasons why acceptance into these social activities was relatively easy was that these groups depended on newcomers for replacements. Children of professional families, after being educated in the Syracuse public-school system or in private schools, often attended colleges and universities in other localities and never returned to the city on a permanent basis. Also, upward social mobility among members of the black community, at least among those who remained in Syracuse, was slight. As an example, only three of the twenty-three members of the local Links chapter in 1986 were originally from the city. The same could be said for Jack 'n' Jill, another middle- and upper-class social club. Most of the members of these social clubs had migrated to the city since 1968. Therefore, it is reasonable to assume that the upper middle and upper classes depended on newcomers for replacement in membership.

Upper-middle-class black incomes ranged from $25,000 to more than $100,000 in the 1980s. This class consisted of professionals with college degrees, some having advanced academic and professional degrees. The upper middle class consisted of educated (college-graduated) ministers, public-school teachers, businesspersons and successful entrepreneurs, college teachers, and high-level city, county, state, and federal employees. Family stability was valued, as in the upper class, but divorce was not uncommon. In two-earner professional families, egalitarian principles prevailed as related to household chores and many child-rearing practices. Family-oriented social and religious activities tended to be dominated by women, whereas nonfamily social activities were more dominated by men. Racially mixed marriages were present among members of the upper middle class, with both spouses participating in social activities in the black community and in the larger society.

Although the upper class was instrumental in establishing the top social clubs in the Syracuse black community, the upper middle class was responsible for the establishment of graduate chapters of fraternities and sororities. This class also played a more active role in political and social-action organizations.

*The Lower Middle Class*

The lower middle class was significantly larger than the upper class and the upper middle class combined in the 1980s. This group made up approximately

28.5 percent of the black community. Its members were clerical workers, salespersons, and skilled blue-collar workers, and among them were high school graduates, technical and community college graduates, and some college graduates. A few members of the lower middle class had not finished high school, but through hard work and respectability had attained status within the black community. A decrease in industrial jobs that began in the early 1960s and accelerated during the 1980s with the closing or employment cutbacks of such companies as Bristol Laboratory, Carrier Corporation, and Allied Corporation hit the lower middle class hard. More than 30 percent of the employment in the community came from the industrial sector (Seely 1987a, A1). Because the lower middle class depended heavily on skilled blue-collar jobs, the decrease in industrial jobs served as a major threat to their social and economic status. Also included in this class were local entertainers (actors, actresses, musicians, artists, etc.) whose artistic work was their primary source of employment.

Family stability was stressed in this class; however, divorce was not unusual. A divorce often meant returning to working or lower-class status because in many cases two incomes were necessary to maintain lower-middle-class status. Incomes within this group ranged from $11,000 to more than $25,000 yearly. Although many individuals in this class had not attended college, they stressed education for their children. Those children who did not earn athletic scholarships at small eastern state colleges attended the local community college or one of the local trade schools. Others attended predominantly black colleges, usually in the home state from which the family originally migrated. Almost no children from lower-middle-class families attended either of the two local four-year institutions.

Home ownership was a goal; however, many lower-middle-class families lived in integrated apartment complexes or rented small single-family dwellings in predominantly black neighborhoods. Upper-middle-class blacks and whites who had relocated to more desirable neighborhoods within or outside of Syracuse owned many of these homes.

Lower-middle-class blacks served as the backbone of black Baptist and Methodist churches, some of which were the largest in the black community. Many also held membership in smaller, more fundamentalist denominations such as the Church of the Word of God, the Cross Church of God by Faith, and the Starlight Holiness Church. These south-side churches, many

of them storefront churches, were carryovers from the days of southern migrants. Lower-middle-class blacks also belonged to the Prince Hall Masons
and other black fraternal organizations. However, few held membership in
black sororities and fraternities because membership in those organizations
was gained in college.

Although social separation was quite distinctive between the upper, upper middle, and lower middle classes, on the one hand, and the working and
lower classes, on the other, individuals within the lower middle class often
vacillated between the two groups when the occasion permitted, especially
native-born blacks who had moved up economically and socially from many
of their relatives and friends. Family and church activities brought them
together with kin and friends from the working and lower classes. Lower-
middle-class males, although associating with professional blacks, also were
more likely to maintain relationships with working- and lower-class friends
and to frequent south-side cafés and bars patronized by the working and
lower classes. The same was not true for lower-middle-class females because
sex-specific norms limited the places they could frequent. Black-owned professional clubs that catered to black professionals were more likely supported
by lower-middle-class blacks, both single and married. House parties with
card playing, dancing, and general socializing occurred frequently among
married persons and singles. Travel was usually restricted to a trip "down
home," the South, to visit relatives or to attend an annual family reunion.

The lower middle class was more politically active than the lower class
or even the upper class; however, their political participation was often restricted to voting. Those few who participated in community activism usually did so through the NAACP or an ad hoc group that was reacting to a
crisis. The Urban League, the Syracuse Minority Professional Action Conference (SYMPAC), and the Syracuse Black Leadership Congress drew membership from the upper middle and upper classes more so than from the lower
middle class.

*The Working Class*

As has been emphasized, the largest division in the Syracuse black community financially and socially was between the top three classes and the bottom

two classes. Upper-, upper-middle-, and lower-middle-class families were more likely to live on the east side of Syracuse and in suburban communities, whereas working- and lower-class families were more likely to be located on the south side of the city. There basically was no socializing between them, save the lower middle class's participation in family and church functions frequented by working- and lower-class kin and friends. Most bars and taverns in the black community were oriented toward lower- and working-class clientele, and were occasionally frequented by lower-middle-class males.

The working class was the largest class stratum within the black community, making up 35.9 percent of all blacks. Because working-class blacks depended heavily on semiskilled and unskilled jobs, decreases in the industrial sector in the city hurt their economic stability. The major differences between the working class, often referred to as the working poor, and the lower class was being employed or not being employed. The community had traditionally witnessed movement between the working and the lower classes, particularly as it related to female-headed households. Working-class females depended heavily on domestic and service work for employment. The availability of these jobs vacillated owing to the economy, seasonal population shifts, and geographical mobility among middle- and upper-class white households.[3] For men and women who held semiskilled industrial jobs, a decrease in the industrial sector often meant a loss in income and a drop to lower-class status. Shifts in employment status (usually from employed to not employed) had a profound effect on family income, especially for males because of the differential in men's and women's annual incomes (Duncan 1984). Incomes for working-class blacks in the 1980s were less than $12,000 yearly.

The working class represented what might be called "ritualistic strivers" in the sense that they worked hard yet were unable to get ahead. They were affected by fluctuations in the economy, seasonal jobs, and the local unemployment rate

3. It is highly likely that the lower class of the black community is represented in higher proportions than depicted in this study because we used the Hollingshead Two Factor Index of Social Position, which utilizes occupation and education to construct classes. We could not place into a class any respondent who did not indicate occupation or education. A portion of the low-income households in which the head was unemployed or on welfare did not indicate occupation. Therefore, they are not included as part of the lower class.

(Duncan 1984; Blackwell 1985). In many cases, both husband and wife worked to make ends meet. Female-headed households depended on kin and friends for childcare so the mother-head could be employed. One domestic worker we interviewed characterized the general attitude of many working-class people in the black community toward work and public assistance:

> I don't understand my sister. She just sits there [at home] all day, won't get a job, don't want to do nothing. Let her boyfriend or some man come by, and she's ready to go. He ain't got no money. She the one have to pay, but she gotta have her a man. Me, I'm nobody's woman. I don't want to depend on nobody and don't want nobody depending on me. When I was sick and couldn't work, I went down to the welfare office. This woman, black as me, looked at me like "What you want?" I said [to myself], let me get well and get me a job, cause I ain't gonna kiss no stuck up black ass just to get some money. It ain't her money no way. She looking at me like I'm asking for her money.

This statement reveals both the independence and the sensitivity that often characterize working-class people. Many of those interviewed felt they were working hard and trying, yet were no better off than some of their neighbors on public assistance.

Like the lower middle class, many working-class black people belonged to the Baptist and Methodist churches within the community. However, the working class, along with the lower class, served as the backbone of the many small churches and storefront churches found on just about every block within predominantly black south-side neighborhoods.

Working- and lower-class blacks participated in the following types of leisure activities, in the following order: socializing and partying, watching television and listening to the radio, participating in sports, and resting/relaxing (Stamps and Stamps 1985, 49). Willie (1974) found in an earlier study that blacks of all classes had only a small amount of time for leisure because of an all-consuming work schedule. This was particularly true for working-class blacks, who spent most of their time working and trying not to slip back into the lower class.

A major conflict existed between the three upper/middle classes and the two working/lower classes within the community in the 1980s. Working- and lower-class blacks often felt that professional blacks had forsaken them and

6.1. Old Timers' Picnic, Thornden Park, 1983. Courtesy of Onondaga County Public Library, Beauchamp Branch.

were concerned only with their homes, integrated neighborhoods, and careers. In other words, they perceived middle- and upper-class blacks as joining the "me generation" spawned by middle-class whites (Lasch 1978). This perception was exacerbated by the physical separation of the two groups; middle- and upper-class blacks lived on the east side of the city, whereas the lower classes lived for the most part on the south side of the city. The lower classes, although supportive of middle-class blacks in their quest for elective office, felt that the latter group, like whites, really did not understand or no longer understood the dynamics of poor inner-city neighborhoods. In actuality, their perceptions were not far from the truth as the remaining analysis shows.

*The Lower Class*

The lower class as characterized here is the same as what has popularly been referred to as the "underclass" (W. Wilson 1978, 1987; Glasgow 1981; Duncan 1984; Murray 1984; Blackwell 1985). The lower class assumed the bottom rung of the black community class structure and, along with lower-class whites and many Native Americans, made up the bottom of the Syracuse class structure. The main difference between the working class and the lower class was that the working class held what were considered permanent jobs, whereas the lower class received a disproportionate amount of their income from public assistance. Approximately 80 percent of black lower-class households were female headed.

Black southern migrant families who poured into Syracuse from the 1930s through the mid-1960s made up and continued to make up the lower class. This fact punctuates the problems faced by the migrants and their offspring over the years. The lower class, with annual incomes less than $10,000, constituted 27.6 percent of the black community in 1980 (U.S. Bureau of the Census 1980, 352). This group was made up of individuals who were the least educated, had the fewest work skills, and hence were the least likely to enjoy social mobility. For the lower class, the loss of industrial jobs had less of an impact because only a few held temporary or part-time industrial jobs. Those who held more permanent jobs usually vacillated between the working class and the lower class, depending on the state of the local economy. During periods of economic prosperity, they were able to obtain somewhat permanent, semi- or low-skilled jobs. During turndowns in the local economy, their employment, when available, was in temporary, part-time, and low-skilled jobs.

In the 1980s, the lower and working classes were highly visible in Syracuse in that they were concentrated in a low-income ghetto that bordered Interstates 690 and 81. Of all class strata within the black community, lower- and working-class blacks were the most segregated (Seely 1987c, A11). Lower-class families formulated neighborhood support groups, whereby kin and friends were bound together by the need to survive on limited resources (Stack 1974).

Church activities played an important role in the lives of many lower-class blacks. Religion served as an escape from their daily problems (Blackwell 1985, 139). Although they felt powerless to alter their worldly circumstances, they also felt that through religion they could better their chances after death. As was the case with the working class, storefront churches and small congregations provided their religious salvation.

According to Dr. Ruben Cowart, director of the Syracuse Community Health Center, which provided health care to poor families in the 1980s, the main health problem faced by the poor was teenage pregnancy (Cowart 1981). For religious reasons and because of subcultural norms, lower-class females tended not have abortions. These teenage girls often viewed children as a source of income. Hence, the "vicious cycle of poverty" was begun and continued from one generation to the next (Seely 1987c, A11). Al Stokes, a married father of three who coached football in addition to being a salesperson, put in perspective the attitude of many working- and lower-class young males: "If I [a young male] leave my family, my family will get her [their] rent paid, gas and light paid, medical bills paid, clothing taken care of, food bills paid—by [Onondaga County Department of] Social Services" (quoted in Seely 1987c, A11). Stokes's statement reflects an understanding of the attitudes and norms that for the most part permeated the thought processes of young working- and lower-class males.

*Lifestyles*

The upper and middle classes maintained a lifestyle that was both black and integrated. Because most members of these classes lived and worked in integrated settings, their social life was often integrated, but it centered more on professional and personal relationships developed on the job rather than on relationships that developed within integrated neighborhoods. Only those blacks who had been the first to move into integrated neighborhoods and had remained there over a period of years developed close social relationships with their white neighbors. These blacks and their white neighbors often invited each other to social functions held in their homes. More prevalent were blacks and whites inviting their professional acquaintances and coworkers, who were white and black, to their homes for social activities. The integration of neighborhoods seemed to facilitate white professional coworkers' being invited to the homes of black professionals. Those few black professionals who maintained residence in or near predominantly black neighborhoods were less likely to have social gatherings in their homes that included whites. Of the blacks interviewed who lived in black areas, most indicated that they did not invite whites to social activities in their homes because they knew professional whites were reluctant to come into the neighborhoods where they lived.

Although by the 1980s blacks were scattered throughout Syracuse, middle- and upper-class blacks tended to move into a large upper- and middle-class Jewish area of the city that had been recently populated by a significant number of Italians. Because both Jews and Italians predated blacks, neighborhood friendships had already been defined along ethnic lines before the entrance of blacks. Italians had been faced with Jewish friendship cliques when they moved in the area. As significant numbers of Italians came into the area, in many cases with siblings or other family members living side by side or in the same block, Italian friendship and kinship groups formulated.

The first black families began to move into this area in the late 1960s during the period when liberal whites felt it was fashionable to include blacks in their social activities. In some cases, true friendship and a sense of neighborliness developed. These types of relationships have continued over the years, with social invitations being extended on a reciprocal basis. However, as the number of blacks moving into the area continued to increase, whites were less likely to include these new blacks in their social networks. Three factors account for this change. First, blacks were no longer a novelty; there were plenty. Second, by the 1970s, blacks were less concerned with social integration. Their reason for moving into integrated areas had to do more with better housing and easier resale than with an integrated social life. Third, as blacks continued to move into the area, their presence began to be perceived as possibly upsetting the statistical majority/minority relationship that had existed.

For many middle- and upper-class blacks, participation in an all-black social setting was also a prominent part of their lifestyle. Not only were all-black parties and dinners held in their homes in integrated neighborhoods, but also more structured forms of social life centered on all-black social clubs and organizations.

## Black Social Clubs and Organizations

Middle- and upper-class social clubs and organizations in the black community in the first half of the twentieth century were controlled by about three families and in their early years observed traditional norms regarding new members. However, the sons and daughters of old families did not return to Syracuse after college, creating a replacement void. By the late 1960s, when significant numbers of professional blacks began to move to Syracuse, these organizations and clubs were in need of new members to sustain themselves. Without a critical mass to draw from, they began bringing in professionals who were relatively new to the community. As this trend continued, the new and younger members soon outnumbered the older original members. The older members, unable to maintain control, soon began to withdraw from the organizations and clubs.

In many respects, these social organizations and clubs, with their new members and constant turnover, were viewed as exciting. Many of the new professional families that moved to Syracuse were highly mobile, staying in the community for only short periods of three to ten years. For the most part, these well-educated and well-traveled blacks brought with them new ideas and new perspectives that assisted in creating an exciting atmosphere. The infusion of new blood into social organizations and clubs, although departing from traditional norms that existed in other communities, allowed these groups to take advantage of new community resources.

Lower-middle-class and working-class social organizations consisted more of lodges and fraternal orders. Because there was a much larger pool of potential members among those who were from Syracuse or had lived in the community for a number of years, local persons maintained control of these groups. Although not very visible within the black community, these organizations and clubs provided a needed social function. Along with black churches, they allowed people the opportunity to control something and make decisions other than within their families. Organizations of all classes served an important political function in that they were often used to pull the community together to back a black candidate or a white candidate who was supportive of the black community.

*Sororities and Fraternities*

With the newly arriving professional blacks to the Syracuse black community during the late 1960s and early 1970s, graduate chapters of black fraternities

6.2. Black fraternal orders parade on Almond Street, ca. 1945. Courtesy of Onondaga County Public Library, Beauchamp Branch.

and sororities became more visible, and new chapters were established. Because the middle- and upper-class population was relatively small, many individuals who belonged to fraternities and sororities also belonged to upper-middle-class and upper-class social organizations and clubs. However, fraternities and sororities represented a wider distribution of blacks incomewise than did the social organizations and clubs discussed thus far.

Sororities and fraternities had less control over the social climate of the community than did the social organizations and clubs; however, they often provided a wider range of community services. Alpha Phi Alpha fraternity set up a program in 1980 for inner-city poor children using their members as role models. They met once a week with these children, telling them how many of their members used education as a mechanism of upward social mobility. By the mid-1980s, many black political leaders began to look upon sororities and fraternities as leadership organizations. Black political candidates sought out their support.

*Barbershops and Beauty Parlors*

An integral part of the social life of lower- and working-class members of the black community was the barbershop and the beauty parlor. These places of business were social centers where former members of the community, upon returning home, would seek out friends and former acquaintances. Gossip, political information, church news, and other types of information were passed on to customers and those who frequented these shops on a daily basis to pass the time of day. Although the number of barbershops and beauty parlors decreased significantly during the 1980s (see chapter 8), their social function remained the same. The ones that were still open by the late 1980s were small, with one or two operators. However, one barbershop, located along the black business strip on the south side, dominated both as a place for men and women to get a haircut and as a recreational and communication center. In this establishment, called Blue Brothers Barber Shop, barber chairs were stationed in an L shape on the left side of the large room as one entered the door. The physical arrangement of the chairs was of social significance in that the barbers with the least status in the pecking order were stationed closest to the door and the farthest away from chairs manned by the two Blue brothers. These two chairs were set off from all other chairs and located on the right side of the room. Their physical placement served a couple of functions. One, the Blue brothers had an undistorted view of the entire room and could observe all activities, and two, by being stationed away from the other barbers, the brothers removed themselves from the jokes and horseplay that occurred throughout the day. Barbers other than the Blue brothers usually serviced young men, new customers, and most women. The Blue brothers were ministers and catered to older well-established black men, many of whom were ministers or held positions of note in the community.

The barbershop also had pool tables and a shoeshine stand. Much of the social activity of younger customers centered on the game of pool. Women friends who came into the shop for money or just to sit and wait for "their men" to get off from work often bestowed status on the young barbers. If the woman was perceived as attractive and shapely, the other barbers and regulars would "carry on" over the barber. High fives would be extended between the barber-boyfriend and the regular customers. New customers and older customers would be amused by these antics.

As a communication center, barbershops and beauty parlors served a community function. National, state, and local politics were often discussed and debated at length. The two-step flow in communication had been at work for years in these establishments, wherein political interpreters would discuss political philosophy and point out which candidate to vote for or against (see, e.g., Lazarsfeld, Berelson, and McPhee 1948). Community political interpreters were well known, and their entrance into an establishment signaled a change in conversation. Regulars who were not getting haircuts or some other service would often leave if they had already heard the discussion or if they were disinterested. The important point is that these conversations did take place, and if an election or an issue was under consideration in the community, the discussions took on another level of significance.

## Social Activities of Black Youth

A major source of conflict between the black community and the white community was social activities for youth. Black and white youth had few things to do in their spare time. White youths tended to congregate at suburban shopping malls and attend private house parties. Black youths from lower-income neighborhoods adjacent to Syracuse University attempted to invade a square block of fast-food places and shops that catered primarily to university students. Given the close proximity of these establishments to where these youths lived, this area was the most logical place for them to frequent, but the university students viewed the local black youths as intruders into their territory (see Suttles 1968). And white shop owners in the area felt that nonuniversity black youths were troublemakers who did not spend money.

Some local black youths attempted to attend parties given by black fraternities and sororities at Syracuse University. Unless the affair was a dance in which an admission was charged and the aim was to make money, however, they were again rejected. So they often experienced two rejections in the university area, and in both cases their presence was perceived as an intrusion into another group's territory. In turn, the local black youths responded to this attitude with hostility and viewed both white and black university students as outsiders.

## Race and Housing

In analyzing data on owner- and renter-occupied housing in Syracuse, we spotted several interesting trends. However, we proceed with caution because, in many cases, what appears to be owing to race was often found to be owing to the disproportionately large number of blacks in low-income categories. In the 1980s, the housing situation in Syracuse had improved vastly over what it was in the 1930s and 1940s, when blacks, wanting to buy housing outside of the Washington-Water Strip district or Jewtown, had to rely on sympathetic whites who would purchase houses from white home owners and resell them to the blacks. Outside of traditional black residential areas, housing for blacks was not to be found in the 1930s and 1940s. During the 1980s, with the exclusion of ethnic neighborhoods, blacks were able to purchase housing throughout the city when they could afford the price. However, as we show later, obtaining a mortgage in Syracuse posed a problem for blacks.

### Race and Home Ownership

Table 6.2 shows the percentage of owner-occupied housing, based on race, from 1960 to 1980. These data indicate that for each of the three decades a higher percentage of whites than blacks owned the houses they occupied.

**Table 6.2**

**Owner-Occupied Housing in Syracuse According to Race, 1960–1980**

| Year | Black (%)* | White (%) | B/W Ratio |
|------|-----------|-----------|-----------|
| 1960 | 15.6 | 50.5 | .31 |
| 1970 | 18.5 | 47.2 | .39 |
| 1980 | 24.5 | 45.2 | .54 |

*Source:* Modified from Sacks and Sacks 1987, 60.

*Percentage of owner-occupied housing within each race.

Table 6.2 also shows that as the percentage of black owner-occupied housing increased, the percentage of white owner-occupied housing decreased for each of the three decades. The increase in the percentage of black owner-occupied housing can be attributed to the increase in the number of middle- and upper-class blacks that began to migrate to Syracuse after the mid-1960s. Of equal importance was the increase in the number of well-paid skill-level jobs blacks obtained during the late 1960s and early 1970s. However, this increase was short-lived as the number of manufacturing jobs within Syracuse declined drastically during the late 1970s and 1980s, for both blacks and whites. For blacks, the effect of the loss of manufacturing jobs was greater than for whites because they held a higher percentage of industrial-sector jobs (Seely 1987c, A15). The decrease in the percentage of white owner-occupied housing occurred in part because of the relocation of middle- and upper-class whites to suburban communities. The result of these changes in housing patterns was that the black-to-white ratio of owner-occupied housing in Syracuse increased from .31 in 1960 to .54 in 1980 (table 6.2).

Utilizing data from the *Urban League Community Survey* (Stamps 1982), table 6.3 shows that 68.5 percent of blacks, 71.1 percent of whites, and 85.7 percent of seven other minorities stated that they were first-time home owners in the earlier 1980s.

Also shown in table 6.3 is the number of years the respondents owned their homes. A higher percentage of blacks (13.8) than whites (9.0) had owned their homes less than one year. For other minorities, 14.3 percent had owned their homes less than one year. At the other extreme, among those who had owned their home sixteen years or longer, the percentage of whites (33.7) almost tripled the percentage of blacks (11.8). This finding supports the conclusion from table 6.2 that home ownership in Syracuse was a more recent phenomenon for blacks than for whites. Looking at types of mortgages in table 6.3, the 127 blacks who stated they had a mortgage represented 25.4 percent of the blacks surveyed; the 74 whites with a mortgage represented 35.6 percent of the whites; and the 7 other minorities with a mortgage were 16.7 percent of the other minorities. It was not surprising to find that a higher percentage of whites than blacks indicated they had mortgages. One reason for this difference was the income disparity between blacks and whites, which would make more whites eligible for mortgages. Another possible reason, of

**Table 6.3**

**Selected Characteristics of Home Ownership According to Race,\* 1981**

| Selected Characteristics | Black (%) | White (%) | Other Minorities (%) |
|---|---|---|---|
| *First Home Owned?* | *(N = 146)* | *(N = 90)* | *(N = 7)* |
| Yes | 68.5 | 71.1 | 85.7 |
| No | 31.5 | 28.9 | 14.3 |
| *Number of Years Home Owned* | *(N = 144)* | *(N = 89)* | *(N = 7)* |
| Less than 1 Year | 13.8 | 9.0 | 14.3 |
| 1–5 Years | 25.7 | 28.1 | 57.1 |
| 6–10 Years | 29.2 | 15.7 | 28.6 |
| 11–15 Years | 19.4 | 13.5 | — |
| 16 Years and Longer | 11.8 | 33.7 | — |
| *Type of Mortgage* | *(N = 127)* | *(N = 74)* | *(N = 7)* |
| VA | 7.9 | 4.1 | 14.3 |
| FHA | 29.1 | 18.9 | 85.7 |
| Conventional (Bank) | 49.6 | 58.1 | — |
| Credit Union | 2.4 | 4.1 | — |
| Mortgage Company | 3.1 | 2.7 | — |
| Private Loan | 7.9 | 8.1 | — |
| None | 4.1 | — | — |
| *Second Mortgage?* | *(N = 130)* | *(N = 79)* | *(N = 7)* |
| Yes | 8.5 | 10.1 | 28.6 |
| No | 91.5 | 89.9 | 71.4 |
| *Rental Income Received from Home?* | *(N = 140)* | *(N = 83)* | *(N = 7)* |
| Yes | 10.0 | 9.6 | 14.3 |
| No | 90.0 | 90.4 | 85.7 |

*Source:* Stamps 1982, 81.

\*Not significant.

concern within the black community, was that local banks were redlining inner-city neighborhoods where many black families lived. The chief executive officer of the local Urban League chapter constantly voiced concerned in the media over disinvestments in inner-city neighborhoods. Local banks, although denying charges that they had labeled certain areas as ones not to invest in, emphasized that profitability was the main criterion in making loan decisions. The data presented here, although indicating that a higher percentage of whites (58.1) than blacks (49.6) had conventional bank loans, do not support a redlining charge. However, a tour of south-side neighborhoods would reveal extensive abandonment and housing deterioration. A black respondent from the south side stated, "[This] neighborhood needs cleaning up, renovate houses or tear them down. Most houses in this neighborhood [are] in bad shape, do you hear me, baddd shape" (quoted in Stamps 1982, 13). Other south-side respondents, both black and white, were concerned about children and the homeless who periodically set fires in vacant houses in their neighborhood. Although these reports and the visual condition of south-side neighborhoods suggested the possibility of disinvestments, additional data are needed before a definitive conclusion can be reached. As shown in table 6.3, a slightly higher percentage of whites (10.1) than blacks (8.5) indicated they had second mortgages on their houses. Again, the data do not reveal significant differences between blacks and whites regarding selected characteristics of home ownership.

Table 6.4 shows the value of owner-occupied housing for blacks and whites. The most obvious finding was that higher percentages of blacks owned lower-priced housing and higher percentages of whites owned higher-priced housing. This table also reveals an inverse relationship between home ownership and the value of houses for blacks. As the cost of housing increased for blacks, the percentage who owned their homes decreased. As the cost of housing increased for whites, ownership increased up to a point (around $45,000), after which white ownership decreased as the cost continued to increase. Of the owner-occupied housing in Syracuse, blacks owned 7.6 percent, and whites owned 92.4 percent. Given that the 1980 population of the city was 16 percent black, owner-occupied housing for blacks was disproportionately low. Only 1.7 percent of blacks lived in black-owned housing valued at $60,000 or more. The percentage of whites in this category more than

Table 6.4
**Value of Housing According to Race, 1980**

| Value of Owner-Occupied Housing Units | Black (%) (N = 1,693) | White (%) (N = 20,485) |
|---|---|---|
| Less than $15,000 | 13.80 | 8.80 |
| $5,000–19,999 | 19.50 | 9.80 |
| $20,000–24,999 | 17.00 | 13.40 |
| $25,000–29,999 | 13.40 | 13.60 |
| $30,000–34,999 | 11.40 | 15.60 |
| $35,000–39,999 | 9.60 | 11.90 |
| $40,000–49,999 | 9.60 | 14.20 |
| $50,000–59,999 | 3.70 | 6.20 |
| $60,000–79,999 | 1.70 | 4.70 |
| $80,000–99,999 | 0.20 | 1.20 |
| $100,000–149,999 | 0.05 | 0.60 |
| $150,000–199,999 | — | 0.08 |
| $200,000 and more | 0.12 | 0.03 |
| Median Value | $24,900 | $30,652 |

*Source:* Developed from census data in U.S. Bureau of the Census 1970/1980.

tripled that of blacks. Based on these 1980 data, only three black families lived in owner-occupied housing worth $100,000 or more. In contrast, 143 whites lived in owner-occupied housing at that value. Thus, not only did the percentage of black owner-occupied housing fall short of the total percentage of blacks in Syracuse, but the black-white discrepancy was even greater for higher-priced owner-occupied housing.

*Owners/Renters and Race*

Table 6.5 compares black and white owners and renters according to their age and income. Summary data in the table reveal that for owners, blacks had a higher median income ($21,669) than whites ($18,443), but a lower median age (44.5) than whites (58.2). For renters, just the opposite was true. White renters had a higher median income ($9,589) than black renters ($7,523).

**Table 6.5**

**Housing Status and Income in Syracuse According to Race and Age, 1980**

| Income | Black | | | | White | | | |
|---|---|---|---|---|---|---|---|---|
| | Owner (%) (N = 2,167) | Median Age | Renter (%) (N = 6,730) | Median Age | Owner (%) (N = 25,705) | Median Age | Renter (%) (N = 30,984) | Median Age |
| Less than $5,000 | 9.4 | 57.6 | 34.8 | 31.1 | 8.2 | 70.9 | 26.0 | 48.3 |
| $5,000–9,999 | 5.7 | 55.8 | 26.5 | 33.1 | 15.7 | 69.7 | 26.0 | 37.1 |
| $10,000–12,499 | 5.1 | 52.7 | 11.2 | 41.8 | 7.4 | 64.5 | 11.5 | 31.2 |
| $12,500–14,999 | 8.0 | 44.1 | 7.1 | 34.4 | 7.4 | 60.8 | 8.9 | 32.6 |
| $15,000–19,999 | 15.4 | 46.1 | 9.7 | 36.0 | 16.0 | 56.0 | 12.3 | 31.1 |
| $20,000–24,999 | 18.2 | 42.2 | 6.4 | 35.4 | 14.7 | 52.1 | 7.8 | 32.9 |
| $25,000–34,999 | 24.6 | 42.2 | 3.1 | 37.5 | 18.1 | 51.2 | 4.9 | 34.3 |
| $35,999–49,999 | 11.4 | 45.0 | 0.9 | 48.3 | 8.1 | 52.3 | 1.8 | 46.8 |
| $50,000 and More | 2.6 | 42.5 | 0.3 | 46.0 | 4.3 | 55.1 | 0.7 | 52.0 |
| Median | $21,669 | 44.5 | $7,523 | 34.0 | $18,443 | 58.2 | $9,589 | 34.6 |

*Source:* Modified from Sacks and Sacks 1987, 62.

The median ages for white and black renters were approximately the same. For both groups, home owners had higher median incomes and a higher median age than renters. Table 6.5 reveals for both blacks and whites that as income increased, the percentage of home ownership increased. In addition, as income decreased, the percentage of renters increased. Low-income (below $10,000) white owners and renters had much higher median ages than low-income black owners and renters. For black renters, the lowest median age (31.1 years) had incomes of less than $5,000 yearly. White renters with the lowest median age (31.1 years) had annual incomes of between $15,000 and $19,999.

These findings suggest that income was related to home ownership and renting for both blacks and whites. However, low-income blacks were less likely to own homes than low-income whites. Although a slightly higher percentage (61.3) of blacks earning less than $10,000 yearly rented than did whites (52.0), blacks and whites had similar trends in relationship to income and renting. Even though blacks and whites differed in income, age, and renting, being older was associated with home ownership for both blacks and whites. The much older median age for white owners (58.2 years) than for black owners (44.5 years) can be explained by the phenomenon of white relocation to suburban communities. Younger whites were more likely than older whites to move to the suburbs. Older whites, in many cases, were "locked in" Syracuse economically and could not move (Sacks and Sacks 1987). It should also be pointed out that older white ethnic families were more likely to remain in their neighborhoods than were white Anglo-Saxon families. Given the supporting role played by ethnic neighborhoods and the availability of cultural, religious, and shopping opportunities, the fact that older people remained is understandable (Light 1983). The data support this statement in that a lower percentage of whites than of blacks in higher-income categories, excluding $50,000 and higher, owned their homes and those home owners had a higher median age.

*Housing and Poverty*

Seymour Sacks and Robert Sacks state that the emphasis of social-science literature has traditionally been on children who live in poverty. The role played by rental housing in families who live below the poverty line has been virtually overlooked (1987, 68). Rental housing and female-headed families have played a major role in urban poverty. In Syracuse in 1980, 48.6 percent of all black families were headed by women. The contrasting percentage for white families was 18.9, according to the data presented in table 6.6. Of the 28.5 percent of black families living in poverty, 82.6 percent were headed by women. Although the percentage of white families living in poverty was less than one-third that of black families, 58 percent of them were headed by women.

Table 6.7 throws some light on this phenomenon. The data reveal that for both black and white families living in poverty, higher percentages lived in rented dwellings rather than in owner-occupied housing.

Of the black renter-occupied housing, 40.1 percent were families living in poverty. The poverty rate for white renter-occupied housing was 24.2 percent. However, when one looks at black female-headed poor families living in renter-occupied housing, one can see that the rate was 50.1 percent, the highest for any group. Table 6.7 clearly shows that for families in Syracuse who were below the poverty line, rates were the highest for renter-occupied housing. This relationship held regardless of race. These findings point to the tenuous status of housing for single-parent families living in poverty, in particular those headed by black women.

Substantial numbers of black female-headed families living in poverty resided in public housing. Considering that 82.6 percent of all Syracuse black

**Table 6.6**

**Race, Poverty, and Household Status in Syracuse, 1980**

| Poverty | Black (%) | White (%) | Total (%) |
|---|---|---|---|
| Female Headed Families as % of | | | |
| All Families | 48.6 | 18.9 | 23.7 |
| Families in Poverty | 28.5 | 9.3 | 12.9 |
| Female Heads Living in Poverty (% of Families in Poverty) | 82.6 | 58.0 | 66.6 |
| All Persons Living in Poverty | 32.6 | 15.1 | 18.4 |
| Females Living in Poverty | 50.1 | 28.4 | 36.1 |

*Source:* From data provided in Sacks and Sacks 1987, 69.

Table 6.7

**Poverty Rates for Families According to Housing Status and Race in Syracuse, 1980**

| Housing Status for Families Living in Poverty | Black (%) | White (%) | Black/White Ratio |
|---|---|---|---|
| *Owner Occupied* | | | |
| Owner | 8.6 | 5.3 | 1.62 |
| Married Couple | 3.3 | 1.9 | 1.74 |
| Male Head | 10.8 | 6.3 | 1.71 |
| Female Head | 25.6 | 13.1 | 1.95 |
| *Renter Occupied* | | | |
| Renter | 40.1 | 24.2 | 1.66 |
| Married Couple | 18.9 | 10.0 | 1.89 |
| Male Head | 31.9 | 24.2 | 1.32 |
| Female Head | 50.1 | 31.1 | 1.61 |
| *Those Living in Poverty* | | | |
| Married Couple | 10.2 | 4.4 | 2.32 |
| Male Head | 29.3 | 20.3 | 1.44 |
| Female Head | 47.6 | 25.5 | 1.87 |

*Source:* Adapted from Sacks and Sacks 1987, 70.

families headed by women lived in poverty, one can determine the dependency of these families on rental housing, especially public housing. In contrast, 58 percent of white female-headed families were below the poverty line. White female-headed families living in poverty were less likely to be found in public housing for two reasons. First, more privately owned low-cost rental housing was available to them, especially in white ethnic neighborhoods. Second, many white families refused public-housing units in complexes that were predominantly black. Pioneer Homes is a good example. Although Pioneer Homes was originally white when it was constructed in 1935, it was 96 percent black in 1987 (Seely 1987e, A16). Other public-housing projects within the city had lower percentages of blacks, but the fact remains that black female-headed families in disproportionately high numbers lived in public housing and other rental units.

Compounding the problem of renting and poverty was the scarcity of affordable housing. Mention has already been made of the inaccessibility of ethnic neighborhoods to blacks. However, few blacks living in poverty could have afforded housing in ethnic neighborhoods had these places been available. Also many black families living in poverty preferred not to venture outside of their informal circle of kin and friends, which provided economic and psychological support. Carol B. Stack, in her book *All Our Kin: Coping Strategies in a Black Community* (1974), provides an insightful description of how poor black female-headed families often came together with kin and friends each month to survive financially.

Even when housing units were targeted to a low-income market, other problems often arose that nullified those efforts. Mulberry Square, built in the early 1970s, serves as an example. As a consequence of mismanagement and poor-quality construction, the 381 units making up this housing project were never fully occupied. By 1986, Mulberry Square had deteriorated to the point that it had to be demolished (Seely 1987e, A16). In 1988, less than twenty years after Mulberry Square was built, work began on 75 new units on the same site.

*Residential Mobility*

Intra- and intercity movement has always been an important ingredient in the growth and development of the black community. During World War I and World War II, droves of southern blacks migrated to Syracuse to obtain jobs abandoned by white men away at war. A similar trend continued with southern rural migrant workers moving into the black community up through the early 1960s. By the mid-1960s, fewer blacks were migrating to Syracuse, and those who were represented a different type of black from the earlier migrating groups. These new black migrants were professional and better educated, and they had much better skills. By the 1980s, however, the entrance of even black professionals into the Syracuse community had slowed considerably.

With urban renewal came a shift from geographical movement into Syracuse to residential mobility, or intracity movement. In chapter 5, we noted that urban renewal—or "urban removal," as the black community referred to it—had an effect on virtually every black household. This section compares the residential mobility of blacks, whites, and other minorities during the 1980s. Table 6.8 shows significant differences between the three groups and the length of time they had lived at their present (1981) address.

For the overall sample, 37.3 percent were more likely to have been living at their present address between one to five years than any other length of

**Table 6.8**
**Residential Mobility in Syracuse According to Race, 1981**

| Mobility | Blacks (%) | Whites (%) | Other Minorities (%) |
|---|---|---|---|
| *Time Lived at Present Address:*[a] | *(N = 498)* | *(N = 207)* | *(N = 37)* |
| Less than 6 Months | 10.6 | 9.2 | 5.4 |
| 6 Months–1 Year | 11.6 | 15.0 | 18.9 |
| 1–5 Years | 38.8 | 30.9 | 54.1 |
| 6–10 Years | 18.1 | 14.0 | 13.5 |
| 10 Years Plus | 18.5 | 25.1 | 8.1 |
| Always Lived Here | 2.4 | 5.8 | — |
| *Times Moved Since 1975:** | *(N = 474)* | *(N = 205)* | *(N = 36)* |
| None | 38.8 | 46.8 | 22.2 |
| One Time | 31.0 | 19.5 | 33.3 |
| 2–3 Times | 21.5 | 20.5 | 33.3 |
| 4–5 Times | 8.6 | 13.2 | 11.1 |
| *Location Prior to This Address*** | *(N = 472)* | *(N = 200)* | *(N = 36)* |
| Another Part of Syracuse | 86.4 | 76.5 | 61.1 |
| Another Part of New York State | 5.5 | 15.5 | 2.8 |
| Another State | 7.8 | 8.0 | 16.7 |
| Another Country | 0.2 | — | 19.4 |

*Source:* Stamps 1982, 75.

*$X^2$ = significant at the .01 level with 10 and 6 df, respectively.

**$X^2$ = significant at the .001 level with 6 df.

time. Broken down by race, blacks and whites were about equally as likely (10.6 percent and 9.2 percent, respectively) to have been at their present address for less than six months. Other minorities (18.9 percent) were more likely than whites (15 percent), who in turn were more likely than blacks (11.6 percent), to have lived at their present address for six months to one year. Other minorities (54.1 percent) were also more likely than blacks (38.8 percent) or whites (30.9 percent) to have been at their present address for one to five years. Among blacks, 18.5 percent were more likely to have lived at the same address ten years or more, and 25.1 percent of whites were more likely to have done so. Only 2.4 percent of blacks had always lived at the same address, but 5.8 percent of whites had done so.

In terms of the number of times that households within this sample changed residences since 1975, higher percentages of white respondents (46.8 percent) indicated stability than did black (38.8 percent) or other minority (22.2 percent) respondents. Of those respondents who moved only once between 1975 and 1982, higher percentages of blacks (31.0) and other minorities (33.3) than of whites (19.5) fell into this category. Blacks (21.5 percent) and whites (20.5 percent) had similar percentages for "who moved from two to three times" between 1975 and 1982. A slightly higher percentage of whites (13.2) than other minorities (11.1) or blacks (8.6) had moved four to five times within this time period. Findings related to times moved between 1975 and 1982 were also significant.

Most of the sample (82.3 percent) in all racial categories were more likely to have lived in another part of Syracuse than elsewhere in New York State, another state, or another country before they moved to their current address. Although significant differences were found between the three groups, blacks (86.4 percent) were more likely than whites (76.5 percent) or other minorities (61.1 percent) to have moved from another part of the city. More whites (15.5 percent) than blacks (5.5 percent) or other minorities (2.8 percent) had moved from another part of New York State. Other minorities were more likely to have moved from another state or another country than blacks or whites. Two factors could have accounted for the higher percentage of blacks who had moved from another part of Syracuse. First, urban removal had forced blacks to relocate to another section of the city. Second, as housing opened up for blacks, many sought out better housing in better neighborhoods. Interviews with black residents clearly revealed that regardless of socioeconomic status, blacks—especially low-income black families—desired better living conditions. Even when they realized that they could not afford better housing, they still hoped to improve their housing some day.

What table 6.8 shows is a slow shift in the residential mobility patterns of blacks from a more mobile group to one with some degree of stability. This conclusion is evident from the data related to "time lived at present address" and "times moved since 1975." The data support national demographic analysis concerning black migration out of the South from 1950 to 1980. More recent national statistics seem to indicate a change in these migration patterns, showing that out-migration from the South has virtually stopped. Some statistics show a modest migration back to the South of middle-class blacks in particular, lending partial support to the findings given here in that from 1990 to 1995 only 7.8 percent of the blacks in this sample migrated from out of state (Marger 1994).

The primary reasons for having moved (see table 6.9) from the previous place of residence were the same for blacks, whites, and other minorities: they needed a larger dwelling and wanted a better residence. Also, for blacks (14.6 percent) and whites (17.7 percent), owning or buying a house was a major reason for moving. As compared with whites (5.5 percent) and other minorities (3.3 percent), blacks (7.9 percent) were more likely to move in order to live in a better neighborhood. Higher percentages of blacks gave lower rent or a less expensive home as a reason for moving, although higher percentages of whites and other minorities indicated "being closer to one's job" as a reason.

Better housing and better neighborhoods were important to blacks in the early 1980s, as respondents clearly indicated to us. A black home owner stated, "It is important that I live in a good neighborhood and that people look out for each other and their children, which they do around here." A black renter stated, "Overall, people in this neighborhood have pride in their houses. All houses are nice except one. There are several houses being painted or repaired. This street is quite like a country back road" (quoted in Stamps 1982, 36).

Table 6.9

**Reasons Why Syracuse Residents Moved According to Race, 1981**

| Reason* | Black (%) (N = 417) | White (%) (N = 181) | Other Minorities (%) (N = 30) |
|---|---|---|---|
| Closer to Job | 6.0 | 13.3 | 13.3 |
| Needed Larger Dwelling | 19.4 | 18.2 | 16.7 |
| Closer to Relatives | 6.2 | 8.3 | 6.7 |
| Wanted Better Dwelling | 18.2 | 16.0 | 30.0 |
| Wanted Better Neighborhood | 7.9 | 5.5 | 3.3 |
| Better Schools | 1.7 | 1.1 | 10.0 |
| Taxes Too High | 0.2 | — | — |
| Lower Rent or Less Expensive House | 11.3 | 5.5 | 6.7 |
| Foreclosure | 1.0 | 0.6 | — |
| Evicted: | | | |
|   Conversion to Condo | 1.2 | 0.6 | — |
|   Private Reasons | 2.6 | 2.2 | — |
|   Urban Renewal | 2.2 | 2.2 | — |
| To Own/Buy House | 14.6 | 17.7 | 6.7 |
| Family Size Increased | 2.4 | 2.2 | — |
| Family Size Decreased | 0.2 | 0.6 | — |
| No Answer | 4.8 | 5.5 | 6.7 |

*Source:* Stamps 1982, 76.
*Not significant.

## Black Community Neighborhoods

Neighborhoods quite often represent communities within a community and provide a better unit of analysis of group life within a city's geographical area than an ethnic group or a racial group. Even in northern industrial cities such as Syracuse where ethnic areas are close-knit and of long standing, ethnic integration is present. In the past, Syracuse's ethnic neighborhoods tended to be related to social-class status because most were working-class areas. A similar statement can be made for racial groups because varying degrees of integration could be found throughout the city. Black residential exposure to whites tended to increase as black social-class status increased, and white residential exposure to blacks increased as white social-class status decreased (Taeuber and Taeuber 1965). In other words, upper- and middle-class blacks were more likely to be found living in predominantly white neighborhoods, and lower-class blacks and lower-class whites were more likely to be found living in predominantly black neighborhoods. The point being made is that racial groups, like ethnic groups but to a lesser degree, live in integrated areas, and integration is class related. In this study, the definition of the black community provided in chapter 1 indicated that some degree of integration existed because the community was not based on a geographical location, but on a common history and an identification of like kind. Given these concerns, a descriptive analysis of neighborhoods occupied by the black community can provide important insights into black life in Syracuse in the 1980s.

*The South Side*

In the early 1980s, the south side of Syracuse was made up of numerous small neighborhoods (intermixed with striplike business areas) that extended south from the central business district (CBD) to the city limits. Also intermixed in the south side were predominately black neighborhoods and businesses. Adjacent to the CBD, a small cluster of black businesses and public housing was followed by an area in which large homes, formerly owned by well-to-do whites, had been converted into white-collar-type businesses and voluntary organizations owned and run by whites. This area was followed by black businesses and predominantly black residential areas that extended to another white commercial business area and finally a white residential area up to the city line.

One of the main streets that ran through the south side of Syracuse was South Salina, an extremely busy street because it was one of the main north-south thoroughfares that extended through the city. North Salina bordered on an Italian working-class neighborhood, and South Salina ran through working- and lower-class black neighborhoods. However, as pointed out, white families and white businesses were intermixed with black families and black businesses in the area. The CBD separated North and South Salina. Of the estimated sixty black churches in the black community, many were located within the area bordering on South Salina, and many were small storefront churches. These churches were intermixed with "mom and pop" stores, small cafés and bars, and an occasional white business, all serving the predominantly black working- and lower-class population that resided in the area. In the middle of the black neighborhood on South Salina, one could see the Starlight Holiness Church with the order of service provided in the window. Right above the Starlight Holiness Church was another church, the Cross Church of God by Faith. The building that housed both churches looked like a former business that had been converted into places of worship. Colored panes had replaced clear panes in the front windows to provide some resemblance of a church. This description fits many of the storefront churches in the area at this time. These churches had been established to provide places of worship for the southern workers and their family and friends who had migrated to Syracuse after World War II. Under different names, these churches had existed over the years to serve black low-income families.

Black businesses were located within the same area as the CBD: Percy Jones Furniture Store, Delight Barbeque, Oasis Fish House, Beauty Supply Store, and the South Salina Food Market. Within the next block and across the street, white businesses and public institutions were located: Mr. Fixit Appliance Shop, the Colvin Station of the U.S. Postal Service, Blue Brothers Barber Shop (black owned and operated), and a branch of Key Bank. Although many businesses within the area were black owned, they did not serve as a source for jobs, nor did they bring significant amounts of money into the black community because they were run by nonpaid family members and barely stayed alive financially from month to month.

Another black business section along South Salina and closer to the CBD reveals similar characteristics, with its small fix-it shops for automobiles, gas stations, taxi stands, liquor stores, and a dry-cleaning establishment, mixed in with a Kentucky Fried Chicken and boarded-up places that had gone out of business. The fix-it shops for automobiles were service stations converted into shops. Automobiles to be repaired were parked outside, for there was no room to park or repair automobiles inside. Such conditions would be tolerable from April through September, but in the severe Syracuse winters service at such places was virtually nonexistent.

Residences on and around South Salina and adjacent to the business areas just described consisted of public housing, apartment buildings, and large two- and three-story houses that had been converted into two-, three-, and even four-family units. Abandoned houses had been boarded up to keep out children and the homeless, who were prevalent on most blocks. Much of the deterioration found on the south side began in the early 1960s with the construction of Interstate 81, which sliced through it. The impact of Interstate 81 on residential housing was the greatest in areas inhabited by the poor. After this section of the south side was broken up by Interstate 81, white lower-middle-class and working-class families that had inhabited the area moved out. The only residents left were lower-class and older whites on fixed incomes who could not afford to move. Lower- and working-class blacks replaced the whites who moved because they could not find affordable housing in other sections of the city. More wealthy whites, who lived closer to the CBD, sold their homes to be converted into businesses. Law offices,

6.3. Shawn Casey Apartments, corner of South Salina and South Warren Streets, 1994. Photograph by Ellen Blalock. Courtesy of Onondaga County Public Library, Beauchamp Branch.

insurance companies, interior decorators, private social service agencies, and AAA moved into the area. Houses not sold to white-collar businesses were abandoned. They tended to be on the edge of predominantly black residential sections, and their abandonment created a barrier between the white businesses and black residences and brought about further deterioration.

Earlier in this chapter we made mention of many black leaders' suspicion that Syracuse banks and financial institutions had disinvested in certain areas of the city. Excluding the conversion of homes near the CBD into white-collar businesses, disinvestment seemed evident in south-side residential areas that had become predominantly black. Within the predominantly black residential areas on the south side, the physical condition of housing was the same regardless of whether the occupants were black or white.

When people in Syracuse talk about segregated black neighborhoods, they usually make reference to the south side. There is no denying that segregation existed within the area; however, excluding public housing, in which apartment complexes were often either 99 percent black or more than 80 percent white, economic segregation was more prevalent than racial segregation (Seely 1987e, A17). The fact that in 1986 only three of eleven housing projects managed by the Syracuse Housing Authority were integrated, with a 50 percent black-white racial mix, makes a strong statement concerning attitudes toward integrated living. Central Village and Pioneer Homes, both south-side housing projects, were nearly all black (Seely 1987e, A17). If poor whites were willing to live in predominantly black areas for economic reasons, as south-side residential housing revealed, they drew the line with public housing. Once public-housing projects reached a critical level of blacks, usually 50 percent, whites were no longer willing to move in regardless of economic conditions or better housing prospects.

Predominantly black neighborhoods on the south side revealed an interesting phenomenon. In non-public-housing projects, the most visible individuals were men. Most visible around public-housing projects were children and women. During warm weather, children could be seen playing in the streets and in the many pocket-size play areas found on the south side. Younger children were supervised by older children rather than by adults. Men hung around bars, cafés, barbershops, service stations, and liquor stores. During warm weather, they hung out on the street in small and sometimes large groups. In bad weather, they moved inside. The vacant lot next to Phillips Liquor Store was a well-known hangout for men. Year round and regardless of the weather, men could be found next to this store. Beer, wine, and hard spirits were purchased and carried to the lot for communal drinking. It was the place where men financially hard up could piece together a bottle. Jokes were told, and "lying on" and "about one's self" was the order of the day. Young men would gravitate to the lot, stand on the periphery, and listen to the tales told by older men. Even before the 1980s, Phillips Liquor Store lot and barbershops represented informal schools were young men were socialized into street corner behavior (Whyte 1943). Because numerous automobiles were always parked around the lot, it could be assumed that many of the men who congregated daily did not live in the area, but drove there to socialize.

Within the south side, the rural southern background of many of its inhabitants was manifested by the many vegetable gardens that could be seen in yards during the spring and summer months. Even in public-housing projects with a postage-stamp-size yard in front of each unit, small gardens were noticeable. Corn, turnips, collard greens, cabbage, pole beans, beets, okra, potatoes, and lima beans were grown most frequently and in larger quantities. These well-tended and geometrically arranged gardens were surprising in the yards of dilapidated houses in need of paint and in general disrepair. In some cases, the rest of the yard needed clearing of rubbish and the grass needed cutting, but the vegetable garden was immaculate.

This seemingly incongruent state of affairs can be explained in part by looking at the ownership of property and the transitory existence of the black community's lower-class residents. Table 6.5, presented earlier in the chapter, reveals that for blacks, home ownership was related to income. The lower the income level, the lower the percentage of blacks who owned their homes. Table 6.7 reveals a much higher percentage (40.1) of renter-occupied housing than of owner-occupied housing (8.6) among black families living in poverty. Based on information received from the Syracuse Public School System for 1983, approximately 50 percent of all children enrolled in school who lived in inner-city neighborhoods moved at least once during the school year. These data help explain the low rate of home ownership and the highly transitory behavior of black south-side residents. It was evident that most did not own their homes and that intracity mobility was prevalent. Such conditions did not lend themselves to higher levels of identification or attachment with one's property, which might be found among home owners or less-transient families. Therefore, pride was often not shown toward one's property. Gardening, in contrast, represented a different kind of identification, one that was closely akin to a southern rural past. It was important for these northern urban transplants to show that they had not lost their heritage.

Rivalry was intense between neighbors and friends as they competed to see who could have the best-looking garden, who could grow the largest of a particular kind of vegetable, and, most important, who had the most success growing vegetables in a season or growing vegetables not indigenous to the upstate New York area. During the early spring and summer, gardening was the major topic discussed in south-side shops and on the streets. People either boasted of their success or gave detailed instructions for early planting of certain vegetables.

From a sociological standpoint, the act of gardening played a functional role in the lives of this group. Gardening provided an avenue for competition among lower-class individuals in which they determined the rules of the games and the skills and knowledge necessary to compete were passed down from generation to generation. Competition was on a more or less even footing. Everyone was a winner in that the products of their labor could be eaten or, for some, sold to neighbors. For groups with individuals who often feel alienated politically and economically, such competitive behavior becomes important to the group's collective well-being. Although it might be concluded that these individuals played small roles in influencing the growth and development of the black community, they perceived themselves as contributing members of society through activities such as gardening and church involvement. This would be especially true for adults living in public housing and receiving public assistance. For many south-side blacks, the neighborhood became their world. It is where they went to school, attended church, recreated and socialized, received medical care, and did most of their shopping.

*The East Side*

Most professional members of the black community within the Syracuse city limits lived on the east side by 1989. Their presence on the east side was in itself a depiction of progress. Prior to the 1960s, only a few blacks lived on the east side of town. Those who did reside in this area at that time did it through subterfuge. Rental housing was not available to blacks, so the only way for them to live on the east side was to purchase a home from a liberal white. As mentioned earlier, blacks would identify a house for sale and evaluate its worth from the exterior and from a description of the interior provided by the white confidant. Based on this information, the white person would purchase the house from its white owner and resell the house to the black buyer.

By the 1980s, contrary to the south side, east-side neighborhoods provided a more integrated lifestyle for black families. East-side housing consisted of well-kept single-dwelling houses and middle-income apartments. However, there were exceptions to this more general characterization of east-side neighborhoods. The neighborhood around Syracuse University consisted of large houses that had been renovated into small apartments to rent to students. A second exception was a narrow strip made up of two predominantly black housing projects that extended east from the CBD for several blocks. Intermixed with east-side integrated neighborhoods was a small area of single-dwelling houses that made up an all-black area named Mountainview after its only street. These small but well-kept homes were inhabited by lower-middle-class black home owners. Mountainview was interesting in that it was the only area within Syracuse where all of the original home owners were black. Although black developments, particularly in the suburban areas, were rather common to southern cities, this was not the case for Syracuse.

The east-side area that perhaps best reflected the city demographically was Salt Springs. Within this area, blacks and whites, young and old, rich and poor came together to make up a neighborhood (Seely 1987e, A17). Harwood Street best depicted the dynamics in the Salt Springs area. Although an outsider's first impression of the area might indicate that the neighborhood was "tipping black," most streets were still predominantly white, as was Harwood Street. When blacks first began to move to Harwood Street, many white residents feared the street would "go black." However, by 1989 the street and the neighborhood seemed to have stabilized racially. Those whites who had been concerned about living with blacks and those who had yielded to the fear of declining house prices had already moved out. Harwood Street, along with many of the neighboring streets, dispelled fears that when blacks move into a neighborhood, the property values fall. In 1987, property prices were escalating at a rapid rate: houses that fell into the $20,000 range in the early 1980s were selling in the $70,000 range by the late 1980s (Seely 1987e, A17).

A close analysis of the trends and people on the east side of Syracuse help explain why this area has somewhat stabilized in the face of integration. Many of the white families stayed in this area because they preferred integrated neighborhoods, even though they could have afforded to live elsewhere in the city. Closely related was the number of Jewish families that lived in the area. Jews have traditionally taken strong stands favoring fair housing laws and integrated neighborhoods. A similar argument can be made for faculty members from Syracuse University and Le Moyne College, who often lived on the east side in close vicinity of their institutions. Also, many large houses around Syracuse University were attractive to college professors, many of whom were into "do-it-yourself" renovation. The first blacks who moved into the east side were as well educated or better educated than many of their white neighbors, thus introducing whites to well-educated blacks with a lifestyle similar to theirs. By the 1980s, when less-educated blacks with well-paid skilled jobs began to move into the area, whites were less likely to stereotype black lifestyles that differed from their own. They recognized that diversity existed among their black neighbors. Because of the low number of starter-price houses that young professionals could afford in Syracuse, many young white professional families purchased their first home on the east side, where housing in their price range was still available.

East-side racial stability was noteworthy because most neighborhoods faced relatively high turnover rates. Streets differed in stability in that on some streets two or three generations of a family lived side by side year after year. Faculty members from the college and the university, interns and faculty from Upstate Medical College, and business executives with large families purchased east-side houses. These families were also the most likely to relocate with their jobs to other cities. Young professional couples purchasing starter houses were also likely to relocate later within the metropolitan area.

## Summary

By the late 1960s, geographical divisions within the black community added to the lines of demarcation between the social classes. Lower- and working-class families lived in certain areas of the city, and middle- and upper-class families lived in different areas of the central city and in suburban communities. Geographical separation of blacks along class lines, although always present in Syracuse, was intensified during urban renewal in the 1960s and continued as southern blacks migrating to the city settled on the south side and incoming professional blacks settled on the east side. The geographical separation of blacks made the black social-class structure more easily recognizable, served as a barrier to interclass communication, and helped create a feeling of "we" and "them" in the black community. As shown in chapter 7, this state of affairs carried over into the political arena as blacks attempted to mobilize their community. Also affected were black businesses as they sought out support from the community.

Although far more difficult to measure empirically, class divisions minimized feelings of shared concern. Many middle- and upper-class blacks in Syracuse had little knowledge of the problems and concerns of poor blacks. The fact that many middle-class blacks had recently reached middle-class status through education and occupation and had come from poor families was not enough to give them a clear picture of local problems confronting poor blacks. Their geographical (east side) separation and possibly psychological separation from the poorer members (south side) of the black community left them without firsthand knowledge. An interview with a black professional woman right after proposed income tax cuts by the Reagan administration in 1982 highlights the type of quandary in which many middle-class blacks found themselves. She felt the need to support the tax cuts because of her family's high tax bracket. Yet she knew that cuts in social programs were being proposed to offset the deduction in taxes, and those families with incomes lower than hers would receive less governmental assistance. She concluded the interview with the following statement, "Oh, what the hell. It is time we [people in her tax bracket] received some relief." This statement does not necessarily reflect the general sentiment of professional blacks on the tax issue. However, it does reflect the different concerns facing blacks in different class strata.

# 7

# Politics and the Syracuse Black Community in the 1980s

CHAPTER 5 DEALT with how American society and the Syracuse community underwent a changed mood in the early 1980s. The more liberal stance of the 1960s and early 1970s gave way to a more conservative stance that prevailed in the late 1970s and throughout the 1980s. As stated in chapter 6, the major question to be answered in the remainder of this book is, What effects did this changed mood have on the black community? This chapter looks specifically at the political arena and how the black community attempted to maintain the political gains made during the l960s and 1970s. For many blacks in Syracuse and in the nation as a whole, black progress in all spheres of life was seen as being closely tied to political power. By the 1980s, blacks in increasing numbers exercised their right to vote. Educational opportunities had been made available to black children on a somewhat more equitable basis. Even some black professionals had moved into occupational areas and positions previously barred from them. However, regardless of these gains, a disproportionately large number of blacks still faced discrimination and poverty (Rhodes 1982, 1).

Starting in the late 1970s, black leaders of civil rights organizations in the community could be heard expressing the view that many local blacks still expected white liberals of the 1960s to wake up and wonder why all those black causes they had fought for had not borne more progress. These black leaders further stated that local blacks seemed to expect that 1960 white liberals would again come to the rescue. Such sarcastic statements were made in an attempt to make blacks realize that they themselves were going to have to come together and fight their own battles and determine their own destiny.

This general feeling was also shared by national black leaders at that time and can best be described by the introductory remarks in the National Urban League's *The State of Black America* (1982): "At no point in recent memory had the distance between the national government and Black America been greater than it was in 1981, nor had the relationship between the two been more strained. Throughout Black America in 1981 there was a broad feeling of isolation, of turning back the clock, of a retreat from civil rights policies and social services programs that were established only after years of struggle" (1).

When a national study of 277 cities rated Syracuse the "seventh most livable city" in the United States in the early 1980s, heads of the local chapters of the NAACP and the Urban League spoke out about the living conditions for blacks. Leon Modeste, executive director of the Urban League, stated, "I say there are people going without food, clothes and housing in this city. When you hear our local Chamber [of Commerce] talking, you wonder if its two separate worlds we're . . . [talking about]" (quoted in Rhodes 1982, 8). Tommie Blount, then president of the NAACP, also stated, "They say . . . [Syracuse] is the seventh most livable city in America, but not for black people. If you walk into most corporations in our city, you will see blacks only in the menial jobs. . . . Even when I try to think of something positive, I have a difficult time" (quoted in Rhodes 1982, 8). These statements highlighted the conditions that prevailed in Syracuse at the time and pointed toward the need for renewed efforts at black political mobilization.

## The Power Structure and the Black Community

In the early 1980s, Syracuse was still controlled by the Democratic political machine of Mayor Lee Alexander, which had replaced the long-standing Republican control of city hall in 1969. Alexander remained in office until 1985, thus having a sixteen-year reign. Given his long tenure, one can hardly question the assumption that Alexander had built up a powerful political machine. In 1969, Alexander had depended on the black, the liberal white, and the union vote, along with other Democrats, to win the mayoral race. However, because of his initial victory in 1969, he had come to a more realistic assessment of the importance of the black vote. Paying close attention to voting trends, the Alexander political machine recognized that the vote in predominantly black precincts and other precincts with sizable numbers of black voters had remained constant over the years. Blacks had consistently voted the Democratic ticket since 1969, but only 30 percent of those registered to vote actually voted. For instance, by 1980 when blacks made up 16 percent of the population, they made up only 5 percent of the registered voters. They had virtually disenfranchised themselves as a result of their lack of political involvement in registration, voting, or participation in the party system. Because they did not participate in the political process, the Alexander administration virtually ignored their needs and concerns. By the early 1980s, black leaders who had attempted to negotiate with the power structure found that local politicians did not feel compelled politically to address themselves to blacks' needs.

Despite low black political participation, some blacks were elected to political office. Clarence Dunham was elected to the county legislature in 1974. Bob Ware was elected to the Syracuse Common Council in the mid-1970s. James Dupree was appointed to an unexpired term on the Common Council during the 1970s, but lost in the general election. Sidney Johnson, after stepping down as superintendent of Syracuse schools, was elected to the Common Council during the late 1970s. Dr. Constance Timberlake, a faculty member at Syracuse University, was elected to the Syracuse School Board in the mid-1970s and served until the early 1980s. Marjorie White, a member of the clerical staff at Upstate Medical College, began serving on the Syracuse School Board in 1980. By forming coalitions with whites, usually in the more liberal precincts around Syracuse University, black candidates were able to gain political office. In other instances, although black and white coalitions were formed, black candidates lost as a consequence of a lack of black registration and the low black turnout on election day.

## Community Participation

As stated earlier, when confronted with problems affecting the black community, local white political figures often did not hesitate to explain that until blacks voted and participated in political and civic affairs in significant numbers, they could not expect their specific problems to be adequately addressed. Within any community, there are individuals who do not necessarily participate in the social, political, and economic processes of that community. In chapter 5, we pointed out that during the 1970s and 1980s the number of black professionals moving into the Syracuse metropolitan area increased significantly. It was also apparent that these new blacks, for the most part, settled in suburban communities rather than in the central city. Their impact on the local black community was lessened by where they lived, and their political impact was basically lost because they could not vote in city elections. Van Robinson, president of the local NAACP chapter in the 1980s and a 1987 candidate for the Common Council stated, "We need their [black professionals'] energies, their resources, their expertise. . . . I wish we could develop homes in [Syracuse] so they could buy here" (quoted in Seely 1987b, A12). Black professionals were also not a political force in county elections because they were spread throughout suburban communities rather than concentrated in any one area. In a city such as Syracuse, where ethnic enclaves and party politics were so important, the lack of a well-organized black political effort was dysfunctional.

To get a better picture of community participation among blacks, we have used data from the 1981 Urban League survey (Stamps 1982). Table 7.1 shows the degree to which blacks, whites, and other minorities held membership in community organizations. It is important to understand that black involvement in the political structure takes on somewhat unique characteristics given their lack of political power and their traditional exclusion from party politics. Political involvement by blacks and by black leaders tends to be organizationally based. As discussed in more detail later in this chapter, one of the most important organizations politically in the black community at this time was the black church. Leadership organizations, aside from churches, included fraternities and sororities, civil rights organizations, and even some social organizations. Therefore, an analysis of membership in the various kinds of organizations listed in table 7.1 provides some indication of community participation.

Table 7.1 reveals that 69.5 percent of other minorities, 50.2 percent of whites, and only 46.1 percent of blacks belonged to at least one community organization in 1981. Most surprising was the low percentage of blacks who stated they belonged to at least one of the kinds of organizations listed. This

## Table 7.1

## Organizational Membership in Syracuse According to Race, 1981

| Organizational Membership | Black (%) (N = 500) | White (%) (N = 207) | Other Minorities (%) (N = 37) |
|---|---|---|---|
| *Holds Membership* | | | |
| Yes | 46.1 | 50.2 | 69.5 |
| No | 58.4 | 49.8 | 40.5 |
| *Teacher Groups* | | | |
| Yes | 8.8 | 8.8 | 8.1 |
| No | 90.4 | 91.3 | 94.6 |
| N/A | 0.8 | — | — |
| *Fraternal (Sorority, Elks, etc.)* | | | |
| Yes | 4.0 | 6.8 | 5.4 |
| No | 96.0 | 93.2 | 94.6 |
| *Political Party** | | | |
| Yes | 7.2 | 20.3 | 21.6 |
| No | 92.8 | 79.7 | 78.4 |
| *Church or Religious* | | | |
| Yes | 29.9 | 29.5 | 35.1 |
| No | 71.0 | 70.5 | 64.9 |
| *Civil Rights* | | | |
| Yes | 6.4 | 5.8 | 16.2 |
| No | 93.6 | 94.2 | 83.8 |
| *Civic** | | | |
| Yes | 7.4 | 15.0 | 27.0 |
| No | 92.6 | 85.0 | 73.0 |
| *Social* | | | |
| Yes | 12.2 | 15.0 | 18.9 |
| No | 87.8 | 85.0 | 81.1 |

*Source:* Stamps 1982, 72.

*$X^2$ = significant at the .001 level with 2 df.

finding is contrary to earlier studies, such as *An American Dilemma*, which pointed out that although Americans were a nation of joiners, black Americans seemed to join in disproportionately large numbers (Myrdal 1944, 952–53). Slightly more than 90 percent of each of the three groups indicated they did not belong to the Parent-Teacher Association or the Parent Teacher Organization for the schools their children attended. There were differences in membership in parent-teacher groups based on income, with middle-income blacks and whites holding membership in larger numbers than low-income or high-income blacks or whites. Even larger percentages of the three groups indicated they did not belong to fraternal groups. Fraternal groups included Greek letter fraternities and sororities as well as the Elks, Moose, and Masonic lodges. Sororities and fraternities were important to the black community in that many blacks looked upon them as leadership organizations. For fraternal organizations, there were differences in membership according to income, with higher percentages of middle-income blacks and whites belonging.

Most important to the current discussion was the degree of membership in political parties for the three groups. As noted, Syracuse politicians did not feel compelled politically to address themselves to the needs of blacks because blacks did not bother to involve themselves in party politics or voting. According to the survey, only 7.2 percent of blacks stated they belonged to a political party. As shown in table 7.1, statistically significantly higher percentages of whites and other minorities belonged to political parties than did blacks.

For those who revealed they held party membership, income differences were found. Higher percentages of middle- and upper-income blacks, whites, and other minorities belonged to political parties than did lower-income members of these three groups. This finding is important from a black standpoint, given the disproportionately higher number of low-income blacks. Without party membership in large numbers among low-income blacks in Syracuse, blacks' participation in the political process will always be viewed as insignificant, and their needs will be overlooked.

Church membership has traditionally been important to the black community's involvement in politics. As a result of integration and the diminution of black institutions, the black church as a political force has become even more important. By 1982, many young black ministers in the community, such as Rev. Larry S. Howard, pastor of Hopps Memorial CME Church, were speaking out about the political inactivity among blacks (Rea 1982, C4). Table 7.1 reveals that church membership did not vary according to race, with almost equal percentages of blacks and whites belonging to a church and only a slightly higher percentage of other minorities belonging. What is most interesting is that approximately two-thirds of each group indicated no church affiliation. Although formal church membership was related to income for blacks and whites, with higher percentages of middle-income groups holding membership than lower-income groups, church attendance was greater for lower-income blacks.

The almost equal percentages of blacks and whites who held membership in civil rights organizations was surprising, but even more surprising was the low percentage of each group that belonged. Other minorities had a much higher percentage of membership in civil rights organizations than either blacks or whites, although that percentage was still rather low. The low percentage of blacks belonging to civil rights organizations further highlighted Syracuse blacks' lack of political involvement in the early 1980s. Organizations such as the Urban League and the NAACP suffered from lack of involvement and commitment from the black community. These findings make it readily apparent that the black community, as a whole, did not pull together in an effort of self-advocacy. One would have to conclude that the community was more reactive than proactive. That is, if a special problem arose in the community, participation in the political process increased somewhat. However, blacks tended not to participate in programs designed for long-range change that would improve the quality of life or ameliorate a social problem. Membership in civil rights organizations seems to be related to income, particularly at the upper-income levels for all groups. This finding is significant for blacks in that in the 1980s blacks with high incomes were a rather recent phenomenon within the black community and were still rather small in size.

In table 7.1, data on membership in civic organizations reveal higher percentages for other minorities (27 percent), followed by whites (15 percent) and blacks (7.4 percent). The same percentage of whites (15) belonged to social organizations. Black membership increased for social organizations, with 12.2 percent indicating membership. Civic and social organization membership was related to income. For each group, there were higher percentages of membership in civic organizations at the upper-income level. Middle- and upper-income levels showed higher percentages of membership in social organizations for all groups.

Overall, table 7.1 indicates that a higher percentage of whites than blacks belonged to at least one organization. More important, significantly higher percentages of whites than blacks belonged to political and civic organizations, the two kinds of organizations that tend to influence public policy. Civil rights organizations showed almost equal percentages of membership for blacks and whites, and that percentage was low for both groups. Income was a factor in organization membership, with middle-income blacks and whites revealing higher percentages of membership than low-income blacks and whites. These findings add further evidence that during the early 1980s blacks were involved very little in the political and civic activities of Syracuse.

## Efforts at Black Political Mobilization

Given the political state of affairs in the black community, black leaders as early as 1978 began making concerted efforts to pull other black leaders and professionals together in a more formalized manner. They recognized that in order to negotiate successfully with the Syracuse power structure, they were going to have to be organized. The community had never launched a united and a sustained effort, save the protest movement of the 1960s when the community's needs were pushed. Certainly, there had been individuals and organizations who at one time or another had attempted to negotiate with the power structure; but a broad-based community effort involving black leaders and leadership organizations had not materialized in the post–protest movement period.

## Black Leadership Organizations

*Syracuse Minority Professional Action Conference*

In 1978, SYMPAC was organized. Black leaders and many blacks in general hailed SYMPAC as the answer to black political mobilization and black economic development. Drawing heavily from the membership of and the ideas originally formulated by the defunct Black Employment Council (1969–72), SYMPAC got off to an auspicious beginning. The Black Employment Council had been designed to bring together newly arrived professional blacks to share employment information, to network, and to provide a forum for ideas. In reality, though, it had been little more than a social club that served the function of introducing resident black professionals to those who had recently arrived in Syracuse. SYMPAC had inculcated from the council the concepts of networking and providing a forum for ideas. In addition, it was designed to bring together minority (black, Hispanic, and Native American) professionals under a structure in which committee formation and assignments would be based on expertise. Educators would serve on the education committee, businesspersons would serve on the economic committee, and so on. In all, SYMPAC was made up of more than ten different committees, each of which was to be semiautonomous. An executive committee to which each semiautonomous committee was to report made up the administrative structure of SYMPAC. The various committees were to provide professional assistance to the black community when problems arose and to monitor citywide activities within their designated area.

The original idea was that professionals would not take it upon themselves to solve problems, but would instead provide technical assistance to nonprofessionals. In this way, the masses within the black community would learn techniques of self-advocacy and problem solving. However, very early in SYMPAC's existence, individual committees began to embark on their own agendas. Many committees initiated agendas that encroached not only on the activities of other organizations such as the Urban League and the NAACP, but on the activities of other committees within SYM-PAC. SYMPAC's effectiveness was compromised by problems with boundary maintenance and by internal and external fighting. Efforts that should have been directed toward dealing with social-economic problems and monitoring activities were diverted to debates about who should be doing what. By 1982, SYMPAC was virtually dead and had accomplished very little within the community. Black political mobilization was in that year still little more than an idea. Despite repeated attempts at mobilizing blacks, nothing really happened.

*Syracuse Black Leadership Congress*

As blacks in Syracuse continued to feel the effects of the more conservative stance exhibited locally and buttressed by a declining industrial base, they realized they needed more influence in shaping public policy. Renewed efforts toward mobilization took shape in the form of the Syracuse Black Leadership Congress. Profiting from the experience of the Black Economic Council, SYMPAC, and even the Organization of Organizations of the 1960s, the Syracuse Black Leadership Congress was started in 1982. Black leaders, in an attempt to establish a stable base for the new organization, sought out the one remaining institution controlled by the black community, the church. This move was logical in that not only did blacks control the church, but the church was a controlling force over the black masses. In other words, the church was the one entity that had access to and influence on the group to be mobilized. The initiators of the Black Leadership Congress sought out black ministers of black churches to assume a leadership role in the organization. They even held their meetings at various churches on a rotating basis in an effort to identify and secure leadership from the church community. Churches provided a strong resource, with more than 60 percent of the thirty-seven-thousand-member black community being associated in some way with more than eighty black churches (Gerew and Seely 1987, A10).

Despite these efforts, however, black ministers were unwilling to assume a leadership role. Although the ministers' reasons were never clearly articulated, many other black leaders felt that competition and rivalry between churches for members and stature in the community did not allow for shared leadership roles. Also, fundamental differences in doctrine and differences in perceptions of the role of the church in community affairs impeded co-operation. Although many of the younger and better-educated ministers saw politics and the pulpit as compatible, many of the less-educated, more fundamentalist, and older ministers saw the role of the church as being limited to preaching God's word and saving souls.

Even with this setback, the Black Leadership Congress emerged as the most powerful organization in the black community during the 1980s. Because it was established as an umbrella organization of all organizations serving the black community, its membership included both Republicans and

Democrats. During its early years, membership was restricted to the heads of other black-oriented organizations, including churches, fraternities, and sororities. By the mid-1980s, it was extended to all black professionals. Although the Black Leadership Congress lost its role as an umbrella organization, it broadened its base among black professionals. Its key tasks included setting up voter-registration drives, networking with black political aspirants and connecting them with the political party under whose banner they wished to run, and advising and developing strategies for political campaigns. However, the Black Leadership Congress came closest to realizing its major goal of mobilizing black voters when it joined the Rainbow Coalition of 1984 presidential aspirant Jesse Jackson.

*Other Black Leadership Organizations*

A revitalized NAACP and the Urban League of Onondaga County continued to play an important political role in the 1980s. The Urban League was involved in attempting to gain solidarity within the black community (Scruggs 1984, 21). Although many new leadership organizations had been instituted within the black community, traditional leadership organizations such as the NAACP and the Urban League were the standard bearers over the years. An accurate assessment of the NAACP as a leadership organization would show, however, that its effectiveness has been closely tied to the strength of its president: during the tenure of strong presidents, it played vital roles; however, when its leadership was weak, it was much less effective. The Urban League, in contrast, has had sustained strong leadership since its inception. Therefore, its presence as a leadership organization has been felt in a more uniform manner.

Members of the black community also considered all local black fraternities (Alpha Phi Alpha, Kappa Alpha Psi, and Omega Psi Phi) and sororities (Delta Sigma Theta and Alpha Kappa Alpha) as leadership organizations. Political candidates often sought out presidents and other officers of fraternities and sororities for support, and other leadership organizations recognized their potential power. However, one would have to conclude that in terms of politics, members of fraternities and sororities worked more through other organizations. Because the black professional class in Syracuse was relatively small in the 1980s, a higher percentage of this class was represented in the membership lists of fraternities and sororities. This was probably true in most urban areas, but was more evident in Syracuse owing to its small number of black professionals.

Of note were two political clubs that had existed in the black community over the years and that were aligned with the two major political parties. The Benjamin Bannecker Democrat Club and the Eagle Republican Club, although of long duration, were never major political forces in Syracuse. The Benjamin Bannecker Democrat Club continued to meet periodically, but was not involved as a group in the Democratic Party or in elections during the 1980s. A few diehard black Republicans still identified with the Eagle Republic Club, but meetings were no longer held. Black Republicans met among themselves and discussed which Republican candidates they would support. However, no attempt was made to mobilize the black vote in support of a Republican candidate. During the 1980s, an attempt was made by black Republicans to organize another political organization, but nothing ever materialized (Clark 1985).

## Democrats, Republicans, and the Black Community

Activity between black Republicans and the Syracuse Republican Party during the 1980s was a response to the dissatisfaction among blacks with the local Democratic Party. Kofi Quay, publisher of *Heritage News Magazine* in Syracuse, stated, "There's much cynicism in this community. People have come along and promise many things—and not delivered. . . . Many people who not long ago would never have considered being a Republican now talk about it. . . . They may not leave the Democratic Party, but they may vote Republican" (quoted in Seely 1987b, A12).

It should be noted that many blacks who ran for office ran on the Republican ticket. Three reasons account for why local black candidates broke away from their traditional Democratic Party alignment. First, local Republicans sought out black candidates in their attempts to attract black voters. Local black voters participated in elections at higher rates when black candidates ran, regardless of party affiliation. Second, the perception within the black community that Democratic officeholders, once elected, did not respond to black concerns had caused local Republicans and Republican candidates to go after the black vote. Third, local blacks who sought political office but were not entrenched in the Democrat-controlled black leadership organizations could sidestep black leadership by running on the Republican ticket. This move initially did not seem to affect black support if the opposition candidate was white. Black leaders who had been sidestepped usually rallied in support of the black Republican candidate, unless the candidate was insensitive to black concerns. The fact that black leaders oftentimes supported black candidates who had gone around them highlighted the fragile relationship that often existed between black leaders, black leadership organizations, and the black masses. Not to support a black candidate without reason other than party affiliation or the lack of prior endorsement would have been the kiss of death for a leader within the black community.

The strained relationship that existed between blacks and the Democratic Party was evident in the campaign and eventual election of Charles Anderson to the Syracuse Common Council. In 1983, Anderson, with support from Jesse Jackson's Rainbow Coalition and the Syracuse Black Leadership Congress, sought the Democratic endorsement during the primary for the Fourth District seat of the Common Council. Keep in mind that between 1982 and 1984, the Black Leadership Congress and the Rainbow Coalition were involved in voter registration in the black community. Anderson supporters attended workshops to acquaint themselves with New York State voter-registration laws and to learn the techniques of fund-raising. The Fourth District was predominantly black and had been represented for seventeen years by Jim McCarthy, a white Democrat who died in office. Although the Black Leadership Congress and the Rainbow Coalition pushed for Anderson to get the endorsement to run on the Democratic ticket, the Democratic Committee endorsed Theresa McCarthy, Jim McCarthy's widow. Mrs. McCarthy had already been appointed to fill her husband's seat by the Republican-controlled council. Anderson thus had to obtain signatures on a petition in order to run in the primary. This attempt was a hard and bitterly fought endeavor. Signatures on the Anderson petition were constantly challenged, and on one occasion blacks were rounded up by Syracuse police and brought to the courthouse to defend their signatures (Seely 1987b, A12). The endorsement of McCarthy over Anderson and the rounding up of blacks did more than anything to point to the need for black political mobilization. Anderson lost the primary by a mere seventy-seven votes (Seely 1987b, A12). The Anderson case caused a larger split between the local Democrats and the black community than at any time since the protest movement of the 1960s. Blacks began seriously to question their relationship with the Democratic Party and to look toward the Republican Party.

Despite the growing discontent among Syracuse blacks with local Democrats, there was a major obstacle to Republicans' efforts to gain black support during the 1980s: Ronald Reagan. When interviewed, many black leaders acknowledged the growing discontent within the black community; however, they felt local Republicans would have to wait until after the Reagan years before they could have an impact on local black voters. The Reagan administration's position on affirmative action, the Voting Rights Act, tax exemptions for segregated private schools, and, to a lesser extent, busing had created a negative image of that administration among blacks (Seely 1987b, A12). Their general feeling can be summed up in the words of a powerful black Democrat in explaining why he had not supported a popular former Democrat who ran for mayor as a Republican: "I just could not see myself working for Ronald Reagan's party" (quoted in Seely 1987b, A12).

### Jesse Jackson and the Black Vote

Although some blacks and whites felt the large local black turnout in the 1984 presidential election was owing more to dissatisfaction with Reagan than to support for Jesse Jackson (Seely 1987b, A12), certain outcomes of this election within the black community cannot be overlooked. At the initiation of Syracuse Black Leadership Congress members, Jackson first came to Syracuse in the spring of 1982. He spoke to an overflowing crowd on Syracuse University's campus. From this initial contact with Syracuse and its more liberal element as represented by students and faculty, a local Rainbow Coalition was started. Spurred by Jackson's visit and the already mentioned joint efforts of the Syracuse Black Leadership Congress and the Rainbow Coalition, thousands of black voters were registered by 1984 (Seely 1987b, A12). In New York State, voter registration can take place in a house-to-house canvas. Thus, on-the-spot registration cannot be overlooked as a positive factor. The efforts of hundreds of workers paid off because in some areas registration of blacks more than doubled. For the first time in Syracuse history, with numerous blacks registering as Democrats, the Democrats exceeded the Republicans in the number of registered voters (Seely 1987b, A12). Before 1982, it had been estimated that blacks made up less than 10 percent of the registered voters. By 1984, this number had increased to 22 percent. Considering that the black population was only 16 percent of the total population in Syracuse, such an accomplishment was a major step toward black political mobilization (Seely 1987b, A12).

In 1984, when Jackson was running, it was estimated that 87 percent of blacks eligible to vote did so. However, by 1986, with a black candidate running unopposed in the general local election, only 48 percent of the eligible voters in predominately black wards voted (Seely 1987b, A12). This low voter turnout revealed that without a national black candidate of Jesse Jackson's stature or without a local black candidate running against whites for office, black voters generally adopted an apathetic posture. The election in these instances had less significance for them; therefore, they did not vote.

Jesse Jackson returned to Syracuse in 1985, held a rally, and endorsed Joseph Nicoletti, one of the Democratic mayoral candidates in the primary, and Charles Anderson, who this time around had received the Democratic endorsement for the Fourth District Common Council seat. Jackson's return was supported by blacks; however, his public endorsement of Nicoletti, the heavy favorite within the black community, caused some concern. Black leaders found themselves in an ambivalent position. Although they welcomed Jackson's support of Anderson as a show of power and as a rallying point within the black community, some were fearful that his simultaneous endorsement of Nicoletti would cause a white backlash (Seely 1987b, A12).

After Nicoletti lost the mayoral primary race, there were two schools of thought in the postelection analysis. Nicoletti himself and strong supporters of Jackson felt that Jackson's public endorsement was beneficial to the Nicoletti campaign. But other black leaders and many whites who had supported Nicoletti felt that Jackson's endorsement and campaigning side by side with Nicoletti was the "kiss of death" as far as white voters were concerned (Seely 1987b, A12). Tom Young, the Democratic candidate Nicoletti lost to in the primary, went on to defeat the Republican candidate. Black leaders pointed out that although Nicoletti lost and even if Jackson's endorsement was a factor, Jackson had been a positive factor in black leaders' effort to mobilize the black community politically.

## Black Officeholders

By 1987, blacks had made strides politically. However, black representation in elected public positions was disproportionately low. Based on 1980 census data, the black population of Syracuse was 15.7 percent of the total (U.S. Bureau of the Census 1980), yet only one of the ten members of the Common Council was black. The Onondaga County black population was 6.5 percent, but there was only one black member in the twenty-four-member county legislature, approximately 4 percent. Within the formal political structure as represented by the Democratic and Republican parties, blacks fared somewhat better. Twenty-one percent (four out of nineteen) of the Democratic ward chairs were held by blacks, and 10.5 percent (two of nineteen) of the Republican ward chairs were held by blacks (Seely 1987b, A12). However, by 1988, with the appointment of Sidney Igesby to the Syracuse Common Council by the councilpersons themselves, black representation increased from 10 to 20 percent (Seely 1987b, A12).

In nonelective positions in city government, only 16 percent of all employees were black. More important, blacks held only three (10.3 percent) of the top administrative positions in city government (Seely 1987b, A12).

The 1987 election of two blacks to municipal judgeships marked a significant step toward political parity for the black community. Langston McKinney, who had earlier been appointed to a vacant judgeship, making him the first black judge in Syracuse, successfully ran for reelection on the Democratic ticket. Sandra Townes, an assistant district attorney, entered the race after being sought out by the Republican leadership. The result was that five candidates, two of whom were black, ran for three judgeships that were up for election (Seely 1987b, A12).

Sandra Townes was selected to run by the Republican power structure in Syracuse. She had close ties with local Republicans through her position as assistant district attorney in a Republican administration. During her years in the district attorney's office, she had gained a reputation as a more than able attorney and had campaigned for Republican candidates. She had paid her dues both professionally and politically.

Republican leaders viewed Mayor Tom Young, a Democrat who had originally appointed Langston McKinney to the bench, as a threat to the party's gaining a judgeship, especially because of the large number of black votes McKinney would draw. To counteract the McKinney threat and diffuse the black voting power, the Republicans chose Townes to run. Once Townes's candidacy was announced, black leaders' perception that Townes was a threat to McKinney's election spread throughout the black community. Many people felt that Townes was running at an inopportune time. They believed that because McKinney was a sitting judge, he had the best chance of being elected. With Townes now in the race, the two black candidates would cancel out each other. Townes countered that her candidacy was independent of McKinney's. She argued that there was a good chance that both could be elected. In the end, she was correct. Townes was the top vote getter out of the five candidates, and McKinney was elected in a close race for third (Seely 1987b, A12).

Townes and McKinney ran different types of races. Whereas McKinney focused more on the black community, Townes ran a more citywide campaign. Middle-class blacks sponsored fund-raisers for Townes, but the target of the campaign was Syracuse as a whole. Both Townes and McKinney were able to draw the black vote. After the election, it was generally agreed within the black community leadership that Townes faired much better in the black community than had previous Republican candidates (Clark 1985).

Townes's candidacy and election bucked the political trend for black candidates in the 1980s. Before the 1980s, black candidates had traditionally been selected by the Syracuse political party leadership, be it Democratic or Republican. Early black political candidates such as Bob Ware and Constance Timberlake had run broad-based campaigns. However, as blacks gained more political power, black candidates sought public office through black political organizations, mainly the Black Leadership Congress. Black political organizations and leaders would support their efforts at the primary level. In cases where black candidates lost in the partisan primary or were denied their party's endorsement, they ran as independents with the support of black political organizations. Townes's campaign, although not out of line with 1960 and 1970 tradition, did vary from newly established norms in which the black candidate would gain support from the black community first.

Although the election of two black municipal judges in Syracuse was a first and black political mobilization played a role in their success, this election showed that whites were willing to support party candidates regardless of race. Black leaders and blacks in general found out that black candidates could run on a Republican ticket and win, even without the support of traditional black power groups (Clark 1985).

## Summary

Within the black community, political participation was very low in the early 1980s. Blacks were still expecting liberal whites to join their efforts in gaining economic equity as they had during the 1960s, when blacks sought their civil rights. Once local blacks realized that outside help was not forthcoming, they started a leadership organization, a ploy used on several previous occasions. The Syracuse Black Leadership Congress became the vehicle in an attempt to mobilize the black community politically. Through its efforts, Jesse Jackson and his Rainbow Coalition were brought to Syracuse. Jackson's two trips to Syracuse in 1983 and 1985 had a major impact in the efforts to mobilize blacks.

The one factor that cannot be overlooked in an assessment of Jackson's involvement in Syracuse politics was that it signaled a new era in local black political behavior. Through voter registration and voter turnout, blacks involved themselves in local politics to a greater degree than at any time since the first blacks had arrived in Syracuse. Furthermore, the organizational ability and influence displayed by local black leaders in the political arena by getting a national figure to endorse and campaign for local black and white candidates were major steps toward black political mobilization. One would have to conclude that during the 1980s the black community reached a new level of political sophistication.

# 8

# Pie in the Sky

*Economic Dilemmas in the Syracuse Black Community*

BLACKS HAVE TRADITIONALLY depended on sources external to the black community to provide income and employment (Newman et al. 1978). As indicated in chapter 5, blacks during the 1980s perceived themselves as losing ground economically since the 1960s and early 1970s. One reason often given in Syracuse for the decline in the economic progress of blacks was that economic structures were not developed during the 1960s to buttress blacks' economic well-being. As Syracuse moved farther into the postindustrial era, many industrial jobs of the past were no longer available (Seely 1987a). Not only were economic structures not developed in the aftermath of the civil rights era, but black businesses were often lost as white businesses opened their doors to blacks or expanded their product lines to appeal to the growing black market (see Gibson 1978). Economic gains made by blacks during the late 1960s and early 1970s were made primarily through an expansion in public-sector jobs, in particular those governmental jobs associated with the War on Poverty and the amelioration of urban problems. As the Reagan and Bush administrations deemphasized or redefined national priorities away from many of the social programs, the post–civil rights economic base of black communities was partially eroded (see chapter 5).

The Syracuse black community was no different from many other black communities across the nation as the shift in governmental priorities hurt an already tenuous economic base. In some respects, it faired worse than many other black communities, in particular those with a larger and more stable middle class—for example, in southern cities where predominantly black colleges were located, such as Richmond and Norfolk in Virginia, Durham and Greensboro in North Carolina, Atlanta and Savannah in Georgia, and Nashville in Tennessee, to name a few. In contrast to these cities, the Syracuse black community has traditionally had a small professional class and only a few black-owned businesses. As was also shown in chapter 5, many black businesses were displaced by urban renewal in the early 1960s. Although some relocated to other sections of the city, many eventually failed primarily because they lost their customers.

Minion K. C. Morrison (1988), in a study of black political leadership in Syracuse, explains that one of the major differences between blacks and whites is how blacks perceived the function of politics as it relates to the economic sphere. In their quest for political gains, blacks have traditionally seen political power as an end in itself. Getting elected to political office or being able to influence who gets elected has been their primary goal. Whites, on the other hand, see the political arena from an economic perspective; it serves as a conduit for the allocation of scarce resources. In this way, whites have traditionally used political power to gain economic advantages, but blacks have not. When blacks have gained elective office, they have attempted to use their position to benefit blacks economically through institutions external to the black community rather than attempting to broaden the economic base within their community. Black politicians and political leaders alike have supported equal employment opportunity programs and social programs for the poor. These politicians have not traditionally perceived as an attainable goal the establishment of mechanisms to assist in the expansion of black businesses or the securing of contracts from the public or private sector for existing black businesses. Atlanta, Georgia, during the regimen of mayors Maynard Jackson and Andrew Young, served as an exception, wherein black businesses prospered and expanded.

During the 1970s and even into the early 1980s, blacks in Syracuse expected help from liberal whites in solving their economic problems, as they had during the 1960s with civil rights. During this period, the political arena went virtually unnoticed as an economic vehicle among blacks. In all fairness, it was also a time when the political power of blacks was rather weak. As the Syracuse black community became more politically mobilized by the mid-1980s, the efforts among black leaders began to shift more toward developing economic structures through black political power.

This chapter begins by focusing on black-white employment and income comparisons. We use these comparisons to determine the economic position of the black community relative to the larger Syracuse community at the beginning of the 1980s. We then focus on attempts by blacks to create a stronger economic base during the 1980s.

## Employment

Employment had become a major concern not only in Syracuse, but also throughout American households as the postindustrial or "high-technology" era fully emerged during the 1980s. During this period, conditions of unemployment and inflation forced many individuals to seek entrance into the labor force who ordinarily would not have sought jobs. The entrance of these individuals into an already depressed labor market served to exacerbate an increasingly bad situation. Groups of women, youths, and older persons who could not afford retirement sought to enter or remain in the workforce in greater numbers. Conditions related to unemployment did not occur within Syracuse in a uniform manner. Various groups, in particular blacks and some other minority groups, were affected by unemployment to a greater extent than were other groups. Although in the early 1980s unemployment rates in Syracuse were high for all groups, they were the highest for blacks.

Table 8.1 shows that the percentage of black and white males employed in 1980 was about the same. Employment differences were revealed between black (60 percent employed) and white (47.2 percent employed) females. However, it is the unemployment rates that reveal the major differences according to both race and sex. The unemployment rates for black males (17.6 percent) and black females (12.3 percent) more than doubled unemployment rates for white males (8.6 percent) and white females (5.9 percent). Even though a smaller percentage of white females participated in the labor force than any other group, they had the lowest unemployment rates. Not surprisingly, black males had the highest unemployment rate. These data coincide with what was found to be true in the nation and in the rest of New York State for 1980 (Sacks and Sacks 1987, 51).

An even closer examination of unemployment statistics reveals that for Syracuse the 16- to 19-year-old age group indicated even greater discrepancies

Table 8.1

Syracuse Employment Status Rates According to Race and Sex, 1980

| Employment Status | Black | | White | | Male | Female |
| | Male (%) | Female (%) | Male (%) | Female (%) | B/W Ratio | B/W Ratio |
| --- | --- | --- | --- | --- | --- | --- |
| Employed | 67.8 | 60.0 | 66.4 | 47.2 | 1.02 | 1.27 |
| Unemployed | 17.6 | 12.3 | 8.6 | 5.9 | 2.95 | 2.08 |

*Source:* From data presented in Sacks and Sacks 1987, 50.

according to race. For this group, which traditionally has had the highest unemployment rates, blacks had a rate of 26 percent, whereas whites had a rate of 15.5 percent (Sacks and Sacks 1987, 52). It is important to note that in Syracuse the 1980 median age for blacks was 21.7 years and for whites was 30.5. This low median age made the black population of Syracuse one of the youngest in urban areas within New York State, save Rochester. Census figures for 1980 further reveal that 23.7 percent of the black community population was between 10 to 19 years old, 57.1 percent was 24 years of age or younger, and 73 percent was younger than 34 years of age (U.S. Bureau of the Census 1983, 34, 316, and 370). Given the age structure within the Syracuse black community, the high unemployment rate among 16- to 19-year-olds takes on added significance. Loss of work experience and training quite often leads to further unemployment and possibly to eventual withdrawal from the workforce. As American society and Syracuse moved farther into the postindustrial era, these young blacks were competing in a job market that required even more skills. How well they fared had significant implications for the economic base of the black community (Seely 1987a, A1).

Of those employed, table 8.2 reveals differences for blacks and whites in employment by industry categories. In professional-related services, a slightly higher percentage of black workers (32.7) than white workers (30.6) were employed.

Specific categories within professional-related services also indicate that a higher percentage of blacks than whites worked in health-related services; however, the opposite was true for education. A higher percentage of whites (14.4) worked in education than blacks (10.8). According to Sacks and Sacks

Table 8.2

**Employment in Syracuse Industries According to Race, 1980**

| Employment Categories | Black (%)* | White (%) | B/W Ratio |
| --- | --- | --- | --- |
| Professional-Related Services | 32.7 | 30.6 | 1.07 |
| Hospitals | 10.6 | 7.0 | 1.51 |
| Health, Excluding Hospitals | 5.2 | 3.2 | 1.63 |
| Education, Including Colleges | 10.8 | 14.4 | 0.75 |
| Manufacturing | 30.5 | 18.9 | 1.61 |
| Service | 10.8 | 7.8 | 1.48 |
| Transportation and Communication | 7.2 | 6.2 | 1.16 |
| Retail Trade | 6.8 | 16.2 | 0.42 |
| Public Administration | 4.4 | 5.1 | 0.86 |
| Finance, Insurance, and Real Estate | 3.9 | 7.6 | 0.51 |
| Construction | 3.0 | 3.1 | 0.97 |
| Wholesale Trade | 1.4 | 4.2 | 0.33 |
| Agriculture, Forestry, and Fisheries | 0.3 | — | — |
| Mining | — | — | — |

*Source:* Sacks and Sacks 1987, 53.

*Percentage of total employed within each employment category.

(1987), the emergence of professional-related services as a major employer of blacks was a new trend within the 1980s. An old trend that had a negative impact on black employment for the 1980s was the disproportionately high dependency of black workers on manufacturing jobs. Frank Wood, in his 1965 booklet on black employment in Syracuse, addressed the issue of the shift from an industrial-based society to a postindustrial era and its impact on the black community. He predicted that this shift, which was well under way in 1965, would displace the low-skilled but high-wage jobs that were attracting blacks from the South to the industrialized North. It should be kept in mind that these jobs had previously allowed European immigrant groups to stabilize their economic position in America (Lieberson and Waters 1988). The massive migration of southern blacks to Syracuse during the 1950s and early 1960s was to obtain low-skilled, high-wage jobs as assembly-line workers (Seely 1987a, A1). The declining industrial base in Syracuse hit the black community hard. Table 8.2 shows that 30.5 percent of black workers were employed in manufacturing, whereas only 18.9 percent of white workers were so employed. The fact that more than 30 percent of the employment in the black community was derived from industrial jobs was unusual in that throughout the United States about only 20 percent of black employment was industrially based (Seely 1987a, A15). The fact that Bristol Laboratories, Carrier Corporation, and Allied Corporation had either cut back or closed out their local operations aggravated blacks' economic base. Not only were black skilled employees hurt, but individuals with some of the highest salaries within the black community were also affected (Seely 1987a, A15). Table 8.2 also reveals that lower percentages of blacks than whites were in retail trade, public administration, finance, insurance, real estate, and whole trade. Given that these industries have traditionally been low in the number of blacks employed, employment changes for blacks during this period presented a difficult transition.

Table 8.3 reveals the sources of employment in Syracuse according race and sex in 1980. A disproportionately high percentage of workers were employed in the private sector. Slightly higher percentages of white males and females than black males and females were employed by private industries.

**Table 8.3**

**Source of Employment for Persons Sixteen Years and Older in Syracuse According to Race and Sex, 1980**

| Type of Employment | Black | | White | | Male | Female |
|---|---|---|---|---|---|---|
| | Male (%) | Female (%) | Male (%) | Female (%) | B/W Ratio | B/W Ratio |
| Private Wage and Salary | 75.4 | 69.7 | 76.8 | 75.60 | 0.98 | 0.92 |
| Federal Government | 5.2 | 4.2 | 3.2 | 2.50 | 1.63 | 1.68 |
| State Government | 4.9 | 7.8 | 4.7 | 6.50 | 1.04 | 1.20 |
| Local Government | 13.5 | 17.3 | 8.6 | 13.10 | 1.57 | 1.32 |
| Self-Employed | 1.1 | 0.7 | 6.5 | 2.00 | 0.17 | 0.35 |
| Unpaid Family Work | 0.2 | 0.1 | 0.3 | 0.33 | | |
| Totals (Number) | 4,285 | 4,953 | 31,641 | 28,128 | | |

*Source:* Sacks and Sacks 1987, 55.

More than 6 percent of white males were self-employed, whereas only 1.1 percent of black males were self-employed. Although the discrepancies were not as great for females, a higher percentage of white females (2.0) than black females (0.7) were self-employed. Table 8.3 further shows that greater numbers of both black males (23.6 percent) and black females (29.3 percent) depended on public-sector jobs than did white males (16.5 percent) and white females (22.1 percent).

## Other Characteristics Related to Employment

Data derived from the Urban League study (Stamps 1982) offer additional characteristics related to the employment situation between blacks, whites, and other minorities in Syracuse. Table 8.4 provides the employment status of respondents and their spouses according to race in 1981. Almost equal percentages of white (47.1) and black (47.9) respondents were employed by someone else. For other minorities, a much higher percentage (66.7) was evident in this category. The major differences between respondents were that more than twice the percentage of blacks (13.8) than whites (5.8) were "unemployed and looking for work," and a slightly higher percentage of blacks (26.1) than whites (21.8) were "unemployed and not looking for work." Also, in the "unemployed and not looking for work" category, the proportions were rather high for all three groups. It should be kept in mind that some in this group were homemakers; however, given the fact that only 41.9 percent of the sample was married, a considerable proportion of the group was probably female household heads who perceived themselves as currently being out of the labor force or who had never been part of the labor force. Last, it is important to note that 15.5 percent of the whites, 7.6 percent of blacks, and 2.8 percent of other minorities were "retired and not looking for work," a significant difference.

For respondents' spouses, the findings shown in table 8.4 are similar across racial categories, except for the "unemployed and looking for work" category. As was true for the respondents, more than twice the percentage of black spouses (9.2) than white spouses (4.2) fell into this category. The percentage of other minorities (14.8) here was even higher than of blacks. For respondents and spouses, those in the "unemployed and looking for work"

**Table 8.4**

**Employment Status of Respondent and Spouse in Syracuse According to Race, 1981**

| Employment Status | Respondent* | | | | Spouse** | | |
|---|---|---|---|---|---|---|---|
| | Black (N = 486) | White (N = 206) | Other Minorities (N = 36) | Black (N = 238) | White (N = 119) | Other Minorities (N = 27) |
| Employed | 47.9 | 47.1 | 66.7 | 59.9 | 54.6 | 51.9 |
| Self-Employed | 2.5 | 3.9 | 2.8 | 5.5 | 3.4 | — |
| Unemployed | | | | | | |
| Looking for Work | 13.8 | 5.8 | 8.3 | 9.2 | 4.2 | 14.8 |
| Not Looking for Work | 26.1 | 21.8 | 19.4 | 14.7 | 15.1 | 14.8 |
| Retired | | | | | | |
| Looking for Work | 0.4 | 0.5 | 1.7 | 1.7 | — | — |
| Not Looking for Work | 7.6 | 15.5 | 2.8 | 4.6 | 6.7 | — |
| Other | 1.6 | 5.3 | — | 11.3 | 14.3 | 18.5 |

*Source:* Stamps 1982, 82.

*X²=significant at the .001 level with 12 df.

**Not significant.

category were individuals who would be included in the unemployment statistics for Syracuse. Both groups, respondents and spouses, were represented
in higher proportions of those unemployed among blacks and other minorities than among whites.

### Characteristics of Those Employed in 1980

Respondents who indicated they were currently employed were asked specific
questions. In table 8.5, it can be seen that there were no differences in 1981
in the proportions of blacks and whites in length of time they had been on
their primary job, except for in the "twenty or more years" and "less than
one year" categories. Higher percentages of blacks (15.4) and other minorities (20.0) than whites (9.4) had been on their main job for less than one year.
In contrast, a higher percentage of whites (7.5) than blacks (2.1) had been
on their main job twenty years or more. None of the other minorities had
been on the same job more than twenty years. These figures point to the fact
that blacks and other minorities were represented disproportionately among
those who were new on the job. Also indicated is the fact that longevity on
a job was more characteristic of whites than of blacks or other minorities.
Whether the respondent's main job was full- or part-time reveals no significant differences between the groups. Approximately 84 percent of the black
and white respondents and 76 percent of the other minority respondents had
full-time jobs.

These data correspond to the trend of increased occupational mobility
in this period in that 82 percent or more of the respondents indicated that
they had previously been employed in a job other than their current one. Job
mobility was revealed in all occupational categories from managerial to unskilled positions. As was the case with current occupational status, prior jobs
revealed that whites were represented in greater proportions in the higher-
status positions, whereas blacks and other minorities were represented in
greater proportions in low-status positions.

Table 8.6 reveals that 94.9 percent of whites, 92.3 percent of other minorities, and 87 percent of blacks were employed in 1980, the year prior to when the
survey was taken. Of those who were employed, higher proportions of blacks
and other minorities were employed for less periods of time than whites.

Table 8.5

**Characteristics of Those Employed in Syracuse According to Race, 1981**

| Characteristics | Blacks (%) | Whites (%) | Other Minorities (%) |
|---|---|---|---|
| *Length of Time on Primary Job* | *(N = 241)* | *(N = 106)* | *(N = 25)* |
| Less than 1 Year | 15.4 | 9.4 | 20.0 |
| 1–2 Years | 18.7 | 17.0 | 20.0 |
| 3–6 Years | 34.9 | 33.0 | 40.0 |
| 7–9 Years | 11.2 | 14.2 | 12.0 |
| 10–20 Years | 17.8 | 18.9 | 8.0 |
| 20 or More Years | 2.1 | 7.5 | — |
| *Primary Job Full- or Part-Time* | *(N = 241)* | *(N = 104)* | *(N = 25)* |
| Full-Time | 83.8 | 83.7 | 76.0 |
| Part-Time | 16.2 | 16.3 | 24.0 |
| *Primary Job, Only One Ever Had* | *(N = 235)* | *(N = 103)* | *(N = 24)* |
| Yes | 16.6 | 17.5 | 12.5 |
| No | 82.1 | 82.5 | 87.5 |
| N/A | 1.3 | — | — |
| *If No, Prior Job** | *(N = 171)* | *(N = 79)* | *(N = 18)* |
| Managerial | 5.8 | 10.1 | 5.6 |
| Professional and Technical | 12.3 | 35.4 | 11.1 |
| Sales | 9.4 | 5.1 | — |
| Clerical | 17.0 | 12.7 | 11.1 |
| Skilled | 14.6 | 10.0 | 16.7 |
| Semiskilled | 24.0 | 19.0 | 16.7 |
| Unskilled | 16.4 | 5.1 | 38.9 |

*Source:* Stamps 1982, 83.

*$X^2$ = significant at the .001 level with 12 df.

*Unemployed Looking for Work*

This section focuses only on an analysis of blacks and whites. For other minorities, the total number looking for employment was so small that any

Table 8.6

**Employed in Syracuse in the Previous Year According to Race, 1981**

| Employment Status | Black (%) | White (%) | Other Minorities (%) |
|---|---|---|---|
| *Employed Previous Year?** | *(N = 231)* | *(N = 98)* | *(N = 26)* |
| Yes | 87.0 | 94.9 | 92.3 |
| No | 11.3 | 5.1 | 7.7 |
| N/A | 1.7 | — | — |
| *If Yes, Number of Weeks* | *(N = 182)* | *(N = 81)* | *(N = 23)* |
| Less than 10 | 1.1 | 1.2 | — |
| 11–19 | 3.8 | — | 8.7 |
| 20–29 | 6.6 | 1.2 | — |
| 30–39 | 1.1 | 1.2 | 8.7 |
| 40 plus | 87.4 | 96.4 | 82.4 |

*Source:* Stamps 1982, 86.

*Not significant.

analysis would be misleading. Because of the low total number of whites in table 8.7, caution is advised in interpreting this data.

For table 8.7, it was found that a slightly higher percentage of blacks (94.5) than whites (83.3) stated in 1981 that they had worked for pay at one time or another. More important, 37.5 percent of the blacks who were looking for employment had not worked for pay between one and almost five years, whereas only 9.1 percent of the whites fell into this category. Higher percentages of whites (18.2) than blacks (10.7) indicated they had not worked for pay within the past five years or more. These findings clearly show that black unemployment, in higher percentages, was more long term than white unemployment up to a point, after which the trend reversed. However, it should be kept in mind that 48.2 percent of the blacks indicated long-term unemployment of one year to more than five years, whereas only 27.3 percent of the whites indicated likewise. It was also interesting to note that 35.1 percent of the blacks indicated their job was part-time, as compared with only 9.1 percent of the whites.

Table 8.8 reveals the reasons given by these respondents for leaving their previous job. Whites were evenly divided between having resigned (45.5

Table 8.7

**Factors Associated with Respondents' Looking for Employment in Syracuse According to Race,\* 1981**

| Factors | Black (%) | White (%) |
|---|---|---|
| *Have You Ever Worked for Pay?* | *(N = 55)* | *(N = 12)* |
| Yes | 94.5 | 83.3 |
| No | 5.5 | 8.3 |
| *Length of Time Since Last Worked for Pay* | *(N = 56)* | *(N = 11)* |
| Less than 1 Month Ago | 7.1 | 9.1 |
| 1–6 Months Ago | 30.4 | 36.4 |
| 7–12 Months Ago | 14.3 | 27.3 |
| 1 Year to Less than 5 Years Ago | 37.5 | 9.1 |
| 5 Years or More | 10.7 | 18.2 |
| *Last Job Was* | *(N = 57)* | *(N = 11)* |
| Full-Time | 61.4 | 90.9 |
| Part-Time | 35.1 | 9.1 |
| N/A | 3.5 | — |

*Source:* Stamps 1982, 87.
*Not significant.

percent) and having been laid off (45.5 percent). Blacks were evenly divided between having resigned (34.5 percent) and "other," which included having been fired (34.5 percent).

These respondents also revealed the various methods they used to find a job (see table 8.9). Of the many methods used, those that reveal differences by race were the higher percentage of blacks (85.7) over whites (69.2) who relied on friends or relatives, and the higher percentage of whites (41.7) over blacks (14.3) who placed ads in the newspaper. Only 25 percent of both blacks and whites stated they registered with a private employment agency; however, 58.2 percent of the blacks and 50 percent of the whites registered with the state employment service. Greater use was made by whites (53.8 percent) than by blacks (41.8 percent) of community job organizations. These data reveal that whites sought out formal avenues when seeking employment in greater

## Table 8.8
### Reason Left Previous Job in Syracuse According to Race,* 1981

| Reason | Black (%) (N = 55) | White (%) (N = 11) |
|---|---|---|
| Resigned | 34.5 | 45.5 |
| Laid Off | 29.1 | 45.5 |
| Other (Fired) | 34.5 | 9.1 |
| No Answer | 1.8 | — |

*Source:* Stamps 1982, 88.
*Not significant.

proportions than did blacks, except for the state employment agency. Higher proportions of blacks look to informal sources, such as relatives or friends.

Table 8.10 provides the concluding set of data for the section on employment: the respondents' perception in 1981 of factors that might prevent them from getting a job. It shows a very interesting trend in perceptions based on race. Higher proportions of whites than blacks perceived personal liabilities such as lack of job skills, lack of education, less than honorable discharge, and transportation problems as barriers to getting a job. In contrast, blacks in higher proportions perceived societal barriers such as race and sex. The exception was age, which was seen as a barrier by a higher proportion of whites than of blacks. Blacks and whites had almost the same perception of having a police record. The fact that blacks identified social-structural factors rather than personal liabilities as reasons for not being able to get a job points to the importance of these factors in the black community. This identification can be explained by looking at the protest period in the 1960s, when the focus was on structural impediments present in Syracuse. Also of significance were Jesse Jackson's visits to Syracuse and the start of a Rainbow Coalition in the community. Both the period of protest and the Rainbow Coalition emphasized social-structural factors as obstacles to employment opportunities for blacks. Whites more often identified personal factors because they did not see structural factors as obstacles in their quest for a job. It is interesting that neither blacks nor whites mentioned the transition to high technology as a reason for not being able to get a job in Syracuse. It is reasonable to assume that neither

**Table 8.9**

**Methods Used in Finding a Job in Syracuse According to Race,* 1981**

| Methods | Black (%) | White (%) |
|---|---|---|
| *Contacted Employers* | *(N = 58)* | *(N = 13)* |
| Yes | 72.4 | 76.9 |
| No | 27.6 | 23.1 |
| *Asked Friends/Relatives* | *(N = 56)* | *(N = 13)* |
| Yes | 85.7 | 69.2 |
| No | 14.3 | 30.8 |
| *Placed Job Ads* | *(N = 56)* | *(N = 12)* |
| Yes | 14.3 | 41.7 |
| No | 85.7 | 58.3 |
| *Answered Job Ads* | *(N = 57)* | *(N = 12)* |
| Yes | 56.1 | 66.7 |
| No | 43.9 | 33.3 |
| *Registered with Private Employment Agency* | *(N − 56)* | *(N − 12)* |
| Yes | 25.0 | 25.0 |
| No | 75.0 | 75.0 |
| *Registered with State Employment Service* | *(N = 55)* | *(N = 12)* |
| Yes | 58.2 | 50.0 |
| No | 41.8 | 33.3 |
| N/A | | 16.7 |
| *Contacted Community Job Organizations* | *(N = 55)* | *(N = 13)* |
| Yes | 41.8 | 53.8 |
| No | 58.2 | 38.5 |
| N/A | | 7.7 |
| *Other* | *(N = 37)* | *(N = 12)* |
| Yes | 8.1 | 25.0 |
| No | 91.9 | 75.0 |

*Source:* Stamps 1982, 89.

*X² significant at the .05 level with df.

**Table 8.10**

**Respondents' Perception of Factors Possibly Preventing Them from Getting a Job According to Race, 1981**

| Reasons | Black (%) | White (%) |
|---|---|---|
| *Lack of Experience or Job Skills** | *(N = 61)* | *(N = 13)* |
| Yes | 47.5 | 69.2 |
| No | 52.2 | 15.4 |
| N/A | — | 15.4 |
| *Lack of Education* | *(N = 62)* | *(N = 14)* |
| Yes | 32.3 | 57.1 |
| No | 66.1 | 42.9 |
| N/A | 1.6 | — |
| *Police Record* | *(N = 62)* | *(N = 13)* |
| Yes | 14.5 | 15.4 |
| No | 85.5 | 76.9 |
| *Other Than Honorable Military Discharge** | *(N = 62)* | *(N = 13)* |
| Yes | 6.5 | 15.4 |
| No | 93.5 | 69.2 |
| N/A | — | 15.4 |
| *Health Problems* | *(N = 62)* | *(N = 13)* |
| Yes | 14.5 | 30.8 |
| No | 82.3 | 53.8 |
| N/A | 3.2 | 15.4 |
| *Race* | *(N = 62)* | *(N = 13)* |
| Yes | 45.2 | 15.4 |
| No | 53.2 | 69.2 |
| N/A | 1.6 | 15.4 |
| *Sex* | *(N = 62)* | *(N = 11)* |
| Yes | 24.2 | 9.1 |
| No | 72.6 | 81.8 |
| N/A | 3.2 | 9.1 |

**Table 8.10 (*continued*)**

| Reasons | Black (%) | White (%) |
| --- | --- | --- |
| *Age* | *(N = 60)* | *(N = 9)* |
| Yes | 20.0 | 33.3 |
| No | 80.0 | 66.7 |
| N/A | — | — |
| *Transportation Problems* | *(N = 62)* | *(N = 11)* |
| Yes | 33.9 | 63.6 |
| No | 62.9 | 36.4 |
| N/A | 3.2 | — |

*Source:* Stamps 1982, 90.

*$X^2$ significant at the .05 level with 4 df.

group really understood what was happening in the city and in society in general. William J. Wilson (1996b), in his study of inner-city Chicago, provides an excellent explanation of how high technology and the move of industry to the suburbs have left blacks without employment opportunities.

**Income**

A 1988 study by the Congressional Budget Office indicates that in 1986 American family income had risen from 1970 primarily because of an increase in two-worker families. However, the study also points out that income gaps had widened between rich and poor families. During most of the 1970s, the income gains made by both low-income and high-income families were similar, but the greater disparities occurred between 1979 and 1986, when more-affluent families' income increased dramatically more than less-affluent families' income (cited in Pear 1988, A1).

The Syracuse family income index for 1986 was most likely similar to the national trend. With a precipitous decline in industrial jobs in the Syracuse area, one would not be surprised to find that the incomes of high-income and low-income families moved farther apart. Table 8.11 indicates the household income for blacks and whites in Syracuse in 1979. Black family median income, $11,902, was 68 percent of white median family income, $17,437. Most interestingly, 21.2 percent of black families had incomes less than $5,000, whereas only 7.6 percent of white families fell into that category. Table 8.11 clearly reveals that there was a major difference between black and white family incomes in 1979.

As family income in Syracuse increased toward $50,000 and higher, the black/white income ratio decreased. Only in the three lowest income categories, less than $5,000, $5,000 to $9,999, and $10,000 to $12,999, did the percentage of blacks exceed the percentage of whites. On the other end of the income spectrum, in the three household income categories that exceeded $25,000, the percentages of whites were greater than the percentages of blacks.

A breakdown of income in terms of race, sex, and type of earners in 1980 is shown in table 8.12. Big differences in incomes can be seen between "all earners" and "full-time earners" for all categories. The "all earners" category, which includes individuals with part-time jobs, accounts for most of

**Table 8.11**

**Family Income in Syracuse According to Race, 1979**

| Income | Black (%)* | White (%) | B/W Ratio |
|---|---|---|---|
| Less than $5,000 | 21.2 | 7.6 | 2.78 |
| $5,000–9,999 | 10.6 | 7.9 | 1.34 |
| $10,000–12,499 | 10.4 | 8.4 | 1.24 |
| $12,500–14,999 | 16.5 | 17.5 | 0.94 |
| $15,000–19,999 | 13.4 | 16.7 | 0.81 |
| $20,000–24,999 | 11.6 | 14.6 | 0.79 |
| $25,000–34,999 | 10.7 | 16.4 | 0.65 |
| $35,000–49,000 | 4.5 | 7.2 | 0.63 |
| $50,000 and higher | 1.1 | 3.7 | 0.30 |
| Median Income | $11,902 | $17,437 | 0.68 |

*Source:* U.S. Bureau of the Census 1980, 34, 352, and 406.

*Percentage of total number of families in each racial group.

Table 8.12

Syracuse Median Income for Persons Fifteen Years and Older with Income, 1980

| Median Income | Male | | Female | | Male | Female |
| | Black | White | Black | White | B/W Ratio | B/W Ratio |
|---|---|---|---|---|---|---|
| All Earners | $8,043 | 9,410 | 5,296 | 5,015 | 0.85 | 1.06 |
| Full-Time Earners | $14,545 | 15,819 | 9,535 | 10,302 | 0.92 | 0.93 |

Source: Sacks and Sacks 1987, 57.

the differences. It should be mentioned, however, that when the part-time earner was the only earner within a household and that earner was female, whether black or white, the economic picture was not good. The biggest differential in income was between males and females regardless of race. According to race, the biggest difference in income was between black and white male "all earners."

## Black Business and the Economic Pie

The battle fought by blacks in Syracuse expanded from a focus on political power to one that also included economic power (Seely 1987a, A1). With this expanded focus, the push for black-controlled economic institutions intensified. Black businesses in Syracuse had traditionally played a minor role in contributing to the economic base of the black community and played an even lesser role in providing jobs for blacks. As pointed out in the section on employment, jobs became one of the most important problems facing the black community during the 1980s (Stamps 1982). In 1980, approximately 450 people joined together to march on city hall to protest the need for jobs within the black community (Seely 1987c, A15). Once the fervor of the march died down, the realization set in that blacks were going to have to create jobs for themselves. It was perceived that only through the expansion of black businesses could black income and employment expectations be met. The Syracuse Common Council focused on black businesses in reacting to the demands made by participants in the job march. It passed a resolution urging that minority contractors be given from 10 to 15 percent of community-de-velopment contracts (Seely 1987a, A14).

Black businesses, although showing some signs of moving beyond the "mom and pop" variety, still consisted in large part of barbershops, beauty parlors, bars and lounges, cafés, liquor stores, fish markets, grocery stores, and funeral homes. An automobile garage or, more frequently, an automobile "fix-it" shop could occasionally be found.[1] These traditional black businesses can be classified within both formal and informal economic sectors (Hart 1973; Sethuraman 1978).

This analysis of black businesses in Syracuse is geared toward provid-ing an explanation of creating and sustaining an economic base in the black community. Any labor force analysis that depends on the crude dichotomy of employed and unemployed does not provide an adequate picture (Light 1983, 361), especially when poor countries or even poor communities within rich countries are in question. Because the overall task of this study is to analyze internal and external factors that influence the growth and devel-opment of the black community, an economic analysis of black businesses seems most appropriate.

In the 1980s, the formal economic sector encompassed traditional no-tions of income- and profit-producing activities whereby businesses, in-dustries, and other institutions, both private and public, operated within at least a loosely defined complex of business principles and activities. Jobs were generated; wages were paid; close ties were maintained with financial institutions (bank accounts, loans, lines of credit, etc.) and related economic institutions; established methods of accounting procedures were utilized; commodities or services were offered to the public; and taxes and civil codes were adhered to by institutions within the formal economic sector. Formal income was derived from public- and private-sector wages and from transfer payments (public assistance, pensions, and unemployment benefits) (Hart 1973, 69). By contrast, the informal economic sector generated income and

1. The fix-it shop differs from the garage in that the fix-it shop carries few parts for re-placement, does not provide oil changes, and so on. It is relegated to mechanical work of a less serious nature. The garage carries a wider assortment of replacement parts, changes oil, has electronic equipment for diagnostic purposes, and takes on more serious jobs.

material needs without wages. Businesses within this sector can be character-ized as: (1) small and offering from part-time to full-time hours; (2) often in violation of civil codes for sanitation, safety, and tax assessments; (3) run by a family; (4) flexible in their operating hours; (5) mobile or temporary in their location; (6) labor intensive, with owner or family providing the labor; (7) operated in a direct-to-consumer fashion; 8) undercapitalized in that they were started and run with personal or family finances; and (9) run by owners lacking in education and skills (Sethuraman 1978).

*Formal Black Business Sector*

Relying on data derived from black and minority business directories from 1981 to 1982 and from 1986 to 1988, we have constructed a realistic picture of formal black businesses within Syracuse. We made comparisons of black businesses between the two time periods. The objective here was to indicate the impact that black businesses within the formal sector had on the perceived need to expand the economic base of the black community during the 1980s.

Table 8.13 categorizes black businesses from 1981 to 1982 and from 1986 to 1988. It is interesting to note that the overall number of black businesses increased by only a single business from the first time period to the second: from 177 for the years 1981 through 1982 to 178 for the years 1986 through 1988. However, major changes took place in the types of businesses that existed between the two time periods.

From 1981 to 1982, contractors made up 17.5 percent of all black businesses, and by the period 1986 through 1988 the percentage of contractors had more than doubled to 37.1 of the total. General contracting showed the largest increase, followed by trucking, painting/signs, and paving. Conversely, retail firms suffered a greater than 50 percent reduction in their numbers. The largest decreases appeared for bars and liquor stores, barbershops, beauty salons, and restaurants/cafés. It should be mentioned, however, that many of the retail businesses listed for 1981–82 but not listed for 1986–88 were marginal at best. Bars, barbershops, beauty shops, and cafés were often quasi-formal businesses, employing only one person or run solely by the owner and family members. Among retail businesses, the most significant change was actually a decrease in the number of car dealers, from two in

## Table 8.13
## Black Businesses in the Formal Sector in Syracuse

| Categories of Business | 1981–1982 | | 1986–1988 | |
|---|---|---|---|---|
| | *No.* | *(%)* | *No.* | *(%)* |
| *Contractors* | *(N = 31)* | *(17.5)* | *(N = 66)* | *(37.2)* |
| Electrician and Supplies | 3 | 1.7 | 5 | 2.8 |
| General Contracting | 11 | 6.2 | 28 | 15.7 |
| Heating and Air Conditioning | 1 | 0.6 | 1 | 0.6 |
| Masonry | 2 | 1.1 | 1 | 0.6 |
| Painting/Signs | 7 | 3.9 | 11 | 6.2 |
| Paving | 4 | 2.3 | 8 | 4.5 |
| Roofing | — | — | 1 | 0.6 |
| Trucking/Moving | 2 | 1.1 | 8 | 4.5 |
| Welding and Fabricating | 1 | 0.6 | 3 | 1.7 |
| *Retail Firms* | *(N = 84)* | *(47.4)* | *(N = 42)* | *(23.1)* |
| Bars and Liquor Stores | 27 | 15.2 | 6 | 3.4 |
| Barbershops | 9 | 5.1 | 3 | 1.7 |
| Beauty Salons | 18 | 10.2 | 9 | 5.1 |
| Car Dealers | 2 | 1.1 | 1 | 0.6 |
| Grocery Stores and Markets | 7 | 3.9 | 6 | 3.4 |
| Furniture Stores | 1 | 0.6 | 3 | 1.1 |
| Independent Enterprises | 1 | 0.6 | 3 | 1.7 |
| Record Stores | 3 | 1.7 | 1 | 0.6 |
| Restaurants/Cafés | 10 | 5.6 | 4 | 2.2 |
| Specialty Stores | 3 | 1.7 | 4 | 2.2 |
| Upholstery Shops | 3 | 1.7 | 2 | 1.1 |
| *Service Firms* | *(N = 62)* | *(35.2)* | *(N = 71)* | *(40.3)* |
| Accounting/Bookkeeping | 1 | 0.6 | 1 | 0.6 |
| Alterations | — | — | 1 | 0.6 |
| Architect | 1 | 0.6 | 1 | 0.6 |
| Auto Repair/Service | 8 | 4.5 | 3 | 1.7 |
| Bowling Lanes | 1 | 0.6 | — | — |
| Car Washes | 5 | 2.8 | 1 | 0.6 |
| Catering | 1 | 0.6 | 2 | 1.1 |

**Table 8.13 (*continued*)**

| Categories of Business | 1981–1982 | | 1986–1988 | |
|---|---|---|---|---|
| | *No.* | *(%)* | *No.* | *(%)* |
| Cleaning/Janitorial | 3 | 1.7 | 6 | 3.4 |
| Consulting | 2 | 1.1 | 15 | 8.4 |
| Dance/Music | 2 | 1.1 | — | — |
| Day Care | 2 | 1.1 | 2 | 1.1 |
| Design | — | — | 1 | 0.6 |
| Driving Schools | 1 | 0.6 | 1 | 0.6 |
| Dry Cleaners/Laundries | 3 | 1.7 | 2 | 1.1 |
| Engineering | — | — | 4 | 2.2 |
| Entertainment/Booking | 4 | 2.3 | — | — |
| Extermination | 2 | 1.1 | 1 | 0.6 |
| Financial | — | — | 1 | 0.6 |
| Funeral Homes | 3 | 1.7 | 3 | 1.7 |
| Insurance | 1 | 0.6 | 3 | 1.7 |
| Karate | 3 | 1.7 | 1 | 0.6 |
| Legal Services | 1 | 0.6 | 1 | 0.6 |
| Limousine Services | 1 | 0.6 | 2 | 1.1 |
| Newspaper Supply | 2 | 1.1 | 4 | 2.2 |
| Nursing Homes | 1 | 0.6 | — | — |
| Photography | 3 | 1.7 | 1 | 0.6 |
| Printing | 2 | 1.1 | 1 | 0.6 |
| Real Estate | 2 | 1.1 | 3 | 1.7 |
| Secretarial | 2 | 1.1 | 1 | 0.6 |
| Security | 1 | 0.6 | 4 | 2.2 |
| Taxi | — | — | 1 | 0.6 |
| Television | 1 | 0.6 | — | — |
| Transport | 3 | 1.7 | 3 | 1.7 |
| Video | — | — | 1 | 0.6 |
| Totals | 177 | 100.1 | 179 | 100.6 |

*Sources:* Data for the 1981–82 period were derived from *Metropolitan Syracuse Black Business Directory* 1981–82. Data for the 1986–88 period were derived from *Central New York Directory of Minority and Women Businesses* 1986–88. Only businesses owned by black men and women were included.

1981–82 to one in 1986–88; that dealership was Syracuse's first black new car dealership, Bill Scott Oldsmobile.

Service firms indicated a slight increase, going from 35 percent of the total to 39.9 percent. Noteworthy increases were in cleaning/janitorial, consulting, insurance, security, and engineering firms, where all were prevalent in the high-technology economy.

*Profiles of the Largest Black Businesses*

By 1988, the largest and most successful black businesses were Bill Scott Oldsmobile, Simmons Moving and Wrecking Company, Metallon Paint Corporation, John Hill Trucking Company, and a recently opened McDonald's. The largest and by far most successful local black business was Bill Scott Oldsmobile. According to *Black Enterprise,* Bill Scott Oldsmobile was ranked as the forty-sixth top black business in America with a 1986 sales volume of $24,296,000 ("List of the Top 100 Black Businesses" 1987, 133). Scott, who went through the General Motors dealership training program, came to Syracuse in 1982 to take over an Oldsmobile dealership that was previously white owned. From that time, his business grew to its 1987 size with a staff of fifty-eight.

Eric Simmons Sr., now deceased, was the original owner of Simmons Moving and Wrecking Company. Simmons got his initial start in the demolition business by working many years for the previous white owner of the demolition company. After learning the business, he eventually assumed control from the owner. With the help of his family, he was able to expand his workforce and began taking on some of the largest jobs in central New York. By the end of the 1980s, Simmons Moving and Wrecking Company was run by Eric Simmons Jr. and thus still a family-run business ("Businessman Trucks Up" 1983).

John Hill, owner of John Hill Trucking Company, began driving trucks at the age of fifteen. By age twenty-eight, he had started his own business. A native of South Carolina, Hill had completed only grammar school, yet he and his wife, who worked with him, knew the only way to expand a business was to reinvest the profits. By the 1980s, Hill's company was unionized, had a fleet of more than thirty trucks, employed more than forty workers, and grossed in excess of $1,000,000 yearly ("Businessman Trucks Up" 1983, 26).

Robert Spencer, who along with his brother started Metallon Paint Corporation in 1983, grew up in a family-owned business. His father had started Sunbeam Welding Company during the 1960s, after arriving in the United States from the West Indies. It was assumed that Robert would take control of family company, but by 1987 Metallon Paint Corporation, with thirty-five employees and plans to expand into Wilmington, Delaware, was much larger than Sunbeam Welding Company, which had only eight employees (Seely 1987a, A14).

Other businesses and their owners might be presented here, but these brief profiles of the more successful black businesses in the Syracuse black community provides insightful information on black business owners, how black businesses operated, and their impact on building up a black economic base. Excluding Bill Scott Oldsmobile, which was more of an exception than the rule, successful local black businesses tended to be family owned and operated by people whose business skills and knowledge were acquired on the job as opposed to through formal training and who grew up in families with businesses. Although by the late 1980s many black businesses listed within the formal sector had expanded beyond being family owned and operated, their economic impact on the black community, although positive, was somewhat limited. One limiting factor was that they still supported family and kin first, then workers outside of the family circle. Because the most successful of them employed between only thirty-five and fifty-five workers, their ability to provide jobs in the black community was restricted.

*Other Black Businesses*

The most successful black businesses were limited in their ability to expand the black economic base and to provide a significant number of jobs, and they were few in number as well. They did not represent the typical black business in the formal sector. Of the 178 black businesses listed between 1986 and 1988, most were small both in terms of revenues and in the number of employees. Most of these businesses were able to support only the owner and his or her family. The profile of Percy Jones provides clues to the operation and impact of a more typical black business in the black community. Jones's businesses, although listed within the formal sector, might better be characterized as quasi-formal because many of its characteristics closely coincided with those that defined the informal sector.

Percy Jones arrived in Syracuse during the mid-1960s from Clarksdale, Mississippi, with eighty-five cents in his pocket. However, he had grown up in his father's small grocery store in Mississippi, so he came to Syracuse with some knowledge of business. Obtaining a loan from the Small Business Association, Jones first opened a coin-operated Laundromat. His financial success from the Laundromat allowed him to start a seasonal snowplowing business. By the 1980s, Percy Jones, his wife, and son operated the Laundromat, the snowplowing business, rental properties, a grocery store, and an appliance-installation business (Shelley 1980, D3, D12).

Many of the businesses listed as a part of the formal sector were not quite as successful, but the black businessperson often operated not one, but two or three businesses within the confines of his or her family. These businesses were often difficult to distinguish from businesses considered part of the informal sector. However, quasi-formal businesses had some characteristics associated with the formal sector. As was the case with Percy Jones, a Small Business Association loan was obtained, some business knowledge was acquired, and daily business activities were carried through legitimate financial institutions.

The expectation that black economic power and jobs for blacks could be attained through an expansion of black businesses had some merit, but the means to achieve it were somewhat limited in Syracuse during the 1980s. The overwhelming number of jobs and incomes for blacks in the city came from public and private institutions external to the black community. As governmental policies shifted funding priorities changed, and, most important, as America continued its transition from an industrial-based society to an information-based society, the economic viability of members of the black community remained tenuous.

*Informal Black Business Sector*

Other studies have shown or provided some evidence that black communities, as well as other poor racial and ethnic communities within American society, often turn to the informal economic sector for incomes (Whyte 1943;

Liebow 1967; Stack 1974). Informal economic activity can be derived from both legal and illegal activities (Valentine 1968; Light 1983). An important ingredient in the rise of informal activity in black and other minority communities is discrimination in lending practices by mainstream financial institutions. Granted, factors such as lack of collateral, lack of business skills, and poor education play significant roles, but discrimination cannot be overlooked. Activity in the informal economic sector in the black community results from blacks' inability to penetrate the formal economic sector, so that they are forced to seek out less-formalized means of initiating businesses and generating incomes. Evidence already provided indicates that many black businesses classified as formal are really quasi-formal.

Many black businesspersons in Syracuse expressed concern and dismay over the results of their efforts to obtain financing from local financial institutions. They stated that lending formulas used by local banks were discriminatory even if discrimination was not the purpose. The owner of Blue Brothers Barber Shop, the largest shop in the black community, was repeatedly rejected for a loan. Trevor White, a local black accountant, purchased a $37,000 computer from a local bank for $3,000, yet he was unable to obtain a loan to purchase the software necessary to run the system. White was denied a loan although he had numerous black and white customers as well as the opportunity to bid on payroll contracts for large local businesses. White stated that he knew of small black businesses that had been offered signed contracts from major corporations for business deals, but were unable to accept the offers because banks refused to grant them loans. Local banks responded to these accusations by stating that granting or rejecting loans was a business decision, not a racial decision (Seely 1987a, A14). Their response was based on what black businesspersons had referred to as discriminatory lending formulas, which included collateral to secure loans, track records of success in business, and business knowledge and skills. Assumptions regarding these criteria were often drawn from traditional ideas of dress and language patterns, in addition to how well the loan application was put together. However, reasons for blacks' concern regarding discrimination in lending practices were justified because even successful black businesspersons, such as Bill Scott, owner of the largest and most successful local black business in Syracuse, was also denied a loan. When Scott attempted to expand his holdings by establishing a dealership in a small suburban town outside of Syracuse, he was unable to obtain a loan after repeated trials. Finally, he was informed on the quiet that the Syracuse business community felt he was moving too fast. The rationale was not that he was getting in over his head, but that his rate of success was too quick.

Our observations and interviews in the black community revealed a range of groups who, for different reasons, participated in the informal economic sector. There were individuals who had been unable to obtain loans from financial institutions because of poor business skills, ill-conceived business plans, and discriminatory practices. These small operators started businesses with money borrowed from family, friends, and personal savings. The following two accounts provide some insights into how these businesses operated. In the first case, when a customer in a small inner-city café ordered a hot dog with mustard, the owner, taking money out of his wallet, sent his cousin to a small grocery store two buildings away to buy a half-pound of hot dogs and a small jar of mustard. The second account tells what took place when an electrical company was hired to repair a light fixture. A young relative of the owner was sent to do the job. After considerable time, the young relative determined that a new part was needed. The customer asked the cost and was told by the young person he did not know, but he would call an electrical supply store and get a price. The customer was then asked to provide the money so the needed part could be purchased. In both cases, the informal business did not carry adequate supplies to sustain a business. The electrical company did not maintain credit privileges at supply houses, nor did it have cash reserves to purchase needed replacement parts. Black accountant Trevor White stated, "Small operations—black or white—can't deal with checks, nine times out of ten. . . . When people get paid, they want cash, certified check or money order. You find few minority [informal] operations with checking accounts. And if they survive the first three years, they are loaded down with judgments, bill problems—liens on this, liens on that. To survive, they can't put money in the bank" (quoted in Seely 1987a, A14).

Many black community members turned to the informal sector when the local economy was unable to absorb them. Southern blacks who migrated to Syracuse during the 1950s and 1960s looking for low-skilled industrial jobs became unemployed during the 1980s as factories closed or had sharp cutbacks in their workforces. Also included in this group were the officially never employed, many single female family heads with children who supplemented their public assistance through the informal sector. This group often exchanged goods and participated in various activities in which there was no exchange of money. Vegetables grown in home gardens, babysitting, sewing, and other activities and goods were often interchanged. The officially unemployed often worked as maids (without benefits) in white and upper-income black homes. Weekend rent parties were given, whereby individuals attending paid a $2.00 to $3.00 admission fee and paid for any drinks served. In some cases, parties extended into illegitimate areas such as poker games in which the home received a share of table stakes. Men and women served as runners for the illegal "numbers" games that competed with the New York State lottery games.

Participation in the informal economic sector was not limited to those officially unemployed or to lower-income members of the black community. Even some members of the formal economic sector attempted to "piece together" an adequate standard of living through legitimate "hustling" buttressed by low-paid employment. Others attempted to better their middle-class lifestyle with one or more "hustles." Take, for example, the laboratory technician at one of the local hospitals who ran a photo service and a driving school from his home in a middle-income neighborhood, or the public-school teacher who also ran a pest control service, or the engineer who converted basements, did plumbing, and electrical work on the side. Many other middle-income members of the black community participated in the informal economic sector as well as in the formal sector.

The one person/one job assumption is risky, especially when individuals are restricted to low-paying jobs or no jobs (Hart 1973, 66). Close observation of the black community in the 1980s revealed that individuals throughout the economic continuum participated in the informal economic sector in varying degrees. Some were forced into informal businesses run out of shoe boxes because of shaky financial underpinnings, and some had no other avenue as the demand for job skills increased to levels beyond their reach. For others, the informal sector served as an avenue where bartering replaced the monetary system and where money could change hands through illegitimate means.

### Economic Prospects

This chapter began by stating that blacks had come to the realization that an economic base was a necessity for the further growth and development of their community. They could no longer look solely to the white community to provide income and jobs. Economic power, like political power, was something that had to be generated from within the community, not from sources external to the community. Both the realization of the need for an economic base and attempts to expand it occurred during the 1980s. As the economic picture of the black community was portrayed throughout this chapter, it became apparent that certain job trends set in motion as early as the 1950s had begun to erode the somewhat restricted economic base that existed at the beginning of the 1980s. As Syracuse's industrial base deteriorated during the 1980s, blacks suffered disproportionately to whites.

It has already been shown that a disproportionately high number of blacks employed in Syracuse depended on these industrial jobs. The entry of blacks into industrial jobs had come about as the result of considerable collective efforts. Many had to relocate from the rural and segregated South to the urban industrialized North. Even then, it took the efforts of a national civil rights movement and the passage of equal employment legislation for blacks to gain some equity in job accessibility and pay. For the black American worker in Syracuse and in similar industrial cities in the 1980s, the American dream they had fought for so hard and so long was again escaping their reach.

It is important to keep in mind that the economic base of the Syracuse black community and of other black communities was predicated on income/salaries external to these communities. As noted, black businesses have played a minor role in contributing to the economic base, particularly in generating jobs and wages. Therefore, entrepreneurial efforts such as those in the Syracuse black community were important to the community's economic well-being. Although the fruits of these efforts had not paid off in significant results as the 1980s came to an end, the prospects offered some hope.

# Education and Syracuse Schools

CHAPTER 8 HIGHLIGHTED the need for a more skilled and more educated workforce in Syracuse as well as in the rest of American society. Decreases in industrial jobs that began in the 1950s and accelerated during the 1980s had a disproportionately negative impact on the black community. Rising unemployment, demands for increased skills and education, and insufficient avenues for retraining were trends that had a negative impact on the community's attempt to expand its economic base. These trends, combined with a longstanding concern regarding discrimination, dimmed the outlook for a brighter economic future for the community.

As the transition from an industrial-based society to an information-based society continued, it was expected that education would play a key role. The concern was not only for the displaced worker or the adult who had never entered the workforce, but also for those young adults who were about to enter the workforce and for their children, who would represent human resources of the future. Those with better education and more skills would have better opportunities for jobs, higher salaries, and a chance for a better lifestyle than those with less education and less skills. Therefore, educational attainment became an important ingredient in the quest for an expanded economic base. Central to educational attainment and the quality of education within Syracuse was its school system and how it responded to its mandate to educate school-age children regardless of race. This chapter analyzes the impact of Syracuse schools on the education of black and white children. We make comparisons between blacks and whites based on the levels of educational attainment, school attendance, attitudes toward the school system, suspensions, expulsions, and parental involvement.

### Educational Attainment

Closely related to the economic and political well-being of a community or a group is the level of education attained by its members. A low level of educational attainment had traditionally been a problem in the Syracuse black community. In the discussion of the history of this community in chapter 2, it was revealed that churches and religious leaders stressed the value of education. This community push for educational attainment had an impact through the elementary school years in that black student attendance often surpassed that of white students. However, as black students reached high school, their attendance decreased, and their dropout rate increased. This trend was accelerated as increasing numbers of southern black laborers migrated to Syracuse. Education was stressed less and less as the pay off of jobs usually did not materialize. Also, the need for every able-bodied person to work in order for the family to survive—regardless of age, type of job, or pay—decreased the emphasis on education.

The data in table 9.1 are indicative of the educational status of blacks in 1980. Evident is the fact that a higher percentage of blacks than whites twenty-five years and older completed seven years of education or less. A higher percentage of whites (9.1) than blacks (6.3) completed eight years of education, and a higher percentage of blacks (28.3) than whites (15.4) completed between one and three years of high school education. Most important, however, is the fact that higher percentages of whites than blacks fell into each of the educational categories beyond one to three years of high school. A much higher percentage of whites (19.1) than of blacks (6.6) had four years of college. For whites, the percentage of high school graduates was 65.8, with the median years of school completed 12.5; for blacks, the percentage of high school graduates was 48.1, with 11.8 median years of school completed (U.S. Bureau of the Census 1983, 316, 370).

Although black educational attainment was below that of whites, federal, state, and local policies enhanced educational opportunities for blacks and other minorities. Max Rubin chaired the Special Task Force on Equity and Excellence in Education within the state of New York, which keyed in on problems faced by large-city school systems, such as Syracuse's, during the 1970s. New state rules and policies in areas such as finance assisted school districts

**Table 9.1**

**Years of Schooling for Persons Twenty-five and Older in Syracuse According to Race, 1980**

| Years of Schooling Completed | Black (%) (N = 11,450) | White (%) (N = 84,017) |
| --- | --- | --- |
| *Elementary* | | |
| 0–4 Years | 5.7 | 3.2 |
| 5–7 Years | 11.6 | 6.5 |
| 8 Years | 6.3 | 9.1 |
| *High School* | | |
| 1–3 Years | 28.3 | 15.4 |
| 4 Years | 29.1 | 32.4 |
| *College* | | |
| 1–3 Years | 12.4 | 14.3 |
| 4 Years | 6.6 | 19.1 |

*Source:* From data in U.S. Bureau of the Census 1983, 48.

in serving all students better (Sacks and Sacks 1987, 79–85). Rules and policies passed as a result of the task force's work brought about a more equitable distribution of state funds to local school districts. Because of these efforts and local programs, blacks faired relatively well throughout high school. However, differences between blacks and whites continued to show in post–high school education levels, particularly college. These data help explain, to some degree, the differences that existed between whites and blacks in the skill levels of jobs held and in job opportunities in Syracuse. With significantly more whites than blacks getting college degrees, it was not surprising that whites in disproportionately high numbers held the high-skilled and high-status positions.

**School Attendance**

*Integration*

For the Syracuse black community, from the time the first move toward school integration was initiated in 1962 through the 1980s, integration had been perceived as being related to quality education. Before integration, Syracuse public schools mirrored ethnic community composition. White neighborhoods meant white schools, and black neighborhoods meant black schools (Seely 1987d, A12). Inner-city black schools were overcrowded and poorly equipped, lacked curricula flexibility, and were usually staffed by inexperienced teachers. Dennis Dowdell, the former head of the Urban League of Onondaga County and later the director of urban affairs at Carrier Corporation, articulated the situation: "We've got to get with the young crowd and encourage . . . scholarship. We've got to put one heck of a lot of energy in training those youngsters so they can match up with the white youngsters that are coming out [graduating]. We've got to tell them that it's going to be a battle. It's not going to be easy. And we've got to be saying this in our churches" (quoted in Cornwall 1987, 112). Blacks realized that the more politically powerful whites would not tolerate such conditions if their children attended these schools. The push for integration, then, was a push for a better quality of education. Even Syracuse School Board president David H. Jaquith, who in the early 1960s had felt the school system should not have the responsibility of solving what he perceived as a housing problem, later became an advocate for school integration. Jaquith saw a significant improvement in test scores for black children who attended integrated schools (Seely 1987d, A12).

By 1980, the integration plan for the Syracuse Public School System was in operation. The plan, largely voluntary, had the magnet school concept at its core.[1] Such a program was begun at the instigation of Sidney Johnson, the first black superintendent of schools in Syracuse. As stated in chapter 4, the appointment of this rather conservative black Republican as superintendent in 1976 was a brilliant move by the Syracuse School Board. Johnson did not support busing to achieve racial integration in schools, which endeared him to many white parents. Although many black parents did not agree with his

1. The magnet school concept was designed as a result of court-ordered attendance plans to remedy segregated schools. Certain public schools were designed to offer students an opportunity to take advantage of their interests and talents in specific subjects in a strong academic environment that fostered equity and diversity. They were usually located in an area where parents might ordinarily object to sending their children if they were bused.

position on busing, they had to take pride in a black person's heading a school system that had hired its first black teacher in 1950.

Syracuse's four high schools were spaced geographically throughout the city. Johnson came up with a plan in which four school districts as quadrants were constructed with a high school in each. He suggested that each quadrant develop its own integration plan with input from both parents and teachers. These efforts resulted in new schools being proposed and magnet programs being devised. In the end, Johnson closed ten elementary schools, opened a new elementary school, and established open enrollment throughout the system. The Johnson plan resulted in all but three elementary schools achieving racial balance (Cornwall 1987, 98).

The magnet school concept was built nationally around the idea that inner-city schools would be made magnet centers, thus attracting white students into the inner-city and integrating those schools. It seems this concept was abandoned somewhat in Syracuse. In reality, all but two-inner city elementary schools were closed. One of the two remaining schools, Danforth, was made a magnet school by providing an early childhood education program that included an all-day kindergarten and an extended-day program. The closing of inner-city elementary schools meant that black students had to be bused to suburban schools. School administrators' earlier rejection of busing as a means to integrate public schools really meant the rejection of the mandatory busing of white students. Under the program that was initiated, black students had to be bused, but white elementary students remained at their neighborhood schools.

Working from a state-mandated formula for racial balance that specified that elementary schools should not have black enrollments lower than 15 percent or higher than 45 percent, school officials in the late 1980s still claimed that students were not forced to ride buses. They argued that they were able to sell parents on the idea of sending their children outside their neighborhood to school (Seely 1987d, A12). However, black children from inner-city neighborhoods were still bused the farthest from their homes to school. The magnet school was designed to bring white students into the inner city, so many black children were unable to attend magnet schools close to their homes because of the racial imbalance it would create. In 1985, when white parents complained that Clary Middle School was becoming all black (the black population was 58 percent), school administrators capped black enrollment by accepting only black seventh-grade students. By 1986, Clary's black student enrollment had dropped to 43.7 percent. However, black eighth-grade students had to be bused to schools in other areas (Seely 1987d, A12).

The rationale behind the thrust for integration is understandable and well intentioned. Integration was expected to provide better resources, facilities, instruction, and opportunities for black children. Although the outcome of integration was debatable within the black community, interviews with black parents indicate that children from professional families received benefits that children from low-income families did not receive.[2] Nottingham High School resembled two separate schools. A disproportionately large number of black students and some white students from low-income families took vocational classes, whereas middle-class students took college preparatory courses. On the surface, such an arrangement would seem to be economic, not racial. And to a certain degree it was economic, but certain other factors entered the scenario. One account provides an illustration of what was often perceived as happening to black students in the Syracuse school system. A black professional family moved to Syracuse with a high-school-age daughter and enrolled her at Nottingham High School. The daughter had been in a college preparatory track in her previous school and had already completed units in science, so the parents were upset to find out that she had been enrolled in a "shop [carpentry] course" her first semester at Nottingham rather than the required science course. After a meeting between the parents and counselor wherein the daughter's transcript was reviewed, the counselor agreed to change the daughter's schedule. Much to the parents' chagrin, however, the revised schedule had the daughter taking "basket weaving" rather than "shop," but no science. After repeated inquiries among black professionals, the mother was directed to the head of the science department, who happened to be black. The head of science intervened, and the

2. Interviews took place when parents attended "role model" sessions designed to keep black children in school. Black professionals from throughout the community would talk to parents and their children about their educational and job-related experiences. These sessions rotated from school to school throughout the school year. Dennis Dowdell, who was at that time head of urban affairs for the Carrier Corporation, initiated this program.

daughter successfully completed her science preparatory requirements. Had this girl, with equal ability and the same academic background, been from a low-income family, the likelihood of the parents' being able to negotiate the system would not have been as great.

Black parents and black students often felt that some counselors and teachers perceived black students as being unable to handle college preparatory courses. These students were usually placed in vocational courses, or if they were enrolled in college preparatory courses, the teachers' expectation for them was different than for white students taking the same course. For many black students, especially those from low-income families, a self-perpetuating racial stereotype of what they were unable to achieve existed (Seely 1987d, A12).

*Enrollment Patterns*

The Syracuse black community population made up 16 percent of the city total, yet in 1987 black students made up approximately 35 percent of the city's public-school enrollment (Seely 1987d, A12). Table 9.2 shows that the percentage of black public-school students increased slightly (by 3.1 percent) from 1978–79 to 1984–85. Over this six-year period, the percentage of Hispanic students also increased slightly; however, the percentage of white students decreased.

The percentage of black students in Syracuse public schools increased from 1970, when the black/white student ratio coincided with the racial composition of the city. Increases in the percentage of black students were

**Table 9.2**

**Percentages of the Total Number of Syracuse Public-School Students According to Race, 1978–1985**

| Race | 1978–1979 | 1984–1985 |
|------|-----------|-----------|
| Black | 32.0 | 35.1 |
| Hispanic | 1.5 | 2.2 |
| White | 66.5 | 59.8 |
| Native American | — | 2.8 |

*Source:* Sacks and Sacks 1987, 83.

a result primarily of four factors: (1) an increase in the black population in the city; (2) a decrease in the white population; (3) a higher birth rate of blacks over whites; and (4) an increasing tendency of middle-income families, most of whom were white, to place their children in private schools. In contrast to the Syracuse School District, the seventeen suburban public-school districts within the county ranged from 0 to 5 percent black. Of the private schools, the Catholic school system had the largest enrollment of blacks. Of those attending Catholic schools, 87 percent were white, and 13 percent were black and Hispanic. Approximately 10 percent of Syracuse's black school children and 30 percent of white children attended private schools. (See Seely 1987d, A12.)

Table 9.3 shows the percentage of students by race and grade level in Syracuse public schools. Larger percentages of blacks than of either whites or Hispanics were enrolled in each grade level from nursery school through high school for 1980. Lower percentages of Hispanic students than black students were enrolled in public schools at all grade levels; and higher percentages of Hispanics than of whites were enrolled at all grade levels. Overall, approximately 91 percent of the total number of black students, 80 percent of Hispanic students, and 71 percent of white students were enrolled in the city's public schools.

Table 9.3

Enrollment in Syracuse Public Schools According to Race and Grade Level, 1980

| Grade Level | Black (%) | Hispanic (%) | White (%) | Total (%)* |
|---|---|---|---|---|
| Nursery School | 60.7 | 59.6 | 43.8 | 48.9 |
| Kindergarten | 85.1 | 73.7 | 69.9 | 74.7 |
| Elementary | | | | |
| School | 92.1 | 77.5 | 70.7 | 77.8 |
| High School | 96.5 | 86.8 | 76.5 | 82.6 |
| Total** | 91.1 | 80.4 | 70.8 | 77.3 |

Source: From table in Sacks and Sacks 1987, 82.
*Total percentage of all students in public schools in each grade level.
**Total percentage of students in each racial category in Syracuse public schools.

One of the reasons behind the higher percentage of the total number of black children enrolled in Syracuse public schools was economic. Private schools, even Catholic schools, charged tuition. Although data are not available, observations indicate that upper-income black families were more likely to place their children in private schools than were lower-income blacks, especially through grade eight and with regard to the more prestigious private schools. However, beginning with grade nine, or high school, many upper-income black families sent their children to Nottingham High School. As was mentioned earlier, Syracuse's high school attendance districts were divided into four quadrants. Nottingham served the quadrants where many faculty members and administrators from Syracuse University and Le Moyne College lived, along with other professional families. Nottingham High's graduates were known for their high SAT and ACT scores, National Merit scholars, and college-bound students. Because most upper-income blacks in Syracuse lived in the quadrant served by Nottingham, they sent their children there.

Hispanic students not enrolled in public schools were sent primarily to Catholic schools. White private-school students attended Catholic schools, other religious schools, and nonreligious private schools. It should be kept in mind that relative to other high school quadrants within the public-school system, higher proportions of white high school students from professional families also attended Nottingham High School.

Table 9.4 reveals the total enrollment, the total number of graduates, and the number and percentage of black graduates in Syracuse from 1966 to 1985. The total enrollment decreased from 30,694 in 1966 to 21,012 in 1985, representing a change of -31.4 percent. Breaking out race, black student enrollment (not shown in table 9.4) increased from 5,450 in 1966 to 7,376 in 1985. The percentage change for black student enrollment was +35.3 percent. Nonblack students, however, decreased from 25,244 in 1966 to 13,636 in 1985, a percentage change of -46.3.[3]

Of the 1,603 students who graduated in 1966, 5.2 percent were black. By 1985, the total number of graduates had decreased to 1,045; however, the percentage that was black had increased to 26.2. The disproportionately large

3. *Nonblack* rather than *white* is used because the number of Hispanic and Native American students for 1966 was impossible to ascertain.

Table 9.4

**Enrollment Data for Syracuse Public Schools, 1966–1985: Number and Percentage of Black Graduates**

|      | Total | | Black Graduates | |
|------|------------|-----------|--------|---------------------|
|      | Enrollment | Graduates | Number | % of Total Graduates |
| 1966 | 30,694 | 1,603 | 84  | 5.2  |
| 1967 | 29,967 | 1,638 | 112 | 6.8  |
| 1968 | 29,583 | 1,822 | 155 | 8.5  |
| 1969 | 29,995 | 1,492 | 152 | 10.2 |
| 1970 | 29,368 | 1,660 | 146 | 8.8  |
| 1971 | 28,600 | 1,504 | 185 | 12.3 |
| 1972 | 27,370 | 1,467 | 216 | 14.7 |
| 1973 | 26,715 | 1,427 | 215 | 15.1 |
| 1974 | 26,314 | 1,485 | 237 | 16.0 |
| 1975 | 26,492 | 1,519 | 236 | 15.5 |
| 1976 | 25,343 | 1,463 | 236 | 16.1 |
| 1977 | 23,818 | 1,554 | 341 | 21.9 |
| 1978 | 22,777 | 1,498 | 283 | 18.9 |
| 1979 | 22,361 | 1,329 | 258 | 19.4 |
| 1980 | 21,665 | 1,287 | 327 | 25.4 |
| 1981 | 21,100 | 1,276 | 285 | 22.3 |
| 1982 | 20,901 | 1,274 | 280 | 22.0 |
| 1983 | 20,881 | 1,105 | 262 | 23.7 |
| 1984 | 20,887 | 997   | 245 | 24.6 |
| 1985 | 21,012 | 1,045 | 274 | 26.2 |

Source: Sacks and Sacks 1987, 85.

number of black students relative to the proportion of blacks in the population has already been accounted for in the discussion regarding public versus private schools. Syracuse public-school officials did not envision a predominately black student body in the near future, mainly because of the baby boom among whites (Seely 1987d, A12).

It is difficult to determine the rate of dropouts or the rate of retention because the black population was highly mobile. Syracuse school officials estimated in 1982 that based on school transfers, approximately 50 percent of inner-city black families changed residences at least once during the school year. Table 9.2 indicates that 35.1 percent of the Syracuse public-school enrollment was black in 1984–85. Comparing 35.1 percent with 26.2 percent (table 9.4) of the graduates who were black in 1985 indicates that the percentage of black graduates was not in proportion to the percentage of black students enrolled in Syracuse schools. Although white students made up 59.8 percent (table 9.2) of the total enrollment, they represented 73.8 percent of the graduates. From these data, one might speculate that the dropout rate for blacks surpassed that for whites.

Interviews with black parents further revealed that many children from low-income families where the parent's/parents' educational level was low had a difficult time in school. Various studies have pointed to the myriad reasons offered as explanations for this complex problem (Cloward and Jones 1965; Henderson 1967; Kozol 1967), including reading behind grade level, poor quantitative skills, poor study habits and skills, low teacher expectation, low parental expectation, and negative peer group pressure. All these factors affected dropout rates and student perceptions regarding their ability to succeed.

For Syracuse, statistical data indicate that black students in the 1980s had narrowed the gap between their scores and white students' scores on standardized tests. Using 1985 to 1986 Science Research Associates tests scores as an example, black students, kindergarten through the ninth grade, had scores in mathematics and reading that averaged 10 percentage points less than white students. Average verbal scores for black students were 13 percentage points below the national average. However, the 1985 to 1986 verbal scores for black students had improved over the 1980 verbal scores, which were 17 percentage points below the national average (Seely 1987d, A12).

Low-income parents indicated that assignments given children in grades four and higher frequently exceeded their own level of understanding, particularly in mathematics, sciences, and English. Furthermore, they revealed that they often felt threatened by the students' request for assistance when the assignment was beyond the parents' comprehension. The parents, not wanting to reveal that they did not know the answer or fearing that they might be wrong, told the child not to bother them with such nonsense. Such a response was counterproductive to the efforts made by teachers and helped to program children for an early failure and an eventual dropout.

In contrast, a black professional mother told the story of her daughter who was taking a course in computer science. Neither the mother, a law student, nor the father, with a master's degree in social work, understood the assignments in the computer course and were unable to help their daughter. To help her daughter, the mother sought out her white next-door neighbor, whose son was in the same class and doing well. The neighbor admitted to not understanding the assignments, but told the black mother that an engineer down the block had been helping her son. The black mother contacted the engineer, and he agreed to help her daughter along with her neighbor's son. Both children did well in the computer course. This story raises a crucial difference between the circumstances for children from educated professional families and those for children from low-income families. Where is the engineer in inner-city or poor neighborhoods?

Such illustrations help to shed light on the differences in dropout rates between black and white students in Syracuse. Higher dropout rates for black students than for white students have had an effect on educational attainment in the black community. It should be remembered that a large proportion of the pre–civil rights era blacks who migrated to Syracuse were rural southern laborers with little education and few skills. With their children and their children's children dropping out of school, a vicious cycle of poverty had developed in the black community and was being perpetuated during the 1980s. Approximately 20 percent of all black students who entered grade nine in 1981 did not graduate (compared to 16 percent of white students for the same year). Of the black students who entered Syracuse schools, two out of five graduated, two out of five transferred to other school districts, and one out of five dropped out (Seely 1987d, A12). These statistics show that there was a relationship between dropping out and doing well in school.

## Parental Assessment of the Public-School System

The Syracuse Urban League study (Stamps 1982) also surveyed the assessment of Syracuse public schools by parents with school-age children in 1981.[4]

*Attitudes*

Respondents' attitudes toward various aspects of public education in 1981 are presented in table 9.5. There were significant differences in attitudes toward student discipline,[5] with a higher percentage of other minorities having more favorable attitudes than blacks or whites; in the other two groups, 41.8 percent of blacks and 39.6 percent of whites felt student discipline was not very good. However, for each racial group, the highest percentage felt student discipline was good.

Among those who felt that efforts made by school officials and teachers to prevent students from dropping out was not very good, blacks had the highest percentage (39.0), in comparison to 34 percent of whites. However, approximately 38 percent of both black and white respondents felt the efforts of school officials at preventing dropping out were good, and 61.9 percent of the other minorities felt likewise.

A sizable proportion of each group stated they did not have any attitudes concerning the prevention of dropouts. Approximately 48 percent of whites had negative attitudes toward the school system's treatment of misbehavior, followed by approximately 38 percent of blacks and only 10 percent of other minorities. In actuality, 85.8 percent of other minorities had positive attitudes toward dealing with misbehavior. More than 60 percent of each group had positive attitudes toward school personnel's effort to improve attendance. Only one-fourth of the black and white respondents indicated negative attitudes toward attendance efforts.

4. These data derived from the Urban League study (Stamps 1982).

5. In the study, *student discipline* referred to more serious behavioral problems (fighting, etc.) and *misbehaving* to less serious behavioral problems (talking in class, etc.).

**Table 9.5**

**Syracuse Parents' Attitudes Toward Efforts Made by School Personnel According to Race, 1981**

| | Black (N = 232) | | | | White (N = 53) | | | | Other Minorities (N = 21) | | | |
|---|---|---|---|---|---|---|---|---|---|---|---|---|
| | Very Good | Good | Not Very Good | Do Not Know | Very Good | Good | Not Very Good | Do Not Know | Very Good | Good | Not Very Good | Do Not Know |
| Toward Student Discipline | 9.5 | 43.5 | 41.8 | 5.2 | 9.4 | 47.2 | 39.6 | 3.8 | — | 66.7 | 14.3 | 19.0 |
| Toward Preventing Dropouts | 9.1 | 37.7 | 39.0 | 14.3 | 11.3 | 37.7 | 34.0 | 17.0 | 4.8 | 61.9 | 23.8 | 9.5 |
| Toward Dealing with Misbehavior | 9.5 | 42.2 | 37.9 | 10.3 | 5.8 | 36.5 | 48.1 | 9.6 | 4.8 | 81.0 | 9.5 | 4.8 |
| Toward Improving Attendance | 10.8 | 52.6 | 28.0 | 8.6 | 11.5 | 50.0 | 23.1 | 15.4 | 23.8 | 47.6 | 19.0 | 9.5 |

Source: Stamps 1982, 94–96.

Note: $X^2$ = significant at the .05 level with 6 df.

*Perceptions*

Table 9.6 provides insight as to how these respondents perceived specific aspects of public education in Syracuse in 1981. As was the case with attitudes toward efforts made by school personnel, other minorities, in higher percentages than blacks or whites, had favorable perceptions concerning the quality of buildings, teachers, equipment, and facilities. Higher percentages of blacks than whites had negative perceptions of the quality of buildings (21.6 to 15.1) and of teachers (15.6 to 9.4); however, high percentages (greater than 70) of each of these two groups had favorable perceptions of both these aspects of the educational system.

A little more than 21 percent of white parents perceived instruction as very good; approximately 66 percent of blacks perceived it as good. On the other end of the continuum, 33.3 percent of other minorities, 21.2 percent of whites, and 18.2 percent of blacks perceived instruction as not very good. Perception of school officials' efforts to inform parents of children's progress resulted was identical among all three groups. Approximately one-fourth of each group perceived the efforts as very good, approximately one-half as good, and the other one-fourth as not very good. Last, table 9.6 reveals these respondents' perception regarding "how well school officials received parents during visits to schools." Eighty percent or more of each group had positive perceptions concerning being made welcome by school officials.

As stated, the impact of integration on black students remained debatable. Furthermore, some evidence was provided to support the contention that black students from professional families seemed to profit more from integration in Syracuse than did those from low-income families (Ginzberg and Associates 1968). The discussion of parents' attitudes and perceptions toward education in the Syracuse system throws some light on how parents were responding to an integrated school system. Although a direct question concerning attitudes toward integration was not asked, table 9.7 shows some indication of overall attitudes toward the school system.

These respondents gave public education in Syracuse good marks overall. In reviewing table 9.7, it can be noted that 75.4 percent of whites were either very satisfied or satisfied with the education of their child/children; 79.5 percent of blacks were either very satisfied or satisfied with the education of their

Table 9.6

Syracuse Parents' Attitudes Toward Efforts to Provide Quality Education According to Race, 1981

| | Black (N = 232) | | | | White (N = 53) | | | | Other Minorities (N = 21) | | | |
|---|---|---|---|---|---|---|---|---|---|---|---|---|
| | Very Good | Good | Not Very Good | Do Not Know | Very Good | Good | Not Very Good | Do Not Know | Very Good | Good | Not Very Good | Do Not Know |
| School Buildings | 15.1 | 56.5 | 21.6 | 6.9 | 20.8 | 62.8 | 15.1 | 1.9 | 9.5 | 71.4 | 14.3 | 4.8 |
| Teacher Training and Expertise* | 12.1 | 61.9 | 15.6 | 10.4 | 28.3 | 56.6 | 9.4 | 5.7 | 4.8 | 71.4 | 19.0 | 4.8 |
| Equipment and Facilities** | 12.8 | 61.9 | 17.3 | 8.0 | 24.5 | 58.5 | 15.1 | 1.0 | 19.0 | 66.7 | 4.8 | 9.5 |
| Instruction | 11.3 | 65.8 | 18.2 | 4.8 | 21.2 | 57.7 | 21.2 | — | 9.5 | 52.4 | 33.3 | 4.8 |
| Efforts to Inform of Child's Progress | 24.3 | 48.7 | 22.6 | 3.9 | 26.4 | 47.2 | 24.5 | 1.9 | 23.8 | 47.6 | 23.8 | 4.9 |
| Receptivity to Parents' Visit*** | 24.5 | 55.0 | 11.8 | 8.7 | 28.3 | 58.5 | 11.3 | 1.9 | 21.1 | 73.7 | 5.3 | — |

Source: Stamps 1982, 98–102.

*X² = significant at the .05 level with 6 df.

**Black (N = 226), White (N = 53), Other Minorities (N = 21).

***Black (N = 229), White (N = 53), Other Minorities (N = 19).

**Table 9.7**

**Syracuse Parents' Satisfaction with Child's Education According to Race,** *
**1981**

| Satisfaction Level | Black (%) (N = 229) | White (%) (N = 53) | Other Minorities (%) (N = 21) |
|---|---|---|---|
| Very Satisfied | 15.7 | 24.5 | 23.8 |
| Satisfied | 63.8 | 50.9 | 66.7 |
| Not Satisfied | 18.3 | 24.5 | 9.5 |
| Don't Know | 2.2 | — | — |

*Source:* Stamps 1982, 103.
*Not significant.

child/children. Other minorities were generally more favorable, with more than 90 percent indicating that they were very satisfied or satisfied.

*Suspension/Expulsion*

In table 9.8, it can be seen that a higher percentage of blacks (22.5) than of whites (13.2) or other minorities (10.5) stated in 1981 that their children had been suspended from school. The differences were even greater for expulsion, whereby 12.6 percent of blacks but only 3.8 percent of whites stated their children had been expelled. None of the minorities stated their children had been expelled. Because the questions related to suspension and expulsion did not inquire about a specific time period, it was impossible to determine if the suspension/expulsion rates were recent phenomena or had always occurred. In 1987, a study of freshmen students attending public schools revealed a higher suspension rate for black students than for white students. Although blacks made up only 38 percent of the freshman class within the Syracuse school system, 45 percent of those suspended were black (Seely 1987d, A12).

The national Black Pulse study revealed that "24 percent of the black parents of school age children reported that at least one of their children had been suspended from school" (National Urban League 1980b, 3). In the Syracuse Urban League study (Stamps 1982), suspensions and expulsions were related

**Table 9.8**

**Suspensions and Expulsions According to Race,\* 1981**

| Suspensions and Expulsions | Black (%) (N = 231) | | White (%) (N = 53) | | Other Minorities (%) (N = 19) | |
|---|---|---|---|---|---|---|
| | *Yes* | *No* | *Yes* | *No* | *Yes* | *No* |
| Children Ever Suspended? | 22.5 | 77.5 | 13.2 | 86.8 | 10.5 | 89.5 |
| Children Ever Expelled? | 12.6 | 87.4 | 3.8 | 96.2 | — | 100.0 |

*Source:* Stamps 1982, 105–6.

\*Not significant.

to income, with low-income households of both races indicating disproportionately higher incidences of both. Although the Black Pulse study found suspensions to be related to income, it also found that 18 percent of the households with incomes of $20,000 a year or more had children who had been suspended (National Urban League 1980b, 3–4). Raymond Vowell (1977), commissioner of the Texas Department of Public Welfare, stated in the late 1970s, "The hickory stick is gone, but the use of suspension in [public] schools has reached mammoth proportions. Figures show that in a recent school year, school districts with a little over one-half of the student population in this country suspended more than one million children. These suspensions represented a loss of more than four million school days and 22,000 school years."

Although suspensions and expulsions were used in Syracuse and nationwide to combat discipline problems, it should be kept in mind that oftentimes during the suspension no learning took place. Society views suspension as a serious punishment that gives students a negative image. Many black parents in Syracuse felt that the high dropout rate among black students was a result, in part, of the relatively high rate of suspensions.

Respondents were asked in 1981 how often they discussed progress in school with their children. Table 9.9 reveals that more than 50 percent of both black and white respondents stated they had daily discussions of school progress with their children. For other minorities, 47.1 percent of the parents

Table 9.9

**Discussions with Child about Progress in School According to Race,\* 1980**

| Frequency of Parent/Child Discussion of School Progress | Black (%) (N = 226) | White (%) (N = 53) | Other Minorities (%) (N = 19) |
|---|---|---|---|
| Every Day | 51.3 | 52.8 | 47.4 |
| 2 or 3 Times a Week | 21.2 | 24.5 | 21.2 |
| Once a Week | 12.4 | 11.3 | 26.3 |
| 1–2 Times a Month | 8.8 | 11.3 | — |
| Once a Month or Less | 6.2 | — | 5.3 |

*Source:* Stamps 1982, 107.
\*Not significant.

indicated that they had discussions with their child/children every day. The major difference based on race was the 6.2 percent blacks and the 5.3 percent other minorities who discussed school progress only once a month or less. Although this difference is not significant, it does seem that a slightly higher percentage of whites discuss school progress with their children more frequently than do blacks.

**Summary**

Educating blacks in Syracuse posed myriad problems during the 1980s. Not only was the dropout rate for blacks high relative to that of other students, but the relatively high rate of expulsions and suspensions seemed to be a contributing factor, especially for black students. Only a disappointingly few black students excelled in school or were enrolled in college preparatory classes. On the more positive side of the educational spectrum, some improvement was seen in the education of blacks in that scores on standardized tests in verbal and quantitative areas improved.

Probably one of the strongest areas of influence for blacks in education was that of making policy. By 1985, three of the seven positions on the Syracuse School Board were filled by blacks. Although blacks had been represented on the school board since 1967, when Mrs. Helen Murphy, wife of the pastor of a leading black church was appointed and then replaced by Robert Warr, also black, their representation had never reached the 1985 level.

One other dimension of education that appeared to be problematic for blacks needs mentioning: the involvement of blacks in the educational decision-making process in the schools themselves. Improvement was seen during the 1980s in the number of black administrators in the public-school system and in the number of blacks serving on the school board. In 1985, Lorraine Myrrick was promoted to executive deputy superintendent, making her second in command and the highest-ranking black since Sidney Johnson served as superintendent (1977 to 1980). Approximately 25 percent of all administrators were black during the mid-1980s, four of whom held positions in the central administration. The 25 percent black administrators represented a significant increase over the 9 percent during Sidney Johnson's tenure. Major problems related to personnel were the recruitment and retention of black classroom teachers. The percentage of black teachers in the Syracuse school system had remained practically constant since the late 1960s.

Although a problem, recruiting black teachers was not as serious as their retention once recruited. Syracuse University, with a large teacher-training program, did not play a major role in the training of local black teachers. Most local blacks who entered Syracuse University's teacher-training program did so to gain postbaccalaureate training or in-service training. Local youth who went away to college did not return to Syracuse, including those who completed teacher-training programs. Unable to draw black teachers from the local community, school officials had to go beyond Syracuse in their search for black teachers. There were three major sources of black teacher recruits: spouses of black professionals hired within the corporate sector or within higher education, single blacks recruited from New York City, and recruits from predominantly black colleges and universities who were also usually single. It was difficult to retain them, though. Spouses of black corporate professionals and black professors tended to move within three to five years because their spouses were transferred elsewhere or better opportunities arose. Recruits from New York City did not like the "small-town" atmosphere of upstate New York and refused to stay. Those recruited from black colleges and universities, most of whom were located in the South, did not readily become acclimated to the cold and snowy winters of upstate New York. Recruits from Texas, North Carolina, and Florida gave the severe winters, feelings of isolation, and the lack of social activities for the young and single as reasons that weighed heavily in their decision to leave.

Education can be seen as an important ingredient in the black community's attempt to reach economic stability. As American society continued its transition from an industrial base to an information base, education became more and more important for those entering the job market. For communities such as the Syracuse black community, a large segment of whose population was originally derived from the rural South and came with few skills and little education, the future lay with the education of its youth. That future did not seem very promising. Those black Syracuse youths who were progressing educationally in the 1980s seemed to be almost entirely from professional families. However, most black youth came from low-income homes, and they, unlike their counterparts from professional families, were not faring well educationally. The most dysfunctional aspect of the educational process for these youth was the fact that many had "come to accept and anticipate failure" (Seely 1987d, A12).

# 10

# The Syracuse Black Community

*A Final Note*

## The Black Community in Retrospect

AS THE 1980S CAME TO A CLOSE, the Syracuse black community had changed significantly in its outlook and in its vision for the future. The community's growth and development from its inception in the early 1800s through the 1980s had depended heavily on external influences. Although blacks played a major role during the period of defiance in their participation in the Underground Railroad, which brought many southern slaves north and into cities such as Syracuse, white antislavery supporters also played a significant role in this period. As the period of exploitation followed, blacks played a lesser role in the direction taken by their community. External forces became more relevant as the white community attempted to exploit blacks economically and politically. Relationships of exploitation laid the foundation for the period of segregation, when the black community was physically separated from the white community. Even though blacks conceived of the idea of a recreational center that became known as the Dunbar Center, forces external to the community initiated and sustained the center because of the community's lack of power and resources. It is clear that the influence of segregation had a lasting effect on the community's growth and development.

It was not until the black community, spurred by local housing and economic conditions, joined in the national protest movement in the 1960s that factors within it began to play a major role in its growth and development. It became apparent that only through conflict would blacks be able to play a primary role in the direction their community would take.

The point being made is that from the time the first blacks arrived in Syracuse until the late 1960s, there were only two time periods when blacks played significant roles in the growth and development of their community: when the Underground Railroad was functional and during the time of protest. Most significant, both periods were characterized by conflict. With the end of the Civil War, the Underground Railroad ceased to function, and when the protest movement ran its course, internal factors diminished in influence.

During the aftermath of the protest movement, in the period from 1968 through the early 1980s, when Syracuse and the nation went through an economic downturn, members of the black community came to realize that their so-called gains of the late 1960s had eroded or had been only an illusion of progress. Frustration spread almost as soon as the local protest movement began to lose momentum. The black masses, whose level of expectation was heightened through legislation such as President Johnson's Great Society programs, affirmative action, and state-mandated fair housing, quickly perceived that they were being left behind. Only blacks with education, strong work skills, and economic resources were able to take advantage of the new economic and employment opportunities. Furthermore, as these professional blacks moved into Syracuse, they either settled in suburban communities or joined the few professional blacks already settled on the east side of the city. The outcome was that they were virtually isolated from the black masses—those with weaker work skills, less education, and a lack of economic resources.

The level of frustration evident among the masses was understandable. However, black professionals, those who supposedly had reaped the benefits of the protest movement, began to recognize in themselves a creeping sense of concern. Their own sense of frustration increased as they found career advancement beyond certain levels blocked, faced hostility from white male colleagues who perceived black progress as an impediment to their own career advancement, and began to see whites who had fought for civil rights less than a decade earlier turn inward and become concerned with their own group and their own personal well-being.

To the dismay of blacks both locally and nationally, a candidate in the 1980 presidential election who made it clear during the campaign that he was not a strong advocate of civil rights legislation was not only elected, but became one of America's most popular presidents. Yet not once during his eight years in office did Ronald Regan meet with black congressional leaders or with national black leaders. Although national political decisions made by the Reagan administration delighted hawks, conservatives, big business, high-income families, and those less enamored with civil rights, blacks of all socioeconomic status witnessed an erosion in their opportunity structure. Poor blacks in disproportionately higher degrees felt the effects of Reaganism.

Although Reaganism represented national politics, the decisions made and the climate it set cut to the core of local black communities such as the one in Syracuse. Exacerbating the economic situation was a movement that had already begun before Reagan's first term of office: the transition of the American economy from an industrial base to a high-technology and information base. As discussed in chapter 8, the Syracuse black community was more adversely affected by the move away from industrial jobs than was the larger community because of its overdependence on those jobs. Working-class and lower-middle-class black families, in disproportionately higher numbers than white families of the same class status, found themselves in a tenuous economic position resulting from job insecurity or job displacement (W. Wilson 1996a, 1996b). These families were the backbone of the Syracuse black community and had enjoyed economic stability during the 1960s and 1970s.

As blacks in Syracuse pondered this state of affairs, their first reaction was to look to white liberals who had come to the rescue during the civil rights era of the 1960s. However, it soon became apparent in Syracuse that blacks were on their own, so black political leaders, working through Jesse Jackson's Rainbow Coalition, organized another new political leadership organization called the Black Leadership Congress. If there was one feature that characterized black leadership in Syracuse, it was the number of leadership organizations started throughout the community's history. Where earlier leadership organizations had not been able to bring blacks together, the Black Leadership Congress had some success in registering voters, networking with black political aspirants, and forming coalitions with local political parties. Its major goal was to attain political empowerment and to translate that empowerment into economic gains. Up until the 1980s, when blacks in Syracuse sought political office, the goal had been the office itself or at the very least the ability to divert public funds and jobs created with public funds to the black community. The new thrust that emerged in the 1980s conceived a connection between political power and private economic advantages. As the 1980s came to a close, this goal had not been reached. With the Reagan-appointed Supreme Court overturning set-aside programs and fair-share economic projects, the ability to attain such a goal was severely curtailed. Despite these obstacles, the direction for Syracuse blacks in achieving political and economic progress had been chartered. What remained was an identification of specific avenues to implement the move toward progress.

## The Syracuse Black Community and Progress

In the 1980s, one factor stood out clearly in the minds of black people on the street, professionals, and leaders: that their future would depend in large part on the black community itself. Recognition that the community would have to take a leadership role in its quest for political and economic progress was a first step. Putting into place measures to implement progress was a difficult next step.

Implementing progress is particularly difficult for collectives of individuals such as the Syracuse black community or black communities in general. Individuals by themselves can plan more easily and move toward accomplishing identifiable goals. The same can be said for formalized groups or even institutions. Although a racial or ethnic community represents a collectivity of people held together by a similar history, individual goals might not be in the best interest of collective goals. In a formalized group or institution, when individual goal attainment interferes with attainment of the group or institutional goal, the behavior is labeled deviant, and the individual can be expelled or coerced into behavior that supports the formalized group or institutional goal. Except in extreme circumstances such as law violation, the same cannot be done within collectivities. Therefore, individual behavior or subgroup behavior can be functional or dysfunctional to the group's collective goals. Looking at racial or ethnic communities, one might say that the goal of economic stability can be attained through consumer support of businesses owned by members of certain racial or ethnic groups. In such a case, when individuals, say blacks, purchase goods from black-owned businesses, they support the community's collective goal. But when the individual goal of being the best dressed among one's peers necessitates purchasing clothes at the top fashion stores that happen not to be black owned, the individual goal can be looked on as dysfunctional to the group's collective goal.

In order for an analysis of individual and group goals to be beneficial, certain prerequisites should be in place, such as comparable outlets for satisfying individual and subgroup goals internally and externally. That is, the individual goal of being best dressed can be attained by purchasing clothes at black- or nonblack-owned stores. Otherwise, the focus of the analysis is on individual or subgroup goal denial or sacrifice in the attainment of collective group goals. A community such as the Syracuse black community that traditionally depended on external influences in its growth and development and had only recently recognized the importance of internal influences would be at the stage of developing prerequisites for competition politically and economically. Political prerequisites can include black candidates running for office and coalition building, thereby offering support to black or white candidates committed to the group's concerns. And the use of public office would provide group equity. Economic prerequisites might include black entrepreneurship or black businesses that provide buying alternatives, financial institutions with loan policies geared toward the black community, and jobs generated by institutions within the black community.

Given this background discussion, this chapter is devoted to an assessment of the black community based on prerequisites for competition. The position taken here is that when the community began to recognize that its future depended on internal influences or black self-help programs, it had taken the first step toward controlling its growth and development. The next step would be to build prerequisites for competition within political and economic arenas. The final step in attaining political and economic stability would be competition to make available comparable alternatives.

In order for political and economic prerequisites to materialize within the Syracuse black community, strides have to be made in the areas of education and technical skill development, family stability, expansion and stability of the professional class, financial development, entrepreneurship, and coalition building. We offer an assessment of the community's past, present, and future in these areas. It should be kept in mind that the emphasis is on internal influences more so than on external influences—in other words, on the black

community's former and future potential to generate its own political and economic prerequisites of competition within the larger Syracuse community.

**Education and Technical Skill Development**

Programs geared toward providing role models for students from disadvantaged backgrounds were started by Alpha Phi Alpha fraternity and Carrier
Corporation in the late 1970s and early 1980s. The Carrier program, started
by Dennis Dowdell, a black executive, involved young black professionals
who met regularly with school-age children and their families and shared
their educational and occupational experiences. Many of these young black
professionals came from similar disadvantaged backgrounds and were able to
recount the obstacles they had to overcome in their quest for success. Black
children and their families were able to relate to these success stories because
they were facing many similar problems.

The Alpha Phi Alpha program was similar to Carrier's except the focus
was more on encouraging black youth to identify professional occupations in
which they might have an interest and to prepare them educationally to enter
these professions. Both the Alpha Phi Alpha and Carrier programs stressed
the rewards of staying in school and studying.

People's Equal Action and Community Effort, Inc. (PEACE), which
has been in existence since 1977 in Syracuse, has had eight neighborhood
community centers, and has played a vital educational role through its administration of Head Start. In 1988, Head Start provided assistance to more
than 510 low-income families with such programs as early childhood education, health services, nutrition, social-service intervention, and services to
disabled children. One of the more innovative programs run through Head
Start was the training and employment of parents of children in the program.
Approximately 20 percent of the parents of Head Start children worked in a
variety of jobs within the program in 1988 (PEACE 1988). PEACE focused its
efforts away from emergency assistance and toward the development of skills
in the young and in adults.

With one-half of the Syracuse's black residents in 1980 twenty-one years
of age or younger and the unemployment rate for black teenagers at 26 percent, efforts such as those just described were crucial to the future economic

viability of the black community. In 1987, an Economic Development Zone was established on the west side of the city, consisting of neighborhoods with some of the highest unemployment rates within Syracuse. Plans in this externally developed project called for extensive job-training and literacy programs within the catchment area (City of Syracuse 1987), for an overall positive impact on the future of the Syracuse black community. Unfortunately, establishing an economic development zone has not brought about the desired results. Attempts are still being made to improve the area and the quality of life for its citizens.

## Family Stability

In addition to the Head Start program described earlier, PEACE ran other programs geared toward family assistance: housing relocation and preservation, job placement, distribution of government food, and emergency clothing. The expectation was that PEACE, with its focus on the family and its extensive coverage of Syracuse, would be able to assist the black community in helping itself.

The Economic Develop Zone (City of Syracuse 1987) had as a major objective the reduction of overcrowded housing, the number of female-headed households under the poverty line, and unemployment and crime. Each of these social problems was highly correlated with family instability. Better skills, higher levels of education, employment, and better housing conditions often meant more stable families. However, unstable families were still a major problem in the black community as the 1980s came to an end.

## Financial Development

*Financial development* here refers to the development of financial institutions controlled by the black community. Attempts had been made since early 1980 to start a credit union in the community. The Syracuse Neighborhood Federal Credit Union, located on the south side of the city, had been slow to grow. Although started in 1980, it suffered from visibility problems. Many southside neighborhood residents were still unaware of its existence as the 1980s came to an end. However, a financial institution such as a local credit union can play a key role in the future viability of the community.

It has long been realized in the Syracuse black community that the black church was in a position to play a pivotal role in the establishment of a black-controlled financial institution. It represented the one institution that was black controlled and that controlled money. When a black church deposited funds outside of the black community, two dysfunctional outcomes occurred: (1) those funds were recirculated outside of the black community, and (2) the church membership was encouraged to continue using nonblack financial institutions. We noted in chapter 8 the fact that black businesses encountered difficulties in securing loans from Syracuse banks and other financial institutions. Compounding the problem was the accusation made by the local Urban League affiliates that these financial institutions disinvested in inner-city neighborhoods.

By depositing funds in a black-controlled financial institution, black churches would be serving their inner-city membership. By investing in inner-city communities and black businesses, black financial institutions would help in recirculating money within the community. As the 1980s came to a close, however, money entered and immediately left the black community.

Assisting the Syracuse Neighborhood Federal Credit Union by joining it or establishing a financial institution in the black community was an area where black professionals could have played a major role. With their advanced education, financial skills, and knowledge, even black professionals who were located in suburban communities or lived in east-side integrated neighborhoods were presented with an opportunity to contribute to the growth and development of the black community by supporting black financial institutions.

However, as the 1980s came to a close, the prospects of building a financial base through the establishment of a viable financial institution seemed bleak. Neither black professionals nor black churches seemed inclined to support a black-controlled financial institution.

**Entrepreneurial Efforts**

Whereas the future looked bleak for the establishment of a viable black financial institution, black entrepreneurship showed more promise in the 1980s. This decade gave rise to some new black businesses. By 1986, *Black Enterprise* ranked Bill Scott's Oldsmobile dealership as the tenth most profitable black-owned automobile dealership in the United States ("List of the Top 100 Black Businesses" 1987). In 1987, Bill Scott Oldsmobile was sold to another black, allowing the black community to continue ownership of one of Syracuse's leading automobile dealerships and businesses in general. In 1987, a new McDonald's franchise was obtained by a black, and Metallon Paint Corporation, a black-owned business, was expanded (Seely 1987a). On a less optimistic note, small black-owned businesses faced major obstacles in their attempts to secure financial assistance.

In the 1980s, the promise of black entrepreneurship was closely tied to the Enterprise Assistance Center and the Economic Development Zone designed by the New York State Economic Development Zone Program. Previously called the Syracuse Minority Business Development Center, the Enterprise Assistance Center was started in 1982 by the Human Rights Council of Onondaga County. With funding from the city and county, the Enterprise Assistance Center (the new name by 1987) acted as a resource office for minority- and women-owned businesses. The center referred them to the appropriate agency for technical assistance. In 1988, when Syracuse received New York State approval to establish the Economic Development Zone, or catchment area, the Enterprise Assistance Center was one of the first agencies to set up an office in the area. Both the center and the zone had as a major objective the creation of new jobs within the catchment area by increasing the number of businesses located in the zone. By providing capitalization assistance, tax breaks, utility fee reductions, technical assistance, and job-training programs for residents of the area, Syracuse hoped to attract small businesses and light industries to the catchment area. Leadership within the black community viewed these efforts as an opportunity for black entrepreneurship. Support services in the form of day-care facilities, housing rehabilitation, and increased police and fire protection were provided. Although a strong infrastructure was what made the area attractive for development, street and bridge reconstruction and recreation development were part of the package (City of Syracuse 1987).

The catchment area was located near the (downtown) west side. Although this area contained a heterogeneous population of white, blacks, Hispanics, and Native Americans, the high percentage of white-owned businesses already in the area and the growing number of Hispanic-owned businesses caused many members of the black community concern (Seely 1987a). Blacks questioned the benefit to the black community. Although blacks were represented in the catchment area, the largest proportion of the black population had settled on the south side of the city.

The concern was not that blacks would not benefit economically, for gains would be made through job-training programs and day care. Rather, it was that without black-owned businesses, external control of the black community would merely continue.

## Professional Expansion and Stability

One of the major problems traditionally facing the Syracuse black community was the lack of homegrown professionals and of stability within its black professional class. Young people from the home community who entered college, usually an out-of-town institution, most often did not return to the community. What this meant was that the professional class depended in large part on a transient professional population. Black professionals entered the black community or the metropolitan area, but remained only a relatively short period of time, before being relocated. As pointed out in chapter 6, most of these professionals lived in suburban communities during their stay in the area and participated only superficially in the black community or in Syracuse affairs. They physically resided in the Syracuse metropolitan area, but they were not a significant part of community activities.

As the 1980s came to a close, two trends emerged that were factors in the projected stability of black professionals in Syracuse. First, an increasing number of local black high school graduates were attending area institutions of higher education. It was hoped that some of these college graduates would remain within the area.

Probably of greater consequence was the establishment of Inroads, Inc., which had thirty-six affiliates nationally in 1989. This privately funded program for college students provided internships at local sponsoring corporations. The Syracuse affiliate was started in 1986 with thirteen firms sponsoring eighteen minority college-bound interns. By 1989, the number of interns had increased to thirty-six, and the number of participating firms had risen to twenty-one. This program was designed to place talented minority college students into careers with local corporations in the areas of business and industry (Inroads 1988). By matching students with corporate sponsors, Inroads provided an opportunity for minority students to intern for pay each summer, starting with high school graduation and continuing through college graduation.

The Inroads program was extremely important to the black community, which traditionally lost its college-educated youth because of a perception that occupational opportunities were not available to them in Syracuse. Increases in the number of black professionals in Syracuse had been almost totally derived from outsiders' relocations to the city. Inroads represented a first step in attracting second-generation local black professionals to remain in Syracuse. Approximately 66 percent of the participating minority youth took jobs with corporate sponsors nationally in 1989.

In the 1980s, as the Syracuse black community attempted to build prerequisites for competition politically and economically, an enlarged black professional group was needed that was committed to its growth and development. As is so often the case with professionals who are in transit, they know their stay is short-lived, so they do not become active members of the community. The attempt by the black community to generate a black professional class from within its own ranks would benefit it politically and economically.

## Coalition Building

During the 1970s, black political aspirants in Syracuse began a move toward coalition building with liberal whites. These often fragile unions usually developed in cases when there was not a strong white candidate within the Democratic or Republican Party. When strong liberal white candidates emerged in either party or there was a white incumbent, blacks found that their attempts at coalition building or gaining support did not prosper. As the 1980s came to a close, black political candidates received mixed signals from the two major political parties. A black female candidate for judge ran on the Republican ticket in competition with an incumbent black Democratic judge and three white candidates. Despite the black community's fears, both black candidates won. During this same period, black potential candidates were constantly challenged when they presented the required signatures to get on the ballot as Independents after being rejected as a party candidate. Black party faithfuls faced stiff competition from white party members when they ran in the primary in districts with sizable black populations. The black political stance shifted from low participation in the late 1970s and early 1980s to a significant increase in the proportion registered and that actually voted with the entrance of Jesse Jackson's Rainbow Coalition into the community. However, the increase in the black vote was not sustained over time, but rose and fell as the black voting population responded to the presence of black candidates or the lack thereof.

Coalition building was introduced when blacks first entered into the political arena. With a small black population in Syracuse, an even smaller proportion actually voted. Black candidates therefore needed support from outside the black community. Coalition building became a necessity if they expected to win. Early coalitions were developed primarily within political parties as black hopefuls joined in with more liberal members of their respective party. Jackson's Rainbow Coalition introduced a new element in coalition building in Syracuse in that the base of the political alliance was expanded. It attempted to attract individuals, regardless of party affiliation or race, who were faced with or were concerned about common problems such as unemployment, poor housing, poor health care, and general alienation.

## The Amorality of American Society

Black communities and their leaders will have to recognize that education as well as economic and political policies and actions have traditionally been driven by amoral principles. They have continually used rationales based on moral principles to justify economic and political equity, yet the decision makers in power and their public-policy statements have addressed amoral rather than moral concerns, particularly relating to race relations. From the time the first African slaves arrived on American soil in the sixteenth century until the civil rights movement in the 1960s, the growth and development of black communities was generated by amoral principles and policies, Christian and Puritan efforts notwithstanding (DuBois 1899). Even the Emancipation

Proclamation signed by President Abraham Lincoln, which freed the slaves, did not constitute a shift from amoral to moral principles because it was not predicated on a Christian or democratic ethic, but was made by the Union in an attempt to gain support from European nations. Only the Confederacy was affected; slavery within border states remained in effect until passage of the Thirteenth Amendment to the Constitution in 1865 (Schaefer 1988).

Black businesses, churches, schools, and healthcare facilities that flourished within black communities during the era of segregation, although providing positive individual outcomes, were also generated by amoral principles and policies. Only during the civil rights era, when the conflict between the races came to the forefront, did moral principles emerge that affected public policy. Even then, without international issues and technological advances in mass communication, it is highly unlikely that the protest emanating from the black community would have been buttressed from the outside by moral concerns (Marger 1994). The civil rights era represented nationally, as it did locally in Syracuse, the first time black communities brought about significant changes for themselves. Although external factors played a major role in the public policies passed during this period, external influences were secondary to internal influences in the conflict generated by the protest movement itself.

As the civil rights and Black Power eras came to a standstill with diminished conflict, amoral principles again began to influence public policy. Because these amoral principles were not tied to an overt base of racism as had been the case before the civil rights era, black communities and black leaders waited patiently for moral principles to again overcome amoral principles. However, the "baby boom" generation, that massive demographic anomaly that followed World War II, had come of age to work, vote, and influence public policy.

As this generation came of age, what Christopher Lasch (1978) called the "culture of narcissism" or the "me generation" emerged within American society. This group cared little about moral principles related to race relations or equity in general. And, if there was concern, it certainly was not to the degree that moral principles would override their concern with themselves and their own ambitions and comforts. Four factors present within American society had a significant influence on the emergence of the "me generation" and hence on the reemergence of amoral principles to guide public policies, in particular those related to race relations. The precipitating factor was the downturn in economic prosperity that had existed in American society from the conclusion of World War II until the early 1970s. As the economic pie became smaller, individuals who had come to expect a certain lifestyle that was now being threatened became concerned with themselves. They perceived that society would not be able to financially support programs for minorities and the poor and at the same time continue to provide the prosperous lifestyle that they themselves had come to take for granted (Stamps 1988). A second related factor was that as this age group expanded the labor pool, competition increased on all levels. For example, post–World War II workers who entered the workforce had experienced accelerated upward occupational mobility until around 1975. By 1975, however, it was estimated that, on the average, there were ten midlevel career candidates for every vacancy. By the mid-1980s, it was estimated that there were from eighteen to twenty midlevel candidates for every vacancy (Snyder and Edwards 1984). A third factor was that as competition for jobs increased, many baby boomers perceived that their stymied occupational mobility was affected by social-justice public policies such as affirmative action, education grants, minority set-aside programs, and so on. These policies had been generated by moral principles geared toward correcting past wrongs. Most important, creating the fourth factor, baby boomers were not immune to racist ideas and assumptions. Their parents, grandparents, and ancestors, for the most part, had been supporters of amoral principles that had buttressed race relations in America before the civil rights era. Although racism had become more covert in society, its seeds were still in place. It only needed an administration led by an indifferent president for it to reemerge. When public policies generated by moral principles were attacked and morality redefined, the ground was plowed for amoral principles to grow and again assume a primary role in determining public policy oriented toward minority issues.

All minority communities need to understand the fact that amoral principles have reemerged and are paramount in determining public policy. Their goal should not be to justify moral principles, for these principles have always been justified and are currently justified, but to take advantage of a pressing issue that can be used to justify public policies that benefit minorities: the state of the economy. The position taken in this book is that the future of black and other minority communities will have to be predicated on assisting the United States in solving any economic dilemma or in maintaining economic prosperity (Hodgkinson 1985).

## Future Implications for Black Communities

Social scientists always run the risk of error when they attempt to extrapolate from single cases or single studies. This study of the Syracuse black community from the 1800s to the end of the 1980s represents a sociological analysis of a single community. It is a study not only of a single community, but of a community that is certainly not representative of black communities in general. In actuality, the fact that the Syracuse black community is somewhat different is a major justification for its study. It developed within a midsize northern industrial community with a relatively new black professional class. The latter phenomenon allowed a look at how the early lack of a black professional class and the later entrance of this new class influenced its growth and development in different periods. Such a history breaks tradition with many southern cities, where a black professional class has been a force since the nineteenth century. Northern cities such as New York, Philadelphia, and Washington, D.C., developed a black professional class with the black migration north following emancipation (Frazier 1939). Despite this difference, our study of the Syracuse black community has revealed many factors, both positive and negative, that are germane to black communities generally. Taking these commonalities, as well as national demographic, political, educational, and economic trends, this concluding section addresses the future of black communities.

It has been demonstrated that technological advances and demographic changes will bring about a new era in the twenty-first century. The century will have its own problems and opportunities related to black communities. Projected demographic changes indicate that as the proportion of the minority population increases, new opportunities will open up. Yet the concomitant technological advances will cause these new opportunities to be predicated on the acquisition of new and advanced knowledge and skills.

America, in its quest to remain competitive or to recapture its competitive posture economically on the global market, will have to have a highly skilled workforce. It is rapidly undergoing a transformation from "production and distribution," which require fewer skills, to "administration, information exchange, and higher-order service," which require higher skills (Kasarda 1985, 33). In the aftermath of the baby boom era, when high birth rates were prevalent for whites, the twenty-first century will see American society seeking out a highly skilled workforce from nontraditional populations. Projections indicate that the traditional entry-level labor-force population will decline significantly as demographic changes take place. Moreover, given the current immigration rates and the higher birth rates, people of color will make up 37.7 percent of the population by the year 2025 (Kendall 2004, 66). This demographic change will result in an older majority population and account for the decrease in the number of traditional entry-level workers.

These technological and demographic changes will mean that America has to turn its attention to groups who have long been ignored. The basis for this concern will not be moral, but economic. Black communities must understand and accept that future public policies that address the status of black Americans will be based on economic concerns. For example, major industrialists, who traditionally have left the education of youth to educators and politicians, save for foundation funding, have begun to address the issue of education.

Black communities have an opportunity to seize the need for an expanded but highly skilled workforce to further their own growth and development. William Wilson (1987) points to a population explosion among black youth that is still of concern, but he makes it clear that this explosion occurred at a time when the need for unskilled labor drastically declined. An employment opportunity unparalleled within U.S. history is projected for minorities and females during the twenty-first century. However, these populations will have to have the education and skills necessary to fill in the vacuum. Although many problems facing black communities are national in scope, their resolution will have to come from local rather than national efforts. Furthermore, the black community will have to play a primary rather than a secondary role in the amelioration of its problems. Throughout the history of black communities, internal factors that have influenced their growth and development have come about only through the majority community. This study of the Syracuse black community clearly demonstrates this phenomenon. When black community influence is secondary, the progress made by individual blacks is often counterproductive for the total black community. Individuals or specific groups might prosper, but the community as a whole tends not to move forward politically or economically. In the period between 1960 and 1975, the black community realized significant economic and political gains. This period was heavily influenced by internal factors buttressed by conflict that arose out of the civil rights movement. It is important to understand, however, that conflict cannot be sustained over a long period of time. Therefore, black community progress cannot be totally dependent on conflict, but must be derived from other alternatives. During the next few decades in which economic concerns spurred by advances in technology and demographic changes influence public policy related to education and the acquisition of high-level skills, black communities must play a primary, not a secondary, role in their own growth and development. They cannot afford to wait on industrialists and business leaders to affect change. National, state, and local black leaders will have to develop a three-pronged approach that includes education, economic development, and political empowerment. Each of these areas cannot be viewed independently, but must be integrated into a concerted push forward.

## Conclusions

Black communities must adopt strategies that take advantage of opportunities and at the same time overcome serious deficiencies brought on by years of systematic neglect. Here, we identify such educational, economic, and political strategies for the twenty-first century. From an educational perspective, black communities must:

• Make sure that an adequate number of black teachers are available and employed. In many school districts, the proportion of black teachers is declining although the proportion of black students is increasing. This goal will require keeping black students in the educational pipeline through college and graduate school. Although the decreased supply of black teachers can in part be attributed to increased opportunities for blacks in other careers, it is also true that educational reforms resulting in increased standardized testing to ascertain teacher competency have also had a negative impact. Colleges and universities who prepare black teachers must take this reality into account and make sure black teachers are prepared to pass these tests. Blacks and whites on school boards must see to it that the financial rewards for teaching are such that the best black and white students choose teaching as a career.

• Make sure that young black children get a strong educational foundation. As an increasing number of black children are born into poverty and born prematurely, there will be an increased need for early-childhood programs like Head Start. Also, as fewer and fewer children in classrooms are white and middle class, innovative and supportive teaching methods that take into account different learning styles and the social problems of culturally diverse groups will have to be adopted in all school systems.

• Make sure that black high school students are properly advised so that they take courses necessary for college entrance or for promising technical careers. Black professionals and role models must see to it that black students are enrolled in either college preparatory courses or in the new vocational education courses, not in general studies that do not prepare them for college or for technical careers.

• Make sure that historically black colleges and universities remain not only viable, but grow and prosper. Black colleges and universities were responsible for educating most blacks who were older than forty by the end of the 1980s, and in 1989 they turned out 34 percent of black college graduates, even though they enrolled only 17 percent of all black college students. Such growth and prosperity can happen only through significant increases in contributions coming from black communities.

From an economic prospective, black communities must:

• Expand the number of black-owned businesses beyond the "mom and pop" variety. During the civil rights era, black businesses began to expand into areas supported by the new global economy: finance, insurance, transportation, wholesale distribution, communication, real estate, and business services (see Sassen 2000 for information on the global economy). Expansion into these fields must continue. However, blacks must also recognize the twenty-first century trends in the global economy that point toward information and high-technology businesses.

• Develop a capital base by organizing and supporting black financial institutions. We have shown that black entrepreneurs have always faced difficult odds in securing loans from white financial institutions. Business loans and home loans secured through black financial institutions help to recycle money throughout the black community and to generate new businesses.

• Support black-owned businesses and black professionals so that they can reach the stage where they are competitive with nonblack professionals and businesses.

• Expand in the area of non-race-dependent businesses such as manufacturing, automobiles, fast foods, information, and customer service (Jaynes and Williams 1989).

• Increase the number of joint ventures with large white-owned corporations through franchising and developing subsidiaries (Jaynes and Williams 1989).

In the area of political empowerment, black communities must:

• Continue the efforts to increase voter registration among blacks and expand efforts to get those registered actually to vote in local, state, and national elections.

• Increase efforts to build coalitions with other oppressed minority groups and with sensitive and politically compatible whites (Browning, Marshall, and Tabb 1984).

• Become involved in the total political process, and not just by voting. Blacks must make financial contributions to and campaign for candidates. They must get involved in party politics and pay their dues so that they can influence candidate selection and platform issues.

• Make the effort to minimize status polarization. Leaders within black communities should emphasize race concerns over class concerns (Campbell 1964). In other words, middle- and upper-income blacks must be willing to support social programs that have little direct benefit to their immediate family, but may have significant consequences for the black masses and other poor groups.

• Look to Congress and the political arena for relief from issues related to justice and equity as the Supreme Court and the federal court system takes on a stricter conservative stance.

Are these suggestions original and groundbreaking? The response, of course, is no. But sometimes we need to remind ourselves of what we already know we should be doing and then do it in order to build a foundation for more exciting and novel endeavors.

# References | Index

# References

Abrams, Charles. 1965. *The City Is the Frontier.* New York: Harper and Row.

Akers, Ronald L. 1963. "Problems in the Sociology of Deviance: Social Definition and Behavior." *Social Forces* 46 (June): 455–65.

"Appraisal of the Croton School Boycott of May 10, 1966." 1966. Community seminar, Syracuse, New York, May 18.

Baron, Harold. 1968. "Black Powerlessness in Chicago." *Transaction* 6 (Nov.): 27–32.

Bartie, Bob. 1970. "The Black Community in Syracuse: 1870–1910." Unpublished paper, May 29.

Battle-Walter, Kimberly. 2004. *Sheila's Shop: Working Class African American Women Talk about Life, Love, Race, and Hair.* Lanham, Md.: Rowman and Littlefield.

Becker, Howard S. 1963. *Outsiders.* New York: Free Press.

Bednarski, Jeanne. 1977. "Third of Pupils Shifted." *Syracuse Herald-Journal,* June 26, A1.

Billingsley, Andrew. 1968. *Black Families in White America.* Englewood Cliffs, N.J.: Prentice-Hall.

Blackwell, James E. 1949. "A Comparative Study of Five Negro 'Storefront' Churches in Cleveland." Master's thesis, Case Western Reserve Univ., Cleveland, Ohio.

———. 1975. *The Black Community: Diversity and Unity.* New York: Harper and Row.

———. 1981a. *The Black Community: Diversity and Unity.* Reprint. New York: Harper and Row.

———. 1981b. *Mainstreaming Outsiders: The Production of Black Professionals.* Bayside, N.Y.: General Hall.

———. 1985. *The Black Community: Diversity and Unity.* Reprint. New York: Harper and Row.

Blackwell, James E., and Philip Hart. 1982. *Cities, Suburbs, and Blacks.* Bayside, N.Y.: General Hall.

Blauner, Robert. 1969. "Internal Colonialism and Ghetto Revolt." *Social Problems* 16 (spring): 393–408.

———. 2001. *Still the Big News: Racial Oppression in America.* Philadelphia: Temple Univ. Press.

Bogdan, Robert. 1971. "Sing for Your Supper: Poverty Programs in Onondaga County Since 1790." *Syracuse Metropolitan Review* (June): 10–16.

Borchert, James F. 1980. *Alley Life in Washington: Family, Community, Religion, and Folklife in the City, 1850–1970.* Urbana: Univ. of Illinois Press.

Bordua, David J. 1969. "Recent Trends: Deviant Behavior and Social Control." *Annuals* 369 (Jan.): 149–63.

Brown, Theodore E. 1943. "Negro Community Relations in Syracuse, New York, as Related to the Social Service Program of Dunbar Center." Master's thesis, Syracuse Univ., Syracuse, N.Y.

Browning, Rufus P., Dale R. Marshall, and David H. Tabb, eds. 1984. *Protest Is Not Enough: The Struggle of Blacks and Hispanics for Equality in Urban Politics.* Berkeley and Los Angeles: Univ. of California Press.

Burgess, M. Elaine. 1960. *Negro Leadership in a Southern City.* New Haven, Conn: Yale Univ. Press.

———. 1964. *Negro Leadership in a Southern City.* New Haven, Conn.: Yale Univ. Press.

Burns, James M. 1978. *Leadership.* New York: Harper and Row.

"Businessman Trucks Up to Success." 1983. *Syracuse National Leader,* Sept. 15, 26.

Calvert, Robert. 1979. *Affirmative Action: A Comprehensive Recruitment Manual.* Garrett Park, Md.: Garrett Park Press.

Campbell, Alan K. 1964. *The Negro in Syracuse.* Syracuse, N.Y.: Univ. College of Syracuse Univ.

Carter, Marjoria. 2003. Interviewed by Miriam B. Stamps and Spurgeon Stamps, Syracuse, New York.

*Central New York Directory of Minority and Women Businesses.* 1986–88. Syracuse, N.Y.: Syracuse Minority Development Center.

"Chaplains Resist Civil Rights Panel." 1963. *Syracuse Daily Orange,* Sept. 25, 1.

City of Syracuse. 1987. *Economic Development Zone: Final Application.* Syracuse, N.Y.: City of Syracuse.

Clark, Kenneth. 1965. *Dark Ghetto: Dilemmas of Social Power.* New York: Harper and Row.

Clark, Lewis. 1985. Telephone interview by Spurgeon Stamps, Nov. 1.

Cleaveland, Carol. 1982. "Center Serves Black Community." *Syracuse Post-Standard,* Feb. 4, B6.

Clements, Nan. 1963. "More of Core Pickets." *Syracuse Post-Standard,* Sept. 21, A1, A9.

Cloward, Richard A., and James Jones. 1965. "Social Class, Educational Attitudes, and Participation." In *Education in Depressed Areas,* edited by Harry Passow, 190–216. New York: Columbia Univ. Press.

Congress of Racial Equality (CORE) Information Committee. 1963. *Syracuse: How Far from Birmingham?* Syracuse, N.Y.: CORE.

Cornwall, Zoe. 1986. "Civil Rights in Syracuse: 1963–1983." Unpublished working document, Human Rights Commission of Onondaga County, Syracuse, N.Y.

———. 1987. *Human Rights in Syracuse: Two Memorable Decades.* Syracuse, N.Y.: Human Rights Commission.

"Court Requires Attorney to Rent to Negroes." 1963. *Syracuse Post-Standard,* July 20, A6.

Cowart, Ruben. 1981. Interview by a student in a seminar on urban research conducted by S. David Stamps, spring, Syracuse, N.Y.

Cromwell, Adelaide M. 1994. *The Other Brahims: Boston's Black Upper Class, 1750–1950.* Fayetteville: Univ. of Arkansas Press.

"Current Geography Selection: Metropolitan Statistical Area: Syracuse, New York." 2004. Available at http://www.freedemographic.com.

Dahrendorf, Ralf. 1959. *Class and Class Conflict in Industrial Society.* Stanford, Calif.: Stanford Univ. Press.

Daniels, Douglas H. 1980. *Pioneer Urbanities: A Social and Cultural History of Black San Francisco.* Philadelphia: Temple Univ. Press.

Darby, Golden B. 1937. *The Negro in Syracuse, NY: A Study in Community Relations.* Syracuse, N.Y.: Dunbar Center.

Davis, Barbara S. 1980. *A History of the Black Community of Syracuse.* Syracuse, N.Y.: Onondaga Community College.

Davis, Shirley. 1990. Telephone interview by Miriam B. Stamps, Oct. 10.

Deutscher, Irwin. 1968. "The Gatekeeper in Public Housing." In *Among the People: Encounters with the Poor,* edited by Irwin Deutscher and Elizabeth J. Thompson, 39–52. New York: Basic Books.

Dollard, John. 1957. *Caste and Class in a Southern Town.* Garden City, N.Y.: Double-day Anchor Books.

Drake, St. Clair, and Horace M. Cayton. 1945. *Black Metropolis: A Study of Negro Life in a Northern City.* New York: Harper and Row.

DuBois, W. E. B. 1899. *The Philadelphia Negro: A Social Study.* Philadelphia: Univ. of Pennsylvania Press.

Duncan, Greg J. 1984. *Years of Poverty, Years of Plenty: The Changing Fortunes of American Workers and Families.* Ann Arbor: Institute for Social Research, Univ. of Michigan.

"Early Black Settlers Processed Salt." 1982. *Syracuse Post-Standard,* Feb. 2, B5.

"Economic Perspectives: Reaganomics and Blacks." 1981. *Black Enterprise* 12, no. 5 (Dec.): 43–44.

Erikson, Kai T. 1962. "Notes on the Sociology of Deviance." *Social Problems* 9 (spring): 307–14.

Federico, Ronald D. 1975. *Sociology.* Reading, Pa.: Addison-Wesley.

Fleischman, Rose Kriss. 1980. "An Exposition of the Syracuse Central Business District: Post World War II to 1980." Unpublished paper.

Franklin, John Hope. 1980. *From Slavery to Freedom: A History of Negro Americans.* New York: Alfred A. Knopf.

Frazier, E. Franklin. 1939. *The Negro Family in the United States.* Chicago: Univ. of Chicago Press.

———. 1957. *Black Bourgeoisie.* New York: Free Press.

Freeman, Linton. 1960. *Local Community Leadership.* Syracuse, N.Y.: Syracuse Univ.

Ganley, Joseph V. 1963a. "City Whipping Racial Housing Woes." *Syracuse Herald-American,* Sunday edition, Sept. 22, A1, A13.

———. 1963b. "Racial Dilemma in City Housing." *Syracuse Herald-American,* Aug. 25, A25, A32.

Gerew, Gary, and Hart Seely. 1987. "Religion and Politics Join Hands." *Syracuse Herald-Journal,* May 16, A1, A10.

Gibbs, Jack P. 1966. "Conceptions of Deviant Behavior: The Old and the New." *Pacific Sociological Review* 9 (spring): 9–14.

Gibson, D. Parke. 1978. *$70 Billion in the Black America's Black Consumers.* New York: Macmillan.

Gill, Gerald R. 1980. *Meanness Mania: The Changed Mood.* Washington, D.C.: Howard Univ. Press.

Ginzberg, Eli, and Associates. 1968. *The Middle Class Negro in the White Man's World.* New York: Columbia Univ. Press.

Gladwin, Thomas. 1967. *Poverty U.S.A.* Boston: Little, Brown.

Glasgow, Douglas G. 1981. *The Black Underclass.* New York: Vintage Books.

Haggstrom, Warren C. 1968. "Can the Poor Transform the World?" In *Among the People: Encounters With the Poor*, edited by I. Deutscher and E. J. Thompson, 67–110. New York: Basic Books.

Hamilton, Norman W. 1946. "A Survey of the Leisure Time Activities and the Social Organizations of the Negroes in Syracuse." Master's thesis, Syracuse Univ., Syracuse, N.Y.

Harrison, Ira E. 1966. "The Storefront Church as a Revitalization Movement." *Review of Religious Research* 7: 160–63.

Hart, Keith. 1973. "Informal Income Opportunities and Urban Employment in Ghana." *Journal of Modern African Studies* 11: 61–89.

Henderson, George. 1967. "Beyond Poverty of Income." *Journal of Negro Education* 36 (winter): 42–50.

Herskovits, Melvin. 1958. *The Myth of the Negro Past*. 2d ed. New York: Harper and Row.

Hill, Robert B. 1978. *The Illusion of Black Progress*. Washington, D.C.: National Urban League.

———. 1981. *Economic Policies and Black Progress: Myths and Realities*. Washington, D.C.: National Urban League.

Hodges, Wayne. 1958. *Company and Community*. New York: Harper and Row.

Hodgkinson, Harold L. 1985. *All One System: Demographics of Education, Kindergarten Through Graduate School*. Washington, D.C.: Institute for Educational Leadership.

Hyman, Herbert H. 1953. "The Value Systems of Different Classes: A Social Psychological Contribution to the Analysis of Stratification." In *Class, Status, and Power*, edited by R. Bendix and S. M. Lipset, 426–42. New York: Basic Books.

Inroads, Inc. 1988. *Annual Report*. Syracuse, N.Y.: Syracuse Chapter of Inroads, Inc.

Jaynes, Gerald D., and Robin M. Williams, eds. 1989. *A Common Destiny: Blacks and American Society*. Washington, D.C.: National Academy Press.

Jones, Alexander F. 1963. "Law and Order or Red Technique." *Syracuse Herald-Journal*, Sept. 20, A22.

Jones, Faustine E. 1977. *The Changing Mood in America: Eroding Commitment?* Washington, D.C.: Howard Univ. Press.

Kasarda, John. 1985. "Urban Change and Minority Opportunities." In *The New Reality*, edited by Paul E. Peterson, 33–67. Washington, D.C.: Brookings Institute.

Katzman, David M. 1973. *Before the Ghetto: Black Detroit in the Nineteenth Century*. Urbana: Univ. of Illinois Press.

Kelly, J. Michael. 1982. "Blacks Have Bittersweet Memories of 15th Ward." *Syracuse Herald-American*, Feb. 21, C3.

Kendall, Diana. 2004. *Social Problems in a Diverse Society*. Boston: Pearson.

Kerr, Douglas. n.d. "The Negro in Syracuse: A Perspective." Unpublished paper.

Kitsuse, John I. 1962. "Societal Reactions to Deviant Behavior: Problems and Method." *Social Problems* 9 (winter): 247–56.

Kozol, Jonathan. 1967. *Death at an Early Age*. Boston: Houghton Mifflin.

Kramer, Judith R. 1970. *The American Minority Community*. New York: Thomas Y. Crowell.

Kriesberg, Louis. 1970. *Mothers in Poverty*. Chicago: Aldine.

Kronus, Sidney. 1971. *The Black Middle Class*. Columbus, Ohio: C. E. Merrill.

Kusmer, Kenneth L. 1976. *A Ghetto Takes Shape: Black Cleveland, 1870–1930*. Urbana: Univ. of Illinois Press.

Lasch, Christopher. 1978. *The Culture of Narcissism: American Life in an Age of Diminishing Expectations*. New York: W. W. Norton.

Lazarsfeld, Paul F., Bernard Berelson, and William M. McPhee. 1948. *Voting*. New York: Columbia Univ.

Levitan, Sar A., William B. Johnston, and Robert Taggart. 1975. *Still a Dream: The Changing Status of Blacks since 1960*. Cambridge, Mass.: Harvard Univ. Press.

Lewis, Hylan. 1955. *Blackways of Kent*. Chapel Hill: Univ. of North Carolina Press.

Lewis, Oscar. 1959. *Five Families*. New York: Basic Books.

Lieberson, Stanley, and Mary C. Waters. 1988. *From Many Strands: Ethnic and Racial Groups in Contemporary America*. New York: Russell Sage Foundation.

Liebow, Elliot. 1967. *Talley's Corner: A Study of Negro Streetcorner Men*. Boston: Little, Brown.

Light, Ivan. 1983. *Cities in World Perspective*. New York: Macmillan.

"List of the Top 100 Black Businesses." 1987. *Black Enterprise* 17, no. 5 (June): 129–37.

Lovett, Bobby L. 1999. *The African American History of Nashville, Tennessee 1780–1930: Elites and Dilemmas*. Fayetteville: Univ. of Arkansas Press.

Lomax, Louis. 1962. *The Negro Revolt*. New York: Harper and Row.

Macionis, John J., and Vincent N. Parrillo. 2004. *Cities and Urban Life*. Upper Saddle River, N.J.: Prentice-Hall.

Mack, William A., president of Organization of Organizations. 1966. Community seminar guest, discussion notes made by Allen Kirschenbaum, recorder for the community seminar, Dec. 7, Syracuse, N.Y.

Marger, Martin N. 1994. *Race and Ethnic Relations: American and Global Perspectives*. Belmont, Calif.: Wadsworth.

Martin, Roscoe C., Frank J. Munger, Jesse Burkhead, and Guthrie S. Birkhead. 1961. *Decisions in Syracuse: Metropolitan Action Studies*. Bloomington: Indiana Univ. Press.

McGarry, William L. 1964. Letter to the editor. *Syracuse Herald-Journal*, Apr. 2, A16.

Meadows, Paul. 1966. "Boundary Problems, Structural or Organizational Problems, and Client Problems." Community seminar, Oct., Syracuse, N.Y.

Meier, August, and Elliott Rudwick, eds. 1970. *The Making of Black America*. New York: Atheneum.

Merton, Robert K. 1957. *Social Theory and Social Structure*. New York: Free Press.

*Metropolitan Syracuse Black Business Directory*. 1981–82. Syracuse, N.Y.: Association of Black Businesses.

Meyer, Jack A. 1986. "Social Programs and Social Policy." In *Perspectives on the Reagan Years*, edited by John L. Palmer, 65–89. Washington, D.C.: Urban Institute Press.

Michels, Robert. 1949. *Political Parties*. New York: Free Press.

Minority Manuscript. 1985. *Class Acts*. Syracuse, N.Y.: Office of Program Development, Syracuse Univ.

Moore, Edward M. 1982. "Steering Street Kids to Success." *Syracuse Herald-American*, Feb. 28, A3, A6.

Morrison, Minion K. C. 1988. "A Profile of Black Leadership in Syracuse, New York Since 1965." *AfroAmericans in New York Life and History* 12, no. 2 (July): 7–18.

Moynihan, Daniel P. 1967. *The Negro Family: The Case for National Action*. Washington, D.C.: U.S. Department of Labor.

Murray, Charles. 1984. *Losing Ground: American Social Policy, 1950–1980*. New York: Basic Books.

Myrdal, Gunner. 1944. *An American Dilemma*. New York: Harper and Row.

National Urban League. 1980a. *The Black Pulse Survey Report*. Washington, D.C.: Research Department, National Urban League.

———. 1980b. *Initial Black Pulse Findings*. Washington, D.C.: Research Department, National Urban League.

———. 1982. *The State of Black America: 1982*. New York: National Urban League.

Nelson, William E., and Philip J. Meranto. 1977. *Electing Black Mayors: Political Action in the Black Community*. Columbus: Ohio State Univ. Press.

Newman, K. D., N. S. Amidei, B. L. Carter, D. Day, W. J. Kruvent, and J. S. Russell. 1978. *Protest, Politics, and Prosperity: Black Americans and White Institutions, 1940–75*. New York: Pantheon Books.

Osofsky, Gilbert. 1971. *Harlem: The Making of a Ghetto, 1890–1930*. 1963. Reprint. New York: Harper Torchbooks.

Palen, J. John. 2005. *The Urban World.* New York: McGraw-Hill.

Pear, Robert. 1988. "Families Better Off." *St. Petersburg Times,* Feb. 26, A1, A16.

People's Equal Action and Community Effort (PEACE), Inc. 1988. *Annual Report.* Syracuse, N.Y.: PEACE, Inc.

Philpott, Thomas. 1978. *The Slum and the Ghetto.* New York: Oxford Univ. Press.

Pinkney, Alphonso. 1975. *Black Americans.* Englewood Cliffs, N.J.: Prentice-Hall.

Portes, Alejandro, and Ruben G. Rambout, eds. 1996. *Immigrant America.* Berkeley and Los Angeles: Univ. of California Press.

Quinney, Richard. 1970. *The Social Reality of Crime.* Boston: Little, Brown.

Rea, Jeff. 1982. "Churches Serving as Beacons for Blacks in a Sea of Troubles." *Syracuse Herald-American,* Feb. 28, C4.

Rhodes, Jane. 1982. "Seems Like Old Times." *Syracuse New Times,* Feb. 1, 8–9.

Rice, Dale. 1976a. "Ask Integration Plan Deadline Extension." *Syracuse Post-Standard,* Oct. 2, A2.

———. 1976b. "Johnson Will Work for Voluntary Plan." *Syracuse Post-Standard,* Sept. 23, A1.

Ropers, Richard H. 1991. *Persistent Poverty: The American Dream Turned Nightmare.* New York: Plenum.

Rossides, Daniel W. 1976. *The American Class System.* New York: Houghton Mifflin.

Roth, A. B. 1966. "Tenant Contract Lacking." *Syracuse Herald-Journal,* Jan. 19, A1, A23.

Ryan, William. 1971. *Blaming the Victim.* New York: Vintage Books.

Sacks, Seymour, and Ralph Andrew. 1974. *The Syracuse Black Community, 1970: A Comparative Study.* Syracuse, N.Y.: Syracuse Univ.

Sacks, Seymour, and Robert Sacks. 1987. *The Syracuse Black Community: 1980.* Syracuse, N.Y.: Syracuse Univ.

Sanders, William B. 1976. *The Sociologist as Detective: An Introduction to Research Methods.* New York: Praeger.

Sassen, Saskia. 2000. *Cities in a Global Economy.* 2d ed. Thousand Oaks, Calif.: Pine Forge Press.

Schaefer, Richard T. 1988. *Racial and Ethnic Groups.* Glenview, Ill.: Scott, Foreman.

Schuyler, George S. 1967. *Black and Conservative: The Autobiography of George S. Schuyler.* New York: Arlington House.

Scruggs, Otey M. 1984. *History of the Urban League of Onondaga County. Urban League: 20th Anniversary Celebration.* Syracuse, N.Y.: Urban League of Onondaga County.

Seely, Hart. 1987a. "The Battle for Economic Freedom." *Syracuse Herald-Journal,* May 14, A1, A14, A17.

————. 1987b. "Can the Sleeping Giant Awaken?" *Syracuse Herald-Journal,* May 12, A1, A12, A13.

————. 1987c. "More Whites in Poverty Than Blacks." *Syracuse Herald-Journal,* May 15, A1, A11, A15.

————. 1987d. "Reading, Writing, and Racism." *Syracuse Herald-Journal,* May 13, A1, A12.

————. 1987e. "Segregation Persists in City Housing." *Syracuse Herald-American,* Sunday edition, May 17, A16, A17.

Sethuraman, S. V. 1978. "The Informal Urban Sector: Concept, Measurement, and Policy." *International Labor Review* 114, no. 1 (July–Aug.): 69–81.

Shelly, Barbara. 1980. "Percy Jones Works to Clean Up in Business." *Syracuse Post-Standard,* May 14, D3, D12.

Smith, Robert C. 1982. *Black Leadership.* Washington, D.C.: Institute for Urban Affairs and Research, Howard Univ.

Snyder, David P., and Greg Edwards. 1984. *Future Choices: An Association Executive's Guide to a Decade of Change and Choices.* New York: Foundation of the American Society of Association Executives.

Sowell, Thomas. 1981. *Ethnic America.* New York: Basic Books.

Spear, Allen H. 1967. *Black Chicago: The Making of a Negro Ghetto, 1890–1920.* Chicago: Univ. of Chicago Press.

Stack, Carol B. 1974. *All Our Kin: Coping Strategies in a Black Community.* New York: Harper and Row.

Staley, Sam. 2003. "Ground Zero in Urban Decline." *Urban Society: Annual Edition* no. 11: 70–76.

Stamps, Spurgeon M. 1982. *Urban League Community Survey 1982.* Syracuse, N.Y.: Urban League of Onondaga County.

————. 1988. "Higher Education and Societal Changes: 1960s and 1980s." In *Proceedings of the Southeast Social Sciences Conference.* El Cajon, Calif.: National Social Science Association.

Stamps, Spurgeon M., and Miriam B. Stamps. 1985. "Race, Class, and Leisure Activities of Residents." *Journal of Leisure Research* 17: 40–56.

Staples, Robert. 1976. *Introduction to Black Sociology.* New York: McGraw-Hill.

————. 1981. *The World of Black Singles: Changing Patterns of Male/Female Relations.* Westport, Conn.: Greenwood Press.

Suarez-Orozco, Marcelo, and Mariela M. Paez, eds. 2002. *Latinos: Remaking America.* Berkeley and Los Angeles: Univ. of California Press.

Suttles, Gerald D. 1968. *The Social Order of the Slum.* Chicago: Univ. of Chicago Press.

Taeuber, Karl E., and Alma F. Taeuber. 1965. *Negroes in Cities: Residential Segregation and Neighborhood Change.* Chicago: Aldine.

Trotter, Joe W. 1985. *Black Milwaukee: The Making of an Industrial Proletariat, 1915–45.* Urbana: Univ. of Illinois Press.

"2 Professors Jailed in Sit-in." 1963. *Syracuse Daily Orange,* Sept. 18, 1.

U.S. Bureau of the Census. 1910. *United States Census of Population.* Washington, D.C.: U.S. Bureau of the Census.

———. 1920. *United States Census of Population.* Washington, D.C.: U.S. Bureau of the Census.

———. 1930. *United States Census of Population.* Washington, D.C.: U.S. Bureau of the Census.

———. 1940. *United States Census of Population.* Washington, D.C.: U.S. Bureau of the Census.

———. 1950. *United States Census of Population.* Washington, D.C.: U.S. Bureau of the Census.

———. 1960. *United States Census of Population.* Washington, D.C.: U.S. Bureau of the Census.

———. 1970. "General Social and Economic Characteristics." In *United States Census of Population,* PC-1 (C-34). Washington, D.C.: Government Printing Office.

———. 1970/1980. *Census of Population and Housing: Census Tracts, Syracuse, N.Y.* Washington, D.C.: U.S. Department of Commerce.

———. 1980. *General Social and Economic Characteristics for New York: 1980 Census of Population.* PC 80-1-C. Washington, D.C.: U.S. Department of Commerce.

———. 1983. *1980 Census of Population and Housing. Census Tracts. Syracuse, N.Y.* Washington, D.C.: Government Printing Office.

———. 1990. *United States Census of Population.* Washington, D.C.: U.S. Bureau of the Census.

———. 2000. *American Factfinder.* Washington, D.C.: Government Printing Office.

U.S. Department of Commerce. 2000. *Summary Population and Housing Characteristics, New York.* Washington, D.C.: U.S. Bureau of the Census.

U.S. Department of Health, Education, and Welfare. Office of Civil Rights. 1976–77. *Directory of Elementary and Secondary School Districts, and Schools in Selected School Districts.* Vol. 11. Washington, D.C.: U.S. Department of Health, Education, and Welfare.

Valentine, Charles A. 1968. *Culture and Poverty: Critique and Counterproposals.* Chicago: Univ. of Chicago Press.

Vowell, Raymond W. 1977. "Child Abuse and Neglect in Issues on Innovation and Implantation." In *Proceedings of the Second National Conference on Child Abuse and Neglect,* edited by Michael Lauderdale. Publication no. (OHOS) 78-30147. Washington, D.C.: U.S. Department of Health, Education, and Welfare.

Warren, Roland L. 1972. *The Community in America.* Chicago: Rand McNally.

Whyte, William F. 1943. *Street Corner Society.* Chicago: Univ. of Chicago Press.

Williams, John. 1966a. "Portrait of a City: Syracuse, the Old Home Town." Unpublished manuscript, George Arents Research Library for Special Collections, Syracuse Univ.

———. 1966b. "Syracuse: A City in Transition." Unpublished article, George Arents Research Library for Special Collections, Syracuse Univ.

Williams, Larry. 1981. "A History of Affirmative Action." *Affirmative Action in Progress* 7 (Nov.): 4–5.

Willie, Charles. 1965a. "Community Leadership in the Voluntary Health and Welfare System." In *Applied Sociology,* edited by Alvin W. Gouldner and S. M. Miller, 207–14. New York: Free Press.

———. 1965b. "The Unfinished Business of Human Rights in Syracuse." *Event: A Journal of Public Affairs* (summer): 6–39.

———. 1967. "Community Organization and Community Development." Community seminar, Oct. 4, Syracuse, N.Y.

———. 1970. "Institutional Vitality and Institutional Alliances." *Sociology and Social Research* 54 (Jan.): 249–59.

———. 1974. "The Black Family and Social Class." *American Journal of Orthopsychiatry* 44: 50–60.

———. 1976. *A New Look at Black Families.* Bayside, N.Y.: General Hall.

Willie, Charles V., Herbert Notkin, and Nicholas Rezak. 1964. "Trends in the Participation of Businessmen in Local Voluntary Affairs." *Sociology and Social Research* 48 (Apr.): 289–300.

Wilson, Frank H. 2004. *Race, Class, and the Preindustrial City: William Julius Wilson and the Promise of Sociology.* New York: New York State Univ. Press.

Wilson, William J. 1978. *The Declining Significance of Race.* Chicago: Univ. of Chicago Press.

———. 1987. *The Truly Disadvantaged: The Inner City, the Underclass, and Public Policy.* Chicago: Univ. of Chicago Press.

———. 1996a. *When Work Disappears: The World of the New Urban Poor.* New York: Vintage Press.

————. 1996b. "Work." *New York Magazine* (Aug. 18): 26, 31, 40, 48, 52, 54.

————. 2001. "The Real Test of Welfare Reform Still Lies Ahead." *New York Times,* July 13, A21.

Wood, Frank T. 1965. "The Negro Employee in Syracuse." Unpublished report, Syracuse, N.Y.

Zeul, Carolyn, and Craig Humphrey. 1971. "The Integration of Suburban Blacks in Suburban Neighborhoods: A Reexamination of the Contact Hypotheses." *Social Problems* 8 (spring): 462–474.

# Index

Italic page number denotes illustration or table.